THIRD TAKE

Australian film-makers talk

EDITED BY RAFFAELE CAPUTO
AND GEOFF BURTON

ALLEN&UNWIN

This book was financially assisted by the Australian Film Commission and Cinemedia, and with editorial assistance from the Australian Screen Directors Association.

First published in 2002

The quote on p 64 is from the Gwen Harwood poem, 'Improptus III', *Poems Volume Two*, Penguin Books 2001.

Every effort has been made to contact the copyright holder of the Ken G. Hall article reproduced in this text. As these efforts were unsuccessful, the copyright holder is asked to contact the publisher directly.

Allen & Unwin
83 Alexander Street
Crows Nest NSW 2065
Australia
Phone: (61 2) 8425 0100
Fax: (61 2) 9906 2218
Email: info@allenandunwin.com
Web: www.allenandunwin.com

National Library of Australia
Cataloguing-in-Publication entry:

Third take: Australian film-makers talk.

Includes index.
ISBN 1 86508 507 3.

1. Motion picture producers and directors—Australia—Interviews. 2. Motion pictures—Production and direction. I. Caputo, Raffaele. II. Burton, Geoff.

791.43023

Set in 11/13 pt Bembo by Bookhouse, Sydney
Printed by Griffin Press, South Australia

10 9 8 7 6 5 4 3 2 1

Foreword

Anthony Minghella

You beauty!

After I'd read the proofs of Raffaele Caputo and Geoff Burton's excellent volume I noticed that I'd written the same word repeatedly in the margins. *America*. What an extraordinary hold America has exerted over the rest of us making films in other countries. Nearly every contributor to this fascinating book defines him or herself by the extent to which they have resisted or succumbed to the cultural hegemony of Hollywood. It's a particular dilemma for those of us for whom English is a first language and where the adjustment to a world audience from a domestic one appears to be minimal, tantalisingly possible and inconsequential. But it is evidently a Faustian accommodation, where seemingly small shifts in taste accumulate and a marginally unreliable compass can take you miles from your original destination.

In the mainstream cinema, the industrial has triumphed over the personal, the dollar over the distinctive. The stupefying costs involved in making and releasing the average Hollywood picture and the concomitant anxiety generated in producers and film-makers result in movies which sandpaper away the contours of an individual voice. And as Rolf de Heer points out in his essay: 'one of the characteristics of Australian cinema has been the contribution of the "auteur"...' Film development, a process which more often resembles film diminution, is increasingly concerned with unearthing franchise projects, event movies and sequels where the distinctive and the morally challenging perspective of the auteur are unwelcome. It appears that there is a perilously direct and inverse connection between the number of dollars spent and artistic merit. To bowdlerise Samuel Johnson, the industrial cinema understands the price of everything, the value of nothing. And it is to Hollywood, the home of the industry, that the Australian film-makers in this volume find themselves turning to or turning away from.

For lovers of film, for students of film, and for makers of film, *Third Take* does what all good books about cinema do—it refreshes our interest in movies we have previously enjoyed and encourages us to seek out those we've missed. I wish this book had arrived accompanied by DVDs of the early Peter Weir films, the documentaries of Dennis O'Rourke and, in particular, a copy of Phillip Noyce's *Newsfront*, the subject here of some entertaining dialectical scrutiny, and—given the dust kicked up about authorship, intention and compromise—essential viewing. Together, the essays collected in this volume offer a vivid snapshot of what some of the current preoccupations in Australian cinema are, as well as for this reader at least, a pungent glimpse of the Australian character.

Nowhere is this more on show than in John Seale's *I'm not an artist; I'm a technician*, the result of a Popcorn Taxi interview, which I attended in Melbourne last year and which is printed in an edited transcription. John's energetic disavowal of his own artistry should not confuse readers. Like many of the contributors to this volume, modest to a fault, John is at pains to assert craft over art, perspiration over inspiration. From a director about to work with John for the third movie running, the truth is that while he is the most hardworking and technically adroit cinematographer—and certainly the most indefatigable—his work is full of beauty. And beauty—a word rarely written in this book, but always I believe lurking in its margins—is, in its most profound, elusive and troubling sense, what we are all here for. *You beauty!* is not only an ubiquitous Australian colloquialism but—as a motif of the true aspirations of the film-makers included in this volume—the most apt.

Ironically, the most powerful and instructive pages of this book come from its final section 'In the margins: documentary'. Curtis Levy's essay, 'The painter, the president and the piano player', speaks of the documentary process in a way that resonates strongly with me as a maker of fiction:

> In truth, I believe that there is no such thing as objectivity. The moment you choose a subject. The moment you point the camera. The moment you make a cut in the edit, all are subjective decisions which effect the audience's feeling for and against the subject of the film. This is where how private space is treated becomes so crucial.

Following Levy's contribution, Martha Ansara's excellent interview with Dennis O'Rourke, 'On the poetry of madness', introduced me to the most compelling and provocative voice in the collection. O'Rourke speaks of documentary practice as the refuge 'for a certain kind of artist *manqué*':

> I look for the madness. If the madness isn't there, then I'm pretty sure they can't quite get it. Joseph Conrad says, 'Before all, to see.' To see, before all else. That's a maxim I carry with me.

I can't think of a clearer maxim for the maker of fiction to contemplate, chiming as it does with Kafka's marvellous war cry: 'Fiction is the axe with which to smash the frozen sea within us.' Perhaps more significant, O'Rourke's observations about the architecture of the documentary collide exactly with the challenges of filmed fiction and describe, too, the method of working with actors as well as with the actual characters collected by documentary:

> The only two things we've really got to work with in all film are *mise en scène* and montage. But how film works, what gives it the extra dimension of meaning is what puzzles people when they say to me, 'How did you get people to be so intimate?'...there's a transformative effect if it's recorded and photographed in a certain way and then placed in a certain context. As my hero Joseph Brodsky, the Russian poet, says, what matters in telling a story is not the story itself, but what follows what.

It is clear to spectators of the Australian cinema that it currently possesses an impressive depth of talent, ranging from the visible and internationally celebrated posse of directors like Baz Lurhmann, Peter Weir, Phillip Noyce and Jane Campion to those actors recognised by a single name, Russell, Nicole, Mel and Cate. It is also true that in less heralded but equally crucial areas—of production design, editing, cinematography—Australians are making a profound contribution to world cinema and I was happy to read here about the work of Don McAlpine and others. It would be interesting in a future volume to hear the views and experiences of Steve Andrews, the legendary Assistant Director, who's been an important ally to almost all of the directors mentioned in this volume, but most of all to me. Indeed, one of the particular virtues of this collection is that it will remind younger Australians, as Phillip Noyce points out in his essay, that the Australian film industry is a recent phenomenon, created in no small part by the film-makers discussed here. In his own childhood, Phillip tells us, he was never exposed to a single Australian film.

Finally, the best thing about film-making is that it shares a common language of miserable predawns—that clay light—of arriving at an inhospitable location, the polystyrene cup of unidentifiable hot liquid, the universal obsessions with what is the warmest wetweather gear, the best insect repellent, the most effective sunblock, the most comfortable boots and the least bad caterers. That camaraderie, and the love of film and the film-making process, is evident on every one of these pages. And if it is generally accepted that making a film is most closely akin to making a war, then what is clear to all of us fighting the good fight is that the comrades of choice would have to be Australian. *You beauties!*

Contents

Illustrations

Acknowledgements

For the unenviable task of having to transcribe a mountain of audiotapes, our greatest thanks go to Kerrie McGovern of Clever Types, Clare Wilmot-Griffiths and Sally Rippin; without their assistance *Third Take* would have taken twice as long to complete. A good load of thanks also goes to Stephen Wallace, former president of the Australian Screen Directors Association (ASDA), Richard Harris and other members of the ASDA work team, particularly for assisting with the articles by Peter Weir and Rolf de Heer, both of which were based on papers they had delivered at ASDA conferences in 1995 and 2001, respectively.

To the crews of the Research & Information Centre of the Australian Film Institute, Cherub Pictures, Film Australia, Palm Beach Pictures, Top Technicians, Vertigo Productions and Village Roadshow, all of whom gave support whenever they could—we need you more than you know. Also, a little nod goes to Michael Agar, Patricia Amad, Philippa Hawker, Sally Jackson, Cassius Matthias, Janette McAlpine, Louise Seale, Peter Tapp and Debbie Withers for various odd jobs.

For reprint permission thanks are due to: Martha Ansara and Dennis O'Rourke for their interview, which first appeared in *Metro*, no. 126, Summer 2001; the organisers of Popcorn Taxi and Paul Harris for the article 'I'm a Technician; Not an Artist' by John Seale; and again to Popcorn Taxi for the interview with Don McAlpine, 'Selling Nuts and Bolts', a part of which was conducted at one of their regular events.

Acknowledgements

To be singled out for special mention are Kate Ingham and Julie Regan, formerly of the Australian Film Commission, who showed an enormous amount of faith in this book series right from the word go. Nor would the series have much of a life without the steady cultural support of the Australian Film Commission and Cinemedia—to them we are always indebted. Finally, a book of this nature owes much to all of its contributors, particularly to Frans Vandenburg and Phillip Noyce, with whom we are fortunate to have shared interests.

Them are fightin' words

Raffaele Caputo and Geoff Burton

In David O. Russell's *Three Kings* (1999), which is set at the climax of the Gulf War, the pre-title sequence opens with the rather enigmatic words 'March 1991. The war just ended'. It's the first indication of an absurd inversion of things for here begins a war film without a war. Then we see an American soldier, Troy Barlow (Mark Wahlberg), who, while on patrol in the middle of a desert, comes across a lone Iraqi soldier waving to him from a distance. We actually do not know whether the soldier is surrendering, or even if he is an Iraqi soldier; he could be an Iraqi dissident. Barlow turns to his fellow troops and delivers the first of a series of pulverising lines of dialogue, 'Are we shooting?' The question volleys back and forth at least three times more without a conclusive answer. Instead one group of his comrades is more interested in haggling over a piece of gum, while another group is engaged in the task of getting a speck of sand out of someone's eye. Seeing that the soldier in the distance is brandishing a weapon, Barlow takes the initiative and shoots him down. They all race over and then Barlow's buddy, Conrad Vig (Spike Jonze), delivers another stinger of a line: 'Damn, I didn't think I'd get to see anybody get shot in this war.' The scene doesn't end there, however, for another soldier steps up and takes a Polaroid snapshot of the dead Iraqi soldier (?) as a memento!

When in *The Lexus and the Olive Tree*[1] Thomas Friedman proposed his unappetising 'Golden Arches Theory'—'that no two countries with McDonald's have ever fought a war against each other since they each got their McDonald's'—he fell slightly short on defining an important ingredient

1

of his theory: war.[2] If, as Friedman makes evident, globalisation is an international system that has directly or indirectly influenced the way people live and think about their daily lives in almost any country in the world, then by that all-encompassing claim so too has globalisation redefined war as one fought between two countries.

Although Friedman in some way had first hand experience of the Gulf War, and certainly understood the deeper purpose of the American military,[3] it seems he did not, could not, penetrate the surreal aspects of that war. Not so for the makers of *Three Kings*, of which the pre-title sequence punctures any expectations or sense of conventional warfare—even a war between a country with McDonald's and a country without one.

What the pre-title sequence points the audience towards is a war where the entanglements of telecommunications, state interests and the global interests of multinational corporations create unmitigated confusion on the ground level. Ironically, in *Three Kings* there are two main characters associated with the media who are the most vocal siphons for this confusion. The first is a military media aide, Major Archie Gates (George Clooney), who demands of his commanding officer, 'Just tell me what we did here?' Then Adriana Cruz (Nora Dunn), reporter for the fictional NBS network, in a moment of self-evaluation says to nobody in particular, 'The war is over and I don't fuckin' know what it was all about!' Why such questions when 'the war just ended' was clearly represented as one fought between a country unjustifiably on the offensive and another righteously on the defensive? In short, the answer given by *Three Kings* is because the invasion of Kuwait and the liberation of Kuwait are forged from the same spirit: economic expansion.

In another scene our 'three kings' witness Iraqi soldiers blow up a tanker that at first we believe to contain oil. The tanker actually contains milk, and the action of the Iraqi soldiers is carried out to effect a policy of quelling any possibility of rebellion by starving the people. In yet another scene Troy Barlow, while under interrogation, has crude oil forced down his throat to bring home the point of America's presence in Kuwait. (Incidentally, the crude oil is taken from a drum that is simply labelled 'Oil' but is stencilled in the same typography and with the familiar red, white and blue of the Mobil logo.) And here is the crunch: every conflict in *Three Kings*, whether large or small, comes down to a choice between oil and milk, or what these two terms symbolise. What is the interest of the Iraqi state? Oil. What is the interest behind the actions of the American military? Oil. What is the interest of the Iraqi people who may rebel against the state? Milk. For the 'three kings' the choice they make determines who their allies and enemies are. The question of ally or enemy is no better realised when we discover that

Barlow and the Iraqi Republican guard (Said Taghmaoui) interrogating him share something in common: they both joined the military for a chance at a better life (in a word, milk). Confusion reigns when behind the stated objective for milk is the wellspring of oil.

What did you do in the war, Daddy?

Who is one supposedly fighting? What ideology or belief is one fighting for? And, importantly, what kind of war is being fought? These questions are Friedman's greatest omissions *in the absence* of a war between a McDonald's country and a non-McDonald's country. For not only has globalisation effectively redrawn the battle fronts—and a lot more fronts have proliferated since he wrote the book in 1999—globalisation has given war a facelift. In other words, globalisation may form partnerships between former rival countries though it may also create its enemies within each. Friedman's chapter titled 'The Golden Arches Theory of Conflict Prevention' might also include an appropriate and realistic sub-title, 'And the Theory of Conflict Redistribution'.

Testimony to this redistribution is the emergence of the new anti-corporate activism or anti-globalisation movement, as we have seen with protests such as the S11, M1, G8 and others around the world, a movement that continues to gain greater public awareness and popularity through the publication of books by such activists as Naomi Klein and Noreena Hertz.[4] These phenomena of dissent are war, not between countries, but war all the same, an undeclared war as something akin to civil war or, as Umberto Eco would call it, the guerrilla warfare of the electronic age.[5]

Friedman is certainly not unaware of this 'war'. His book contains two chapters titled 'The Backlash' and 'The Groundswell (Or the Backlash Against the Backlash)',[6] of which the former explains why the movement grew. Friedman boils down the complex 'character' of the anti-globalisation movement in the following way. It is made up of disparate groups of people who feel either financially threatened, unequipped to keep up with the pace of change, hammered by the system, or simply offended by the homogenisation of their culture or the cost incurred by the environment. Moreover, these groups have not identified the real interest of human beings and are without a coherent ideology or sustainable economic alternative that can produce higher living standards.

Yet Friedman warns the movement still poses a very real threat to globalisation, especially if it achieves critical mass, because it 'comes from the depth of people's souls and pocketbooks'. (The word 'pocketbooks' means a healthy wallet, extra cash, profit as the signs of better living standards; when the pocketbook is unhealthy the owner can be a potential threat.) He goes on to explain that for most of the groups within the movement their main purpose is not to slow down the global roller coaster in order to get off, but so they can hang on.

The latter chapter, 'The Groundswell', explains why globalisation cannot be effectively disrupted, and he begins this chapter with a very curious anecdote. On a trip to Hanoi in 1995, every day during his morning exercise around his hotel, Friedman encountered a Vietnamese woman with a bathroom scale, who would offer to weigh passers-by for a small fee. Every morning Friedman paid her a dollar and weighed himself even though he didn't need to know his weight. For Friedman this exchange was his contribution to the globalisation of Vietnam. Why? Well, because what drives globalisation is the basic human desire for a better life (re the pocketbook, extra cash, profits). According to Friedman globalisation comes from the ground level: 'It starts with a lady in Hanoi, crouched on the sidewalk, offering up a bathroom scale as her ticket to the Fast World.'

For Friedman, despite the problems globalisation may create, it also creates benefits for those on the ground level. Admittedly it creates enormous power for those people and multinational corporations way up in the stratosphere, yet a trickle of that power reaches those on the bottom who never had any before, or where the alternative might be worse. This is why Friedman believes the anti-globalisation movement has mistaken agendas and does not pose a real threat. This belief compels him to write: 'When all of *them* [the people on the ground level] give up trying to be in the Fast World, and when all of *them* declare that they would rather go back to their old, closed, regulated systems, and give up trying for a better lifestyle—for them or their kids—then I will acknowledge that globalisation is "finished" and that the backlash has won.'

But this belief shows another weakness. No matter the system, old or new, is the system justified in unconscionably exploiting the human desire for a better lifestyle? It would seem so from the sentence Friedman writes to conclude this chapter: '[I]f you construct an economic and political environment that gives them half a sense that with hard work and sacrifice they will get to Disney World and get to enjoy the Magic Kingdom, most of them will stick with the game—for far, far longer than you would ever expect.' For one thing Friedman sounds suspiciously like an apologist for the faults of the new system. Even more troublesome is that his final sentence sounds like a theory that would be offered to a chief executive officer or politician on how to maintain a loyal workforce or keep the populace in tow—as in, 'Give them just enough so that they'll want more.'

Friedman cannot equate basic human desire for a better life with anything other than the pocketbook. But while the needs and desires of individuals are subject to the global market place, does that necessarily mean that certain moral rights and social values can be expressed in terms of the market? What Friedman fails to recognise is that most manifestations of the anti-globalisation movement are not mercenary; they are driven by beliefs in fundamental values and rights for all. To name a few: fairness, liberty of opinion, equality, health, proper working conditions, fraternity, employment opportunities and freedom of choice.

As Arnold Toynbee once said in conversation with his son Philip, '[I]f you really think there's nothing in common between someone else's system of morality and your own, you're not treating him [sic] as a full human being.'[7] When that commonality is unrealised, misunderstood or miscarried, globalisation is thus an *idolum*—its benefits can be very real, but most of those benefits are phantoms for the majority of the world's population, especially the populations of the Third World.

Is the bathroom scale for the little old lady in Hanoi really her ticket *to* the Fast World? Or is it her meal ticket *in* the Fast World?

September 11 postscript

Contrary to what the reader may be thinking at this point, this book is in no way about war or the representation of war in movies. Nor, we should add, is it about terrorism or the events of September 11.[8] But amid the countless e-jokes that zipped over the Internet in the days, weeks and months following September 11, one was particularly instructive of our concerns with globalisation—apart from being very amusing. It was called 'Afghanistan After the War', and when one scrolled down to find out more, it revealed a new geo-political map of Afghanistan: the whole country looked like a gigantic, yellow-striped parking lot and the names of all its cities were replaced by the Golden Arches of McDonald's. The e-joke seems to be the perfect condensation of Friedman's 'Golden Arches Theory of Conflict Prevention'— if only Afghanistan had a McDonald's, it could have prevented a war.

Now given that the first target of September 11 was the World Trade Center, an unmistakeable emblem of global economic expansion, it would not take much brainstorming to conclude that opposition to globalisation is the prime motive behind the terrorist attacks. Since September 11, it's a belief that has found favour and been echoed by many, perhaps too many, commentators.[9] Lately the routine manner by which globalisation is mentioned in the same breath as September 11—no matter whether globalisation is given negative or positive inflexions—has made them hopelessly entangled.

But are they? Perhaps of greater surprise for the reader would be to claim that this book is not about globalisation per se. In other words, could it be possible that the e-joke is indicative of the extent to which globalisation has gripped and shaped the imagination of the West, rather than a telescoped image of the true state of affairs in the world today?

One of the few commentators to offer a corrective view on recent events has been Noam Chomsky, who has argued globalisation is a convenient excuse for the US and many other Western countries. It is worthwhile quoting Chomsky at some length:

> [T]he *Wall Street Journal* reported attitudes of rich and privileged Egyptians who were at a McDonald's restaurant wearing stylish American clothes, etc., and who were bitterly critical of the US for objective reasons of policy, which are well-known to those who wish to know: they had a report a few days earlier on attitudes of wealthy and privileged people in the region, all pro-American, and harshly critical of US policies. Is that concern over 'globalisation', McDonald's and jeans?[10]

The issue of globalisation is first of all an issue over the *idea* of globalisation, a very powerful idea of course, one we've too quickly embraced, can be read into anything, sometimes unknowingly, and often appears to inappropriately condition our perspective on things. This is not to say that globalisation is a complete fiction, without disastrous or beneficial effects on cultures and economies all over the world. But against the backdrop of a war between a McDonald's country and a non-McDonald's country, in the West the idea of globalisation tends to leave unsaid that which should be spoken.

Planet Hollywood?

The greatest danger of globalisation, certainly as it regards film-makers in this country—actually the film-makers of other countries including America— has been unknowingly best summed up by Thomas Friedman: 'For all I know, I have eaten McDonald's burgers and fries in more countries in the world than anyone, and I can testify that *they all really do taste the same.*'[11] Today it is quite conceivable that *Planet Hollywood* is not merely the name of a restaurant chain owned by a small group of Hollywood's A-list actors, but the metaphor for a way of life that is deeply felt by the local film community and tempers the make up our films. Admittedly it is a way of life that has brought forth a mixed bag of welcomed benefits—greater employment opportunities, better technology, more skills and expertise, and of course more money. Yet the accelerated pace at which these benefits arrived or were embraced in this country has also stirred up unexpected fears from all corners of the film industry.

At the 1999 Australian Film Institute Awards a 'war' of sorts was enacted when Bryan Brown stepped up on stage to receive a Best Supporting Actor award for his role as Pando in Gregor Jordan's *Two Hands* (1999). His acceptance speech derided the official opening of Fox Studios in Sydney, which had happened a week earlier, describing the event as a celebration of American film culture and of little significance to Australia. He then went on to laud a number of performers who had contributed to Australian cinema as well as to the identity of the nation. Brown's speech gave rise to a counter-response from Russell Crowe, who was something of an overseas guest, having flown in from between film commitments in the US to present awards at the ceremony. Crowe responded that Australian performers who crossed the Pacific Ocean to Los Angeles were no less Australian for having done so, suggesting instead that such crossings signal the varied international interests in and of the local film industry.

The incident reminds us of a humorous little Chinese tale about two men wanting to form a partnership to produce rice wine. One says to the other, 'You provide the rice and I'll supply the water.' The second man asks, 'But if all the rice comes from me, how do we divide the finished product?' The first man, who made the proposal to begin with, thinks a moment and then says, 'I'll be absolutely fair about the whole thing. When the wine is finished, each gets back exactly what he put in—I'll siphon off the liquid and you can keep the rest.'[12]

Like Brown, many in the industry believe globalisation *in the end* siphons off our identity and therefore leaves us with an unequal say in determining our culture. But for those like Crowe, *at root* globalisation means a welling-up of resources that maintain and foster the diversity of Australian film culture.

If the metaphors of the Lexus and the olive tree were this clear-cut, and if their opponents were seemingly equally balanced, then there wouldn't be much of a problem. Neither our feelings of distress nor wonder would be as profound and irresolute as they are experienced in today's world. This is because the Lexus, or globalisation, does not draw a dividing line nor does it seek balance; it is pervasive.

In a section of our first volume, *Second Take*, titled 'What Price, Hollywood?' we wrote: 'From its very beginning the Australian film industry has had, inevitably, to turn its face towards the mecca of movie-making,

Hollywood—and this is true even when facing in the opposite direction'.[13] The latter clause suggests that even if a film-maker deliberately chooses to make a non-Hollywood film, he or she must look towards Hollywood and is still defined by Hollywood. There is no escape because their *otherness* is characterised by a negative relation to Hollywood.

Thus the image of one side against another might be an illusion that merely conceals the schizophrenic condition in which the Australian film industry finds itself. In this instance film-makers are the servants of two gods, and placed in the disorienting position of having to obey conflicting rules. If you do not globalise, you perish; globalise and you perish just the same— and that choice is ever shifting.

Third Take is the second volume in a series that opened with *Second Take*. Revisiting many of the articles and interviews of *Second Take* today, it should be to no one's surprise that the seeds of this present volume were planted in the first. *Third Take* only slightly mitigates, but deepens the concerns of the other by taking globalisation as a fine thematic thread that weaves its way from start to finish. The articles and conversations that follow present a 'war' that gets played out between the lines and in the margins of the authors' thoughts set on paper. At face value Australian film-makers may not directly confront the issues of globalisation as, say, environmentalists or trade unions would on the steps of Parliament House in Canberra, though they still face its challenges daily. How they face the challenges is expressed in the type of films they choose or wish to make, or are forced to make, in their working methods, in how they deal with funding bodies or studios, in the tactics they use to get a distribution deal, in the very identities film-makers present of themselves, which, it has to be remembered, are never only in and of them-selves, they are always in relation to the *other*.

PART I

CUT! HOW WAS IT FOR YOU?

John Seale and Don McAlpine are two of the most seasoned and influential cinematographers to emerge out of the Australian film renaissance of the 1970s.

The pieces that follow chart similar career paths from humble beginnings at the Australian Broadcasting Corporation (ABC), through their personal experiences working in a buoyant local film industry in the 1970s and 1980s, on to the present day, working exclusively on Hollywood productions, or what is also termed the international film arena. Their paths raise a complexity of issues, not least of which are what happens to the development of one's work when situated within a cultural context different from your own, and how does one evaluate the original culture when conditioned from afar? Both Seale and McAlpine seem to suggest that in the current globalised world the Australian cinema is like a satellite industry, in that it becomes a training ground for launching oneself into the international film market.

Selling nuts and bolts: an interview with Don McAlpine

Raffaele Caputo

Let's start with a simple question: what do you consider to be the role of the cinematographer?

That is a simple question and there's a very simple answer: the role is basically to photograph the film. But the old cliché that you are the 'eyes of the director' is only partly true; you have to be more than another set of eyes if you are going to survive in this industry. A director of photography (DOP) is an interpreter who approaches film as though it is a foreign language and translates the scriptwriter's and director's hopes into a language the audience can understand. Every definition must be a simplification by nature, and that's cinematography in a nutshell.

Career-wise, however, what I normally do is assess the type of director I'll be working with. They've all become directors for different reasons, some because they are great scriptwriters, some because they're infatuated with the technicality of film, others because their great love is the performance of actors, and others for a combination of those reasons. What I do then is to look for where the gaps are. For example, if a director is technically oriented and not much involved in supporting the actors, then I will try to give greater support to the area of performance. That situation is very rare and can be a dangerous game to play, but sometimes I have to do it.

A lot of work comes to me from the fact that I work very well with writer-directors. They are a pretty odd lot because they come out of the world of literature and usually they are visually illiterate. They've read books about

11

the camera but they genuinely do not understand the camera or what I might be talking about. I'm therefore given an incredible freedom, but also obligation to actually teach the director what the camera can do for interpreting the story. I've come to realise that I've worked with too many writer-directors because of the fact that I'm paid a lot of money to do that work.

Do you mean you actually feel the greater responsibility for the film?

No. For me the poor old director is my boss and has the greater responsibility. He or she is the person I'm working for and whom I'm trying to really please. I'm number two on the ladder when the film is shooting. When the film moves into areas like editing, I have a very minor role to play or I just vanish. In pre-production I have a stronger part, but that phase is mostly the work of the production designer, whom I have to watch closely to make sure what they do is best for photographing. But once shooting starts, the director is number one and I'm number two.

To what extent have you supported a performance?

I have had the occasion where I've approached an actor and said very subtly, 'Why don't you play the scene a bit flatter, just let it die a little in the next take and I think it might work a lot better on camera.' That's the sort of support I tend to give to a performance, which is what a good director does with his actors anyway. I've watched some really good directors at work over the years and have seen them get great performances even out of bad actors. I've learnt from those experiences, and when I make suggestions I use my intuition because I'm also politically aware of the dangerous path I'm walking along.

In a normal situation I always keep a distance from the actors because getting involved can be a real trap and it's where a lot of good DOPs have gone down the drain. They get too close and get dragged into their world, which is a world that's out of this world. Most actors live in a world that's a little beyond where I live and so I am very aware of not crossing over the line. I'm very friendly and very cooperative when doing the work, but when the day's work is finished I deliberately avoid invitations because you can get distracted from what you're being paid to do.

Let's go to the start of your career at the Australian Broadcasting Commission (ABC) and at the Commonwealth Film Unit (now Film Australia). What do you remember of those years?

Lots of beer drinking! [Laughs]

I started as a stringer for the ABC while I was still a schoolteacher in a little town in New South Wales. The Department of Education, via the headmaster, pointed out I was in breach of my contract as a teacher by taking outside work. When I told this to the ABC, they offered me a job and I jumped at the chance. The pay was less money but I made it up fairly quickly by working overtime. I was an assistant cameraman with ABC Television News and I shot a lot of material for very early programs like *Four Corners* (1961–), *This Day Tonight* (1957–78), and *Weekend Magazine* (c. 1950s–1970s). Then eventually I got a job at Film Australia. I went there because they used 35 mm cameras. It was a technical fascination that took me over there, but I must admit Film Australia is where I had something like an epiphany or revelation: film could do more than report on events, it could be an art form. While working on documentaries with people like Peter Weir and many other talented directors, I discovered that film could be a very powerful emotional tool.

It seems quite a number of now-established names went through the ABC and Film Australia, people like Dean Semler, Geoff Burton, and you mentioned Peter Weir. Were the ABC and Film Australia the only games in town?

To a degree they probably still are. Basically we were all of one family and a very incestuous group because most of us had our 'birth' at the ABC. Peter Weir didn't, he started at Film Australia as far as I can remember. John Seale used to be my driver-assistant when I was at the ABC—and that's when I was an assistant cameraman! I was actually a cameraman for only a short time at the ABC before I moved on. Then after a couple of years at Film Australia I was made chief cameraman in charge of about eight cameramen, and Dean Semler was the first guy I appointed when a vacancy came up. He was a great talent then and he's a great talent now.

Could you see then these people becoming film-makers of note?

It's amazing the number of talented people I worked with who haven't become a 'Peter Weir'. I'm just using Peter as an example here, but what's interesting to me when I look back is the number of 'Peter Weir' types— one wouldn't have been able to distinguish between Peter and them. I can remember so many directors, cameramen and editors who had great talent but for some reason never made it. I guess one can put it down to personality. They may have made it in another career; I don't know what happened to them. But being self-centred—as we all are in this business—if you don't make it in the film industry then you haven't made it.

Don McAlpine on the set of The Time Machine

What about yourself?

It's very hard to look at myself. I can much more easily look at other people and evaluate their careers. Not many, but some of the people I worked with at Film Australia obviously had a killer instinct. Persistence is perhaps the better term because failure over a five-year period does deter a few people, and when I say 'Peter Weir' types, I'm meaning Peter Weir as I knew him back then. Peter has developed as a film-maker and it has been his persistence—and the opportunities that have come his way because of his persistence—that has aided his development.

With regard to my career, luck has had a lot to do with it—no two ways about it. Now let me tell you about a little bit of luck I had. I basically got to shoot my first big American film, *The Tempest* (1982), because of an odd circumstance: *'Breaker' Morant* (1980), *The Getting of Wisdom* (1977) and *My Brilliant Career* (1979), three films I'd shot, all came to be released in New York over a one-month period. A New York film critic eventually looked at these films and discovered I was one of the connecting links, and these were films that had quite an impact on American audiences. Paul Mazursky[1] was looking for a DOP at the time and a woman in his office said to him, 'Have you seen the films this Australian guy has shot and that people are

14

talking about?' Mazursky said, 'No, I've never heard of him.' But on that same day from two o'clock in the afternoon through to midnight he managed to watch all three films. He rang me at three o'clock in the morning Australian time—Mazursky is a Jewish New Yorker and has got no idea that the world is round and that the sun goes down on the other half. [Laughs]

Anyway, I was pretty drowsy when I took the call but I was clever enough to say, 'Paul, I'm thrilled that you've called, but it's three o'clock in the morning, why don't you ring back in a quarter of an hour when I've had a coffee.' I didn't really have too much of an idea of who he was, so I did have a coffee really quickly—I used to drink instant coffee in those days—got the film books out and had a little look at who this Paul Mazursky guy was. The outcome is that Paul and I did four films together. That's the sort of luck I'm talking about, and the kind of break people need to get in this industry. If those three films had maybe just drifted into New York, then who knows what might have happened? I might be back at school teaching physical education.

Unlike today, was there a luxury and freedom at the ABC to go out and shoot thousands of feet of film, allowing you to experiment and to 'make your bones', so to speak?

Yes and no. Like anywhere else I had a job to do at the ABC. However, even as an assistant cameraman I was allowed to shoot material for broadcast. For instance, when the ABC ran out of cameramen I would be handed a little hand-held, clockwork-motor camera, a 16 mm Bell & Howell with three lenses on the front, I'd be given a duty sheet from the newsroom, and they'd say, 'You're going to be allowed seventeen seconds on the news and you've got fifty feet of film to shoot the story.' It was the perfect teaching assignment because one had to visually construct the whole story and virtually edit the shots in your mind before you actually did it. The real buzz was when you made a good twenty-one-second story even though they only gave you seventeen seconds. Then, of course, you were heartbroken when they used only five seconds, but that's the way it was.

I never really sensed any excess of freedom. Maybe that happened after I'd left. I have a terrible feeling we were pretty conscientious about what we had to do. I can remember only one stupid thing we'd do when we suffered some abuse from management. We used to play a game with 16 mm film: going along in a car at 60 mph we'd have a competition to see who could get the most film to stream out from the windows. [Laughs]

Cut! How was it for you?

Around this point in your career you went to Vietnam during the war and shot a documentary.

That was for a *Four Corners* story and it was a very unusual thing to do for television, and *Four Corners* was a great program back in those days. I went over to Vietnam a couple of times with *Four Corners*, but I had no great wish to keep going back. The really frightful part about being there during the conflict was that you never knew who the enemy were. It could have been the Vietnamese soldiers walking alongside of you who could very quickly change sides. It wasn't a nice place to be.

You also took lessons in Italian. Can you explain why?

There was no film industry in Australia when I was with the ABC and it occurred to me that if I wanted to get involved in film I couldn't go to America because I wouldn't have been able to get a work permit, especially not at that stage in my career. The only place that I thought would be acceptable and would allow me to work was Italy, and so I thought of getting over there and working on those spaghetti westerns, probably starting out as an assistant cameraman or focus-puller. With that in mind I had about four or five lessons in Italian, but then the ABC sent me to one of the four corners of the world and that idea just collapsed. I was trying to find some way to move on from where I was in the industry. Not that I minded what I was doing at the time, I really enjoyed working in television—I guess it was a young man's desperation to move on. It wasn't until I got to Film Australia that I really caught on to the idea of film as not so much a technical challenge as a form of expression. So my wanting to go to Italy wasn't because of a burning creative desire, it was a career hope.

Though you must have admired Italian cinema, particularly popular Italian cinema, to even consider a way of working in their industry?

Absolutely, I was very admiring of their films. And when I think back, the Italians had the most interesting commercial cinema around at that point in time. There wasn't much coming out of America that was as challenging as Italian cinema—and there still isn't.

What inspired you to get into film-making in the first place?

Do you know what? I really do not know. I can remember getting electrocuted at the age of eleven while wiring my own darkroom—that may have had something to do with it. [Laughs] And I was exhibiting stills by the time I was sixteen years old. I guess I was a very keen still photographer and that grew into a fascination with motion pictures, just the pure fact that one could record a story on film.

I should also mention that I did a Diploma in Physical Education and when I started teaching I realised the movie camera—an 8 mm camera first of all—was a great teaching aid. I used to make little 8 mm loops of gymnasium activities and had them projected on the gym wall while I supervised six other activities. But I cannot remember having the grand ambition to be a James Wong Howe, for instance. Each step I've made in my career has been the jumping of a hurdle. When I leaped over one hurdle then there would be another one to jump. I've been jumping hurdles all my life—although there haven't been many in the last few years.

You weren't a film buff or scholar?

No. I've always liked the movies but I was certainly never an academic student of film. I admire people that are and I've learnt a lot from them, but film scholarship is not for me a satisfying study. I've never had a formal lesson in film-making or communications and I've probably been to eight universities in my life. Never to receive lessons, only to give them.

It's hard for young people to believe but there was no such thing as a film school when I started out. They just didn't exist in this country, and not in many other places in the world either. Not to my knowledge, anyway. The first time anything carried the stamp of a school in film-making was when the Australian Film and Television School started, and I can remember that was considered a real phenomenon in those days. What is a little disconcerting now is when I realise there are about 200 to 500 students graduating each year in film or communications. Where can they all be absorbed? That's a bigger question. It puzzles my mind a bit.

Let's move on to the 1970s and your association with Bruce Beresford. How did you meet Beresford?

I was chief cameraman at Film Australia by the time I met Bruce. The line producer on *The Adventures of Barry McKenzie* (1972), Richard Brennan, was dispatched to ask me who on my staff could shoot a feature film. There hadn't been any feature films shot by Australians in ages, probably since *Sons of Matthew* (1949) or *Jedda* (1955). I recommended three guys to Richard and then went and pulled out a few dramatic documentaries they'd made about foot-and-mouth disease or something along those lines. I gave those films to Richard and he came back about three days later. I still hadn't met

Bruce by this stage, and Richard said, 'Bruce has looked at all of those films, but he's seen a documentary you've filmed called *No Roses for Michael* (1970).' Chris McGill directed the film and it's about drugs, which were beginning to become a noticeable problem in Australia at that time. Anyway, Richard went on to say that Bruce would very much like to consider me, but thought I wouldn't leave my cushy government job at Film Australia. I said, 'Richard, you're standing in the doorway, that's a dangerous place to be.' Two weeks later I was off to England to shoot *The Adventures of Barry McKenzie*. That was my first feature film and it was a wonderful experience because I felt like I was inventing everything, but of course I eventually found out it had all been invented already.

As a little point of interest, on *Barry McKenzie* I got paid an eighth of what I get paid for living allowances now. [Laughs]

Hadn't there been a string of Australian film comedies just prior to Barry McKenzie?

Actually there was *Barry McKenzie* and *Stork* (1971), and I think *Stork* was the first one to be released. These two films were actually the precursors to the successful Australian cinema of the 1970s. There were a number of other films around but none made it to the cinema screen, whereas *Stork* and *Barry McKenzie* had massive financial success. Maybe critically they lacked a little. [Laughs]

In the past Beresford has distanced himself from The Adventures of Barry McKenzie *and the sequel,* Barry McKenzie Holds His Own *(1974). How do you feel about those two films?*

I'm very proud of them. Bruce did distance himself a little, but without them we wouldn't have made *'Breaker' Morant* and *The Getting of Wisdom* and *The Club* (1976) and so on. We ended up doing eleven films together and I think that's a bit of a world record for an association between a director and a DOP. Eventually we got to the stage where we didn't talk to each other, not because we had nothing to say but because we sort of understood what each was expected to do and we just did it.

Why did that association come to an end?

The honest truth is that I eventually outpriced myself. As I got more and more into bigger-budgeted films I couldn't afford to work with Bruce. That's how our association really ended, apart from the fact that our partnership wasn't a marriage and we both felt we'd done enough.

You've not come close to matching that number of films with any other director?

No. I did four films with Paul Mazursky, and I've done two or three films here or there with a few other directors. Unless a director has something genuinely new, doing repeat films can be wonderful but not very rewarding.

Do you feel you will ever work with Beresford again?

'Never' is a word one should never use. If there were a project that intrigued me then, yes, we'd probably work together. Maybe because we've had such a long break from each other it would be fun again. But we just worked too long together, and from my point of view I think a long association can, after a while, destroy the creative process a bit.

Many of the 1970s generation talk about those early days with great excitement and pride, when one was grateful not only to be working but also to be enjoying the whole experience.

Yes, that's spot on. Now I have the luxury and the problem of getting a script, reading it and saying, 'Oh no, I don't want to do this.' In those days if someone offered me a script, I shot it! There wasn't much work around, you weren't paid much, and so you had to keep working. If I wasn't doing a feature film then I had to shoot documentaries and commercials to survive. Now I can do a feature film every year and live happily ever after.

There was definitely an excitement, and a nationalistic streak to our films. I don't know if many people realise it but the Australian film industry in the first ten or so years—considering the amount of money invested into the films—was the greatest world promotion Australia ever had. One of the biggest problems for Australia back in those days was, first of all, that nobody knew too clearly where Australia was located and, second, Australia was considered to be just one big sheep station. One still comes across a bit of that attitude in certain parts of the world, but before the film industry was kick-started, the rest of the world didn't respond to the concept of Australia having any other type of industry, or even having a culture approximating Western civilisation. The films changed those perceptions, and subsidising a film industry was a deliberate move by then Prime Minister John Gorton, which was later carried through by Gough Whitlam. Both Prime Ministers could foresee the financial kickback to the country from the film industry.

At Film Australia, for instance, we spent an awful lot of time and money doing short film-reports on Australian industry and tourism generally that would be screened in cinemas all over the world. What these short films were trying to say is what the feature films actually did say—that Australia was more than a giant sheep station, that it was a vibrant, Western cultural identity tucked away just south of Asia. The film push was terribly important for a guy who was just selling nuts and bolts to, say, a Spanish company. They would say, 'You come from Australia? Oh yes, we've seen the films, and you can make nuts and bolts.' Before that time the attitude was, 'What do you mean nuts and bolts from a sheep farm?' That's a simplification of things, of course. But it's true that the identity of Australia was more strongly established in the world by the film industry, and that's the proudest claim I can make for the work I was involved in back then.

It's ironic that John Gorton appears in The Club, *though the film is very pro-Labor.*

Yes, but it's a Williamson script. I'm sure he has changed a little—like all of us. [Laughs]

Of the films you've shot in America, a favourite is your first, The Tempest, *and one of the reasons is because it has a string of great character actors all in the one film—John Cassavetes, Gina Rowlands, James Hardin, Paul Stewart and Vittorio Gassman. Can you tell us about working on that film?*

Well, they had you in mind when they cast the film. [Laughs]

Seriously, it's a film that meant a lot to me too, because it was my first big American adventure. We shot first in New York, then we moved off to Greece, and we finally did a lot of stuff at the Cinècitta studios in Rome. If you remember the film, there is a line that John Cassavetes screams, 'Show me the magic!' Well, for Paul Mazursky that line is his life's catch-cry. He wanted magic all the time. I don't think he knows what magic is, but he does have some idea of how to get it.

Paul was one of the writer-directors I talked about earlier. The weird thing is that I guided him over the first film, basically ran a camera course, but by our fourth film together I was smiling a lot because Paul was coming over and telling me all the stuff I had told him in the beginning. He was a very up-student and did indeed develop a good visual sense over the four films. I like to think that one can actually see a progression of his accepting of film as a visual medium.

John Cassavetes was not only a great actor, he was also a great director and there are moments in that film that look like they have been lifted from one of his films. Were you at all aware of Cassavetes as a film-maker in his own right?

I knew he was a director and although his films personally intrigued me, I wasn't much in love with them at that point. Maybe if I saw them now I'd change my mind. But Cassavetes certainly didn't offer any advice on how to direct or shoot any of the scenes in *The Tempest*. He was a very centred actor and he took no part at all in the structure of the film.

There is a scene sequence near the end of The Tempest *which is a single shot that lasts approximately six to seven minutes, with the camera continually moving up and down and characters coming in and going out of frame. How did you achieve that shot?*

That shot was done at Cinècitta, although we actually cheated. If you look closely you'll notice there's an edit and so the sequence is composed of two shots, not one. We started the sequence downstairs outside a villa where I think there is some father and son business going on at that point; we crane up and the camera goes over a wall, and then we repeat the move and that was the first piece. Then in the second part, which is about four minutes long, the camera moves upstairs and looks through the window of a room and from then on it's a whole continuous boom shot that goes right out into a garden. The sequence was totally choreographed, plotted and shot; we used a massive truck-mounted crane that we had to elevate about three metres off the studio floor. For most films if you get two minutes in the can you are doing well. The theory behind those types of shots is that if you can spend two days devoting a lot of time to rehearsal and preparation and be ahead of schedule, then that's film in the can.

Another favourite is Predator (1987) *with Arnold Schwarzenegger.*

Arnold is a great character. John McTiernan was the director on *Predator*, and I can remember there had been a rewrite of the script and Arnold came in one morning waving the pages at John, saying, 'John, there are four words here, I do three!' [Laughs] *Predator* was a wonderful film to work on, and I think it's a special film in terms of the evolution of the action/science fiction genre.

An interesting story is that we shot *Predator* over an incredible hiatus. Joel Silver was the producer and I remember the day he took me to see the monster suit, which he was very proud of. We were in Mexico at that stage and the suit had just been flown in from the States and it was hanging up in a motel room, which was not the most glamorous way to present it. When I saw the suit I said, 'I'm sorry, Joel, but it just looks like a big rat to me.' I knew he was very upset because his knee started to shake—his knee always shakes whenever he gets nervous. Anyway, we shot with that suit and then the studio saw the rushes and—I say this genuinely—sent back a note that read, 'It looks like a big rat!' They canned the film right away and the whole cast and crew were pulled out of Mexico in two days. The philosophy behind the studio's decision was that the film wasn't going to work if that big rat suit was the monster, and so they got John to come back to the States, edit all the material we'd shot, which was about 70 per cent of the film, and present it to them. On the basis of that edit the studio would then decide how much money they were prepared to invest in a new monster. Almost a year later we reassembled in Mexico and finished the film.

Another interesting fact about *Predator* is that I shot the film with zero lighting. You simply cannot put a light up in dense jungle because all that you are doing is lighting the jungle immediately in front of the camera. It looks so incredibly false, so I shot the whole film in the jungle with available light, which really did end up suiting the film—necessity showed me the direction to take.

As a side issue, Joel Silver is one of the greatest producers in Hollywood and possibly the world's greatest liar. He would come up to me and we'd have a discussion and I'd say, 'Joel, you've told me three supposed facts and I'm totally confused because normally you tell two and so I know one's a lie and one's the truth and I can work it out. But with three I can't quite get the equation.' He'd just laugh at that. Joel will lie about anything and everything to achieve his aim. Once you know this, however, you just accept it because it seems to work.

You've worked with Harrison Ford on Patriot Games *(1992) and* Clear and Present Danger *(1995).*

I've worked with two Harrison Fords. On the first film, *Patriot Games*, he was great and we got on really well together. On many a night shoot around 3.00 a.m., he'd come over to me and say, 'Oh, you Australians drink tea, don't you?' He'd hand me a cup and of course it was full of malt whiskey, which at that hour does one a world of good. On the second film, *Clear and Present Danger*, it was quite a sad situation. He seemed to have lost some of his enthusiasm for the process. Like us all, he was having a really bad patch.

The reality of Hollywood as it relates to me was reinforced at a dinner I had with Mace Neufeld, the producer of *Clear and Present Danger*, and the director, Phil Noyce. Phil was having some difficulties—that's the best way to put it—with Harrison, and the problems were being aired, argued and discussed back and forth over the dinner table. Eventually, Mace Neufeld, an old, very gentlemanly type, a fellow I really do like, leaned over and said, 'Phil, you've got to understand one thing. I can finish the film without you, I can't finish it without Harrison.' That's Hollywood, that's the truth of it.

The studio had $70 million invested in the star; if the problems were to fall to a choice between the director and the star, then Phil became expendable.

But when working with a star of Harrison's stature one comes to realise there is something magical about their personality. I think their work is made up of craft and gift. The gift is something I can probably identify and judge immediately, yet the craft is something I see the result of but do not know how that gets them to the point of becoming a star. I'm sure they all get there in a million different ways. Some of them are bad ways, some of them are good ways, but they get there.

And what's it like working with Phil Noyce?

Phil is great, and mad as a proverbial cut snake. One day I was sitting with Phil and his arms were covered with nicotine patches. He was trying to give up smoking, but at about four o'clock in the afternoon he just snatches a cigarette out of someone's mouth and starts puffing away. He was hopeless—but this is a neurotic business. I enjoy working with Phil immensely. We haven't been able to get back together since *Clear and Present Danger,* but I'm sure we will one day. We're very good friends.

Is it true that in a day's shoot he will spend most of the day shooting a third of it and then try to cram the rest of it into the last few hours?

All directors sometimes suffer from a condition that was best described by a dear old cameraman I used to assist: 'A cameraman who never made a shot never made a mistake.' That's true of nervous directors, especially early in the morning when they are trying to decide which way the day should go. A lot of the time you do find that you do a fraction of the work in the first half of the time available and the bulk of it in the second half when panic has set in. Phil would sometimes do anything to avoid doing a shot, but it's been worse with other directors.

Is The Man Without a Face *(1993) the first time you had worked with Mel Gibson?*

Yes, Mel directed and starred in that film. I found him quite good as a director, obviously far more concerned with performance than most other directors, but still he had quite a vision of what he wanted. He had a vision but no real concept of how to achieve it, which I guess is why he asked me to do it.

Was there any intention of continuing the association on Braveheart *(1999)?*

Yes, there was. The interesting thing is that I was at a dinner with Mel about a month or two before he started *Braveheart* and he was virtually making noises that he wanted me to shoot the film. Then he obviously changed his mind, and for what reason I've never found out. But that's the nature of this business.

You've worked with some American directors who could almost be described as old school— apart from Paul Mazursky, there was Alan J. Pakula and Martin Ritt.[2]

The film I did with Marty Ritt, *Stanley & Iris* (1990), I think was his last film. He was not well at that stage in his career. He was a diabetic, which is what finally killed him. But working with Ritt was a great personal experience if not a cinematic one, because Ritt was a living piece of history. My greatest regret is that I didn't have a tape recorder rolling all the time, because the stories he told me are just amazing, about working with Paul Newman, and about the McCarthyite era when he was blacklisted from working in television.[3]

Alan was sufficiently removed from that period to have avoided the communist witch-hunt. He was a wonderful gentleman who came from a poor background, and he always seemed to be trying to come to terms with his background in some way. Which seemed to me to be weird, but still he was a great guy to work with.

Paul Mazursky, of course, was my American mentor. He is the guy who really got me established in Hollywood as an A-grade cinematographer. Baz Luhrmann is a little bit like Paul in as much as they have a similar war cry: 'Show me the magic!' It's what I had to do with Paul and that's what I have to do with Baz too. I think Paul was using that line way before we made *The Tempest*. You've got to produce magic with most directors anyway, but Paul would demand it.

You spoke before of shooting Predator *solely with natural light. As a personal rule, do you prefer using whatever there is of available light before you actually start to light a scene?*

Not as a rule, there's no rule. On *Moulin Rouge* (2001), for example, there was no available light because all of it was shot in the studio. It depends on the story you're telling—some films require glamour, some require enhancement in the dramatic sense, others the realism of naturalistic lighting or no lighting. To me good storytelling is telling a believable lie, but if the lighting is false the audience senses that straight away and will not believe in the story. Relying on available light is often part of a basic desperation philosophy. That is, if you cannot find any dramatic motivation for the lighting, then fall back on nature.

Do you see big differences in terms of working approaches between what you do in the States and what you do here?

Well, *Moulin Rouge* is an American film in the sense that Fox has invested the money and, to be blunt, the film has been made in a way that an Australian audience is considered peripheral to its success. It's made for a world audience. You cannot make a film for the amount of money invested in *Moulin Rouge* and hope it's going to be made only for an Australian audience and still be a success.

However, when I work in America I do sense that certain obligations or limitations are placed upon me. If one looked at American films without the sound and credits, most of the time one can sense they are American. That's because there are unwritten laws, a certain film grammar or language that has been established and become acceptable in the States. If you don't understand that you will not work in America for long. It's highly limiting, there are no two ways about it. But so too is working in Australia—one is limited by finances, for example. Having said that, however, ignorance is a great source of freedom. That's almost universal when you think about it. When film-makers really understand and analyse a problem, they then have a way of restricting what they do; but you have great freedom whenever you don't really understand what you're supposed to do.

Okay, let me put to you a related question. When the guests arrive at the start of Don's Party *(1976), for example, Don (John Hargreaves) has to go to open the door four or five times and yet there's not one shot that's repeated. He essentially performs the same action but from so many different angles and lengths. Now I've noticed something similar happening in a string of American films you've shot, where, say, in a dialogue scene between two characters one might expect a conventional shot–reverse shot situation, you rarely go in tight and again each shot is always at a different angle and focal length.*

To me that's the fundamental difference between the extravagance of film as opposed to television. In television you just set up the camera and the direction would be something like, 'Okay, Charlie, open the door for Fred and say, "Hello, Fred". And, Fred, you say, "Hello, Charlie".' That would be done for every other character that arrives and then one would shoot the farewells in the same shooting sequence. That's often the case when working in television or shooting high-pressure work, but the situations you are talking about are examples of the indulgence we allow or demand of ourselves in cinema. The rules I'm talking about are unwritten and they're felt. A simple explanation of what goes on is that it's almost impossible to get a rear, extreme low- and wide-angle shot in an American film. That's a simplistic answer.

There are exceptions to the rules and in exceptional scenes you can get away with bending the rules. But on day-to-day stuff one has to work down a reasonably narrow visual path. I cannot explain it much more than that because it's something I feel rather than think about.

Are the limitations partly a consequence of the fact that in Hollywood a DOP is rarely allowed to operate the camera, which can create a tenuous relationship between the camera operator and the DOP?

Not necessarily, and it depends on the type of battle you are fighting. If you are fighting a battle in which you are sure that the enemy is not going to arrive at your back all of a sudden, then you can operate the camera. But generally on American films, where one never has that security, I have to be like a general standing on a hill, keeping my eyes open and looking in all directions for where problems are coming from. And to keep the army simile going, the operator has to be the captain down in the midst of the battle.

Moreover, communication between the DOP and the camera operator has become more solid now because the authority of the operator has been castrated to a degree by the video-split. I just sit there all day watching minutely what the operator is doing, suggesting and correcting, and the operator soon gets into the pattern of my work and soon gets a feeling for what the director is on about. Otherwise we get another operator. This is a business in which you do not fool about—nobody has a right to a job on a film.

To what extent do you rely on the video-split?

For me the video-split is only a device for the framing. That is, to check that the operator is including and excluding what needs to be included and excluded in a shot. That's a massive simplification of the video-split, but I essentially use it for the framing, not for the lighting or the performance or anything of that nature.

Do you still operate?

I still operate on a lot of hand-held work because it's always too late to tell an operator what to do. If I have to tell them, then I've lost it. Anyway, there are few operators who can operate a Don McAlpine hand-held shot as well as Don McAlpine—and that's a bit of truth. That's why I chose to do most of the hand-held material on *William Shakespeare's Romeo + Juliet* (1997), which is a fair bit, and so too the hand-held material on *Moulin Rouge*. The big trouble is that I'm sixty-six years old and as I've gotten older the camera gear has gotten heavier. When you have a 15 kg lens on the front of a full 35 mm sound blimp camera, it's a bloody monster and you really know you're working. The weight of the camera gear marks the degree of my limitations nowadays. [Laughs]

How did you get to shoot Romeo + Juliet?

It was quite odd. I was back in Australia at the time and I received a phone call from Baz Luhrmann, who I vaguely knew existed, and he wanted to talk to me about a film. I had no idea what the film was about and because I had no real intention of working back in Australia, I went along to meet him more out of perverse curiosity than job-seeking. I arrived at this little office above a rather sleazy Chinese restaurant, went up the stairs and there was a room filled with a bunch of young, bright people. We all sat around an old kitchen table and Baz started telling me about how he was going to do Shakespeare's *Romeo and Juliet*. Eventually I asked, 'Who is going to do the rewrite?' Baz said, 'We're doing Shakespearean dialogue,' and I said, 'Well, you're losing me!' Basically because Kenneth Branagh had twice considered me for Shakespearean films and, although I admire his work, his films are destined for a very limited audience. Even Branagh's most successful things are just one step above art-house, which is great but not what I really want to do.

Anyway, my meeting with Baz went on and he eventually said, 'On top of that I'm making the film for kids to get them involved in Shakespeare.' I was saying, 'Yeah, yeah, yeah,' in honest disbelief all the way along. Then Baz told me that Fox Studios—who were going to finance the film back then— were prepared to spend money to do a full 35 mm shoot of the scene in the swimming pool. I said to Baz, 'Look, I've been around a little while and I know that's wrong. Shooting an actual scene from the movie brings corruption into the whole system because people will start to judge everything you don't want them to see at this stage, and the script ideas will turn into minor things and it will become much harder to sell your concept.' I then suggested he should shoot a wide selection of bits and pieces of the film on video so that Fox could get some idea of it. I said, 'I'll help you out, I'll shoot the video and you get the best sound recordist you can get to ensure the dialogue is audible.'

So over three days we improvised a whole series of tests under the Anzac Bridge in Sydney, which was under construction then, with Leonardo Di Caprio and a team of very fine Australian actors in the supporting roles. Baz then edited the material in the style that is something like the final film. At that point, not only Fox Studios but I too could see there was something worthwhile, and that's when I genuinely became interested in the film. It was a very slow learning process for me, which turned into a phenomenal experience working with the creative team of Luhrmann and Martin.

Romeo + Juliet begins with a highly choreographed gun duel at a gas station, which looks like a dance sequence rather than action sequence.

Actually, a lot of people have asked why the film starts in that heightened fashion. It's a deliberate ploy, a way of asking the audience whether they are going to come along with us or are going to get up and leave. A few people did get up and leave, but the majority did come along with us on that film. In other words, we wanted to transport the audience to a make-believe world and the way we did it was to shock them into it.

There are many more successful scenes in *Romeo + Juliet* and so much of that success goes back to Catherine Martin's visualisation and the unity of her design throughout the film.

How do you feel about Moulin Rouge?

It's very hard to talk about because I've been so close to it. But I remember when my wife and I had the opportunity to see two rough cuts of the film—which had great slabs missing because they still had to complete the computer-generated material and the sound was not quite right—and she said that you walk out as though you've seen a wonderful live performance rather than a film. That's something I'd partly echo. Cinema normally affects one in a quite different way, but this film is so energetic and lively and the dynamic is so phenomenal that one gets the weird feeling of having watched a live production. I've deluded myself once or twice before, but most times I've picked films that audiences have liked and I'm sure this will be one of them.

How would you compare it with Romeo + Juliet?

Romeo + Juliet was really a rehearsal for *Moulin Rouge*. It is the uncut diamond while *Moulin Rouge* is the polished stone—I hope!

What are the criteria you apply when choosing to do a film?

How close the location is to good restaurants. [Laughs]

The script is probably not the most important factor in whether I choose to do a film or not—the director is. Even if I get a script that seems disjointed, maybe a bit pathetic in plot, if it comes from a director who has told brilliant plot stories then I know that he or she is going to sort out the script's problems. And if the production is far enough advanced that they're casting the talent, I then get a pretty good visualisation of how the actors are going to play their roles and I start to see a reasonably concrete film. That's the way I do it: the combination of those three factors, but my picking order would be the director first, probably talent second, and the script almost always third. That's because the script, although a tangible thing, is also a variable thing, and it's what the director reads in the script that is important, not what a cinematographer reads.

Are there any films you've knocked back that maybe you shouldn't have?

There are stacks of them. The most memorable one is *Terms of Endearment* (1983), which is about the biggest hit I knocked back. But it would be silly for me to worry about the mistakes.

There are no regrets?

None.

Then of the films you've shot, which are your favourites?

That's a bit like talking about your children. I think the most rewarding was *The Getting of Wisdom*. It was the first film after the two *Barry McKenzie* films, which were wonderful things to do, but here we had an emotional story to tell and it felt like I was actually making a real film. *Wisdom* wasn't just a fluke like *Barry McKenzie*, it was a straight, honest, dramatic piece of film-making and a very successful piece, in my opinion. I love that one. *Down and Out in Beverley Hills* (1986) is another favourite, as much for the association as the film itself. Then there's *Romeo + Juliet*, which has now been superseded by *Moulin Rouge*. Until *Moulin Rouge*, *Romeo + Juliet* was maybe not a personal favourite, but certainly a favourite in terms of pure cinematography.

Actually, my wife and I still have *Don's Party* evenings at our place during elections and we screen the film out in the back yard, so I guess that's a favourite film as well.

When I mentioned Cassavetes earlier, I was actually suggesting a little the idea of taking inspiration from other visual sources. For The Fringe Dwellers *(1986)[4] one can be forgiven for thinking immediately of the paintings of Russell Drysdale,[5] particularly when seeing* Justine

Saunders dressed in that heavy coat and period hat on her head because the 'look' is very similar to Drysdale's The Drover's Wife *(1945). Do you take inspiration from other visual mediums?*

In that instance I didn't. I'm actually very loath to borrow and that's because I think it's too restricting. Critics have written my name alongside one great artist after another, which is very flattering but totally wrong. One is affected by everything that happens in one's life and I just went out and saw the story of *The Fringe Dwellers* for what it is, and I believe what you have seen is my interpretation of what is there. The fact that my interpretation happens to be similar to some gentleman who was there before me is somewhat irrelevant. In retrospect I can see what you are saying, but in truth that's not what I happened to see.

The other thing is that as a cinematographer I am incredibly dependent on having a great production designer. Half of the credit I have received throughout my career should rightly go to the production designers I've worked with. I'm very aware of the importance of the production designer's work to the work I have to do, because they are the people who in many ways actually structure a scene. I can place people around the set but the production designer puts up the buildings, the walls, puts in the windows and decorates the set. *Moulin Rouge* is an absolute classic example of the production designer's art. Catherine Martin is unbelievable in her sets and the compulsion to do great work in them is overpowering. I walk onto her sets and I'm motivated way beyond my normal self just because of the magnificence and appropriateness of what she has done. Inspiration is probably too weak a word to attribute to her.

Earlier you essentially attributed getting the job on The Tempest *to a critic who realised the cinematographer as the connecting link between three films. Are you aware of a 'Don McAlpine' style across a variety of films?*

I've toyed with that question for some years and I think I must have some fundamental conditioning that presents a certain degree of style, whatever that may be. But what I really like to think is that I just develop the style based on the script, the director, and the edge the actors give to the story. For me there is certainly some direction or development of those three elements that gives a film its particular style. In other words, maybe I'm more of a chameleon than a stylist. I've consciously avoided ever working on or doing the same sort of film in succession, and what I resent the most is a director referencing other films. Sometimes referencing another film can be a means of communication, but if the director is using the reference as an interpretation of the style the film requires, then the director is really just aping somebody else. That's obviously something I don't like to do and I'm very wary of consciously developing a personal style. I love to just open my mind up. When I recently committed myself to *The Time Machine* (2002), for example, there began a stage in which I opened up my mind and really searched for what the director wanted and what the script called for, and even if I hadn't seen much of the acting work, that stage was simply a process of absorption and a building-up of interpretative ideas.

What kind of preparation would you do on something like The Time Machine, *which has been made twice before, once in 1960 with Rod Taylor and then a 1978 television remake? Would you look at the earlier versions as part of the preparation?*

I will admit I did have a quick look at the Rod Taylor version, basically to avoid unconsciously lifting anything from it. Because it's a film I saw way back when it was first released and it was lodged somewhere in my subconscious, I just wanted to get it out of my mind more than anything else. I've seen it and I've written it off. The television version I've not seen and so it's not a problem.

Perhaps the term style is something that's overused today, because you've pretty much worked through the 'four seasons', so to speak, of film genres, which anyway require different approaches.

Style certainly is a term that is overused today. Phil Noyce sent along quite a witty little note for the Popcorn Taxi evening I had in Sydney, and the point of his note was that I've actually reinvented myself endlessly. He listed all the reinvention processes, saying that I deliberately go along a different tangent every time I do a movie, which is my reason for doing *The Time Machine*.

Do you think you'll ever make an Australian film again?

As I said earlier, I've learnt never to say never. But the reasons for me to make an Australian film are diminishing pretty quickly. First, there are a host of good people shooting here, so why would anyone need a Don McAlpine? Most of the really good directors here come through with their cameramen and they are going to stick together, and so it would have to be an exceptional situation for me to do an Australian film because of where I've been working for most of my career. Inevitably I'd come back unbalanced and bring too much baggage with me.

Of course the other question is that while we can make great films in Australia with Australian themes, we have to remember that the audience is the world. It's hard to rationalise making a very expensive thing like a film for a limited audience. A film like *The Dish* (2000) throws that argument out a bit, yet the exception may prove the rule. I don't think *The Dish* has done well anywhere else but in Australia because it's a good example of a very parochial and fun film with a particular audience in mind. But let's take a film like *'Breaker' Morant*, on the other hand—here is an Australian film with an Australian subject, but it was incredibly successful internationally. *'Breaker' Morant*, or something similar, would now cost $20–$30 million to make and that's virtually saying the film-makers must have an international audience in mind.

I think that what I'm about to say applies to a film like The Dish, *which is that the term 'Australian cinema' has been redefined in a global environment, but it's unclear and somewhat meaningless nowadays, unlike the seventies when the term did have resonance within the wider community because there was a greater sense of identity building at that time.*

I've had this discussion with many people and I think that's wrong. Obviously the first two or three films made in Australia in the seventies were amazing efforts, but I think history has given the period splendour it didn't have. The *Barry McKenzie*s and other films like that were just buy-and-ply and a few years later we had the very basic skills to make good movies. Inevitably, though, I guess all the talent that evolves here will be consumed by the world market.

That's what I'm getting at in a way: the sense of this thing called 'Australian cinema' is 'empty currency' in a global environment. Are we still selling nuts and bolts?

Perhaps, but what's our gladiator friend[6] going to do? Come back here and do what? [Laughs] Or you can look at it this way: the first version of *The Time Machine* had an Australian star and this new version also has an Australian in the starring role, Guy Pearce. What I'm saying is that I think there should always be some sort of backing for new talent in this country, which will evolve with all of its own set of problems, but one always has to remember that the film industry is an international business.

Most people don't agree, but I really believe that filming a US production like *Mission: Impossible II* (M:I2, 2000) in Australia is a plus all around. It has given a lot of work to a lot of people, and crews have developed skills they didn't have before. There was a time when we tried to prevent anyone coming here to make films, but we were just burying our heads in the sand because—and I'll keep emphasising the same point—the film industry is an international business.

More than ever before?

Yes, and it's amazing that Hollywood is doing it. You obviously know how the American film companies came down here and essentially closed down the Australian film industry back in the 1920s and '30s. Well, so far they haven't looked like they are doing that. In fact, there is an awful lot of union pressure in America to get film productions back. Only a little bit of film production is coming here, nothing really of major consequence, but work of considerable consequence is going to Canada. The film unions in America are really driving hard to get government backing or tax breaks to keep production in the States, but they can't get them, particularly not with George W. Bush in power. If the Democrats had had a better run, the unions probably would have got some minor protection.

Early in your career you shot a rather anarchic 16 mm feature called Surrender in Paradise *(1976) in which you also played a name part.*

Oh yes, a character called Raw Meat.

Did you have aspirations of becoming an actor?

No, the whole thing was a bit of fun. I went up to Queensland and a guy came up to me and said, 'I'm the grip. What is it that I do?' [Laughs] It was great! We would all go swimming in the nude at the end of the day and everybody lived happily.

I'm not an artist;
I'm a technician

John Seale

GETTING STARTED

After high school I went up to central Queensland and jackarooed, and it was out there that I first saw fantastic images of the outback. Over eighteen months of pushing sheep around, I thought how terrific it would be to travel the world as a documentary film-maker recording these wonderful corners of the world for people who may never get there. I actually took along a little 8 mm camera to the outback, basically to record the life out there so that my parents could see what I was doing. It was through that little camera and the visuals I saw that I decided to dump everything and head back to Sydney and try to get into film-making. It took me a year to get a job at the Australian Broadcasting Corporation (ABC) and I ended up staying there for seven years.

But I couldn't just roll up and say, 'Hey, I want a job as a cameraman.' My first job at the ABC was actually located in the basement of a Pitt Street building in the stationery department, handing out biros, sharpeners and the like to ABC personnel. After eighteen months in Queensland where it's all sky, to then suddenly go to work in a basement in Sydney was a pretty hard thing to take. Over the years people have often asked me how it is possible to get into the industry and work your way up to a well-respected position. The one word I push at them is perseverance, because even though I was working in a basement, every week I would ring Mr Bert Nicholas, head of cinecamera over at Gore Hill, and ask, 'Have you got a job over

34

there for me yet, Mr Nicholas?' I think it took almost two years before finally he said, 'For God's sake, give that kid a job and get him off my back.' They then sent me to another department, I've forgotten which, but it wasn't much better.

Finally my first opportunity to work with film was in newsreels. Back then the ABC cameramen had drivers and I was one of them. I had to look after the car and make sure we didn't run out of fuel while we were out on assignment. But I also got to do sound and support the camera crew. It was a long ladder to climb but I never look back on my early years at the ABC as a waste of time, because as I climbed the ladder, slow as it was, I managed to be involved in all facets of newsgathering, and that included the likes of straight hard news and *Four Corners*-type documentary.

And most of the ABC cameramen I was working for were old Australian combat cameramen, and I've got to say that they were amazing guys. They constituted the generation of cameramen portrayed in *Newsfront* (1978), which is a wonderful example of how those guys worked. They were glad to be alive and they played everything to the hilt. Newsgathering with those guys was like a war and they taught me to work at high speed, such as pre-setting all of the focuses on a fixed three-lens turret camera. That meant that right in the middle of a take you could swing the lens around and get into a close-up. The editor would later cut out the turret rolling over and only lose about eight frames but suddenly you're back into continuity. Some of the early skills of newsgathering at the ABC have put me in good stead right up to now with *Harry Potter and the Philosopher's Stone* (2001).

It's interesting that quite a number of DOPs came out of documentary and newsgathering. At the ABC, there were Dean Semler, Don McAlpine, Geoff Burton and others. Then there were a lot of other cameramen, such as Russell Boyd, Peter James and David Gribble, who came out of the other newsgathering situations, Cinesound and Movietone News. Newsgathering was a training ground in lieu of the fact that there wasn't any full-fledged feature film movement in Australia at that time. There was only a trickle of feature film production in the late sixties, but as the film industry eventually got the big wheel turning that generation of newsgatherers went on to be the backbone of the Australian cinema renaissance in the 1970s.

CAMERA OPERATING

I must confess that during this time all the other guys of my generation basically hopped straight up to lighting, but I had fallen in love with camera

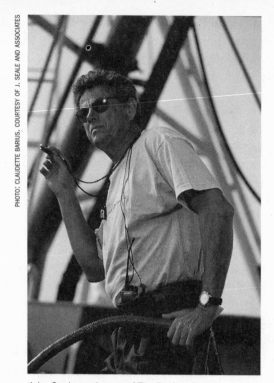

PHOTO: CLAUDETTE BARIUS. COURTESY OF J. SEALE AND ASSOCIATES

John Seale on the set of The Perfect Storm

operating. I found that operating the camera was just the most exciting job ever, and so I stuck with camera operating for about seventeen years. It wasn't until I was suddenly the DOP on a very low-budget film by Brian Trenchard-Smith that I got a real fright.[1]

Back then the light meter wasn't digital; it had a little needle that moved and I couldn't work out what the needle was doing. It wouldn't stop moving and I'd be saying, 'What the heck is going on here? It won't stand still!' I realised I didn't know a thing about lighting and felt pretty silly because here I was having worked seventeen years with the greats of Australian cinematography. They were so calm and cool about it and I was stressing out while I watched this needle do what it wanted to do. I just enjoyed operating so much that it never occurred to me to learn what the light meter was doing.

So I went back to operating the camera and over the next three years and three feature films later, I had learnt what the needle was doing. I closely watched the lighting guys do their job, asked questions that I thought were quite intelligent, and I was ready. By the time *Fatty Finn* (1980) came along

I started to thoroughly enjoy lighting while also operating the camera. I actually continue to operate. I get into a lot of trouble with unions overseas for doing both simultaneously, even to the tune of being fined $50 000. Yet operating is still a very satisfying way for me to make films.

THE DOP'S JOB

Aside from having a good understanding of the craft and the technical side of cinematography, I feel there are a number of aspects that are essential to my doing a good job.

Loyalty

The first and one of the most important roles for a cinematographer is to show loyalty to the film and the director. I'll stand by every word of that. It's all part of the learning process as you get to make different films and work with different people. It was those combat cameramen at the ABC who instilled in me that loyalty to your director, good or bad, is of paramount importance and no matter how hard the film actually is, you are employed to make the film to your utmost ability and never lose sight of quality.

Too many times I've heard on the grapevine that a particular film-in-production is believed to be crap, and yet that film turns out to be a winner. There's a lesson to be learnt there: nobody on set can ever predict how a film will perform until it's finished. Although most of a film's key personnel are assembled on the set, there's at least one key person waiting in the background who hasn't even started to work—the editor. When shooting stops there is still a long way to go before a film is released, and some of the most phenomenal films have come from what happens between a director and the editor in the post-production phase. They can sometimes change the whole concept of the film you thought you had shot. When you know that can happen, I believe there is no way in the world a cameraman, or anyone else on a set, can pass judgement on whether a film is good or not.

Reading the Script

I love to read the script; I think that's essential. Funny things can happen on sets and I feel that if you've read the script, you not only know the characters, you're open to magical things happening for them that you didn't count on. For example, one of the luckiest mistakes of my career happened on *Rain Man* (1988); it's the moment when Dustin Hoffman and Tom Cruise come down an escalator after a montage of them getting ready to go gambling. We were on location in a casino in Las Vegas and I'd not been to the top of the escalator, so I didn't know what was up there. I said to my gaffer, 'Put a lamp up there and bounce it off something to get a top light over their heads so the boys look god-like and full of confidence.' Several minutes later I watched the stand-ins descend the escalator and thought, 'How lucky can I be?' What had happened was that when they were halfway down the escalator, the lamp light hit a very bright piece of steel and caused a flare to appear on their bodies, moving up and over their heads as they descended. The gaffer, who is actually a great gaffer, turned around and said, 'Don't worry about the flare, I'll get rid of that.' I said, 'You get rid of that flare and you are fired—six times!' In that moment the little flare was the best thing that could have happened because here are the boys dressed up and ready to go gambling and it adds a 'stinger': they look like they've been given the Midas touch just as they are about to enter the gaming room.

Communication

Because I've never believed that a DOP can just blast off one production after another with the same style or attitude even, good communication is an all-important part of the job. If you go plunging into a new project with a director you haven't worked with before, you have to spend a lot of time listening and talking to find out where he or she is coming from. And because it's a new script and different director with a different pace and rhythm in mind, a good line of communication with all members of the crew can save your life. Especially when you are moving along very quickly and your brain just doesn't log on properly, you sometimes throw a camera or lamp in the wrong spot but they correct you and make you pull back, the continuity person in particular, to keep the rhythm or flow of the film going.

Speed

On *Rain Man* Dustin Hoffman is quoted as saying, 'This guy John Seale is so fast I don't have time to get out of character.' It's very hard for an actor to stay in character when it might take a couple of hours to set up the next take. An actor might go off and sleep for about an hour and then come back and find they've lost the thread of their role. So, inevitably, an essential part of a cinematographer's role is to work fast and keep the film on schedule.

Part of the reason Australian cinematographers are respected around the world is because they can think on their feet and are not subject to the politics on film sets in America where the atmosphere can become quite paranoid. A lot of people in the film industry believe that with bigger budgets they can be more indulgent. But I disagree with that attitude. You are actually paid reasonably well on international films to keep the film on schedule. That's your job, and for me speed is part and parcel of making a better film.

Technical Independence

There is reliance at all times on technical means—filtration, desaturation, computer or laboratory work—for a film to suddenly change gear photographically. But I found that from *Witness* (1985) onwards, you often do not need to rely on technicalities.

The English Patient (1996), for example, may look like an overly technical film but it really isn't. The film has two stories running alongside, one is set in postwar Italy and the other in the North African desert, which is a memory or flashback. Now the film had to be edited in such a way that we could cut from Italy straight to the desert and back again without having to superimpose any titles like 'Meanwhile back in Italy'. But our survey showed us that Italy was under the plough and looked just like the desert except hilly. The director, Anthony Minghella, was beside himself because in the story the Germans are retreating, they've mined and booby-trapped everything, the place is burnt and bombed out, and so Italy had to look bleaker and have hues of greys, blues and blacks.

At first we thought that technical things would do it for us; in preproduction we talked about desaturating Italy either on the computer or on the optical printers. In the end what we needed was achieved by an osmotic process involving all the heads of departments from production design through to wardrobe, who listened and understood that the scenes in Italy had to look cool and bleak, and those in the desert were to look warmer and happier. So even though it was winter in the desert, wardrobe kept the actors in shirts, the art department pumped up the colour because the flashbacks represent good times, while I overexposed a little and used coral grades where necessary to make the sand look more golden.

Then for Italy the art department thought not to use primary colours, brought in black soil to give Italy a slightly cooler colour and make it contrasty, and I didn't overexpose, shooting instead at a fairly standard negative density. We used a minimum of lab work for the final result, but the fact that Italy and the desert had to look completely different just infiltrated all departments and they quietly did their job. The audience knew exactly when the film had gone back to present time in Italy.

Simplicity

As you get older and greyer you realise that the fewer lights you use the better, because the film looks more natural. Many regard the scene of Juliette Binoche swinging around the abandoned church as their favourite scene in *The English Patient*. And there are only three lights in all: a 20 K light[2] up top, which looks like the last vestiges of sun hitting the window and the ceiling of the church, the flare in her hand, which is actually her key light, and a 'chicken' fill[3] on the ground that I turned on and off a few times because I really couldn't make up my mind whether to leave it on or off. As I chickened, it went on; when I didn't chicken, it went off. I wish I had left it off all the time.

In a couple of lectures people have asked how I could have lit that gorgeous woman with two sharp, pinpoint lights and no diffusion? I was a bit staggered by the question because I simply had to. The script called for a flare in her hand, and of course we couldn't put a real Smith and Wessex period flare in her hand because it would have filled the set with carcinogenic smoke. We had special effects build an electrical light that looked like a flare, and rigged it to have heaps of smoke coming from it. The cable with which Juliette is swinging around the church is actually an umbilical cord of power and water-based smoke, which we kept as thin as possible to make it look like rope.

At first I thought I'd embed soft lights with some diffusion around the walls of the church, but in that scene Juliette is swinging around at will and we would've ended up with shadows all over the place. It would have taken two days to shoot and I don't think it would have looked any better. As it turned out, because we built a key light to stand in as the flare, it only took us half a morning to shoot and it worked brilliantly. I think it's one of the most memorable scenes for people because of the simplicity of the lighting combined with brilliant writing and music to make a beautiful moment between two people.

HIGH-SPEED NEGATIVE

I fell in love with high-speed negative after my experience with it on *The Mosquito Coast* (1986). That was twelve years ago and I haven't used low-speed negative below 500 ASA since. I love high-speed negative because as a technician it enables me to keep shooting right up until the last ray of light. I must confess that a few American producers have been amazed that I've kept shooting into the night and still produced a consistent look. When doing *Harry Potter* at Kings Cross station in London in the middle of winter, the light only lasted for five hours. We then had to change the whole of Kings Cross station, which is pretty big, over to artificial lighting and match it to daylight. After the dailies the American producer came up and said, 'I can't even tell which shots are night and which are day!' As I said earlier, to keep the production going is exactly what I'm there for, and not to just throw my arms in the air and say I can't do it.

And there is a shot in *City of Angels* (2000) where Nicolas Cage and Denis Franz are sitting on a construction beam on top of a building. When you see the shot you can understand why I don't find it logical to use low-speed stocks. It's a crane shot that comes up behind and moves over the top of them, but the high-speed negative picked up the ambient blue tone in the midnight sky and silhouetted them on the beam. It's not a CGI [computer generated image]. I don't know whether it could have been done as a CGI—they would have had to paint in something like the moon. I did that shot for real and it's extraordinary, the kind you often dream about.

PERSONAL STYLE

I love what I'm doing but I would never use the word artist when it comes to what I do. I don't believe I am an artist; I feel I'm a technician. I think each film you do enhances the films you'll do in the future, but I don't believe you should take a certain approach from one film into the next, not even a simple thing like a photographic 'look'. If people feel that my results are artistic, good! But it was a technician that created them.

Cinematography is a continuous learning process. You may start off with a certain approach, but as different films pass through the camera your attitude and approach towards the making of films tend to change each time. You never lose your love of watching a director work with actors, you're there to record and try to help that process, but there are a million variables within that process that are different to the last film you worked on.

To be honest, over the years I've realised that I'm simply a realist cameraman. I look for the 'reality' of the images and then I either enhance the period, the location or the climatic situation in accordance with the story. *The Mosquito Coast* and *Gorillas in the Mist* (1988), for example, are two films shot in jungle settings. For *Mosquito Coast* Peter Weir didn't want a postcard-type, pretty jungle because he felt the character of Ally Fox (Harrison Ford) would see the jungle as beautiful no matter how bad it looked to the audience. I actually shot that film on Fuji high-speed negative all the way through, day and night, and degenerated the negative as much as possible to give the whole film a grainy, nitty-gritty look.

But the jungle in *Gorillas in the Mist* is a place that the main character, Diane Fossey (Sigourney Weaver), loves and respects. We decided to go for the prettiest jungle we could produce so that the audience could identify with her, and her plight to save the gorillas from extinction. Thus, despite similar attributes, every film is so different in its original concept, writing and location that every film should be approached in a completely new and fresh manner, as though it is the first time you have ever photographed a film.

THE FUTURE

Editing and sound have already gone digital, but cinematographers are basically using the same technology today as Thomas Edison was using back in late 1800s. However, I'm interested enough in the future to know that change is coming on very quickly in the camera department.

The DOP had it lucky right up until the introduction of the video-split: we had greater control and an air of mystery about us. We used to walk around the set with a little back box that had half a ping-pong ball on it, saying, 'Flood that, spot that', etc. The director would be looking at you wondering what you were doing and why you were doing it. Then when we'd go to dailies there'd be little surprises and people would say, 'Gosh that worked well!' But now we see everything before we go to the dailies, and that's a bad thing because it's good to have mystery and surprise, they keep creative juices going.

With the video monitor a director can just yell across the floor to the camera operator, 'Pan left, tilt up, zoom in, I like that. Shoot it!' The DOP doesn't exist in a way, he or she is just there to light the set. But it won't be long before that changes too. Already a lot of little tricks have come along, such as the digital camera that Panavision has interfaced with a laptop, which is programmed with all the modern Eastmancolor and Fuji negatives. On that camera you can click a frame and download it into the laptop and then change the printer lights according to how you want the shot printed. In the very near future that'll be interfaced onto a video monitor and then the director will be able to change the idea of the shot—darken it, lighten it, whatever—right then and there on the set.

That type of scenario is in the future but I don't think it should be ignored. As technicians we should be ready to accept the challenge of new technology, even though I worry about it because, sadly, the DOP might not have the creative control that he or she wants or was used to. Of course that type of scenario will definitely happen on big-budget American films where studios want the greater control. Studios really want to see what they are getting beforehand because they tend to feel there are too many people who have their fingers in the pie of creativity. I just hope for the lower budget Australian films that it doesn't get to that scenario for a long time.

WHY DON'T I WORK IN AUSTRALIA ANY MORE?

I haven't worked in Australia at all since the time of *The Empty Beach* (1985) and I have legitimate reasons why I don't work on Australian films any more. On average, films take five months out of a DOP's life and that includes pre-production and shooting time. It doesn't matter if you're offered three or thirty films in a year, you discover you can only work on one and a quarter films per year, and you always need a break in between.

Nowadays some international films take even longer. On *The Perfect Storm* (2000) I was away for nine and a half months, I was home for about three months and then I went away for another eleven months on *Harry Potter*. The last thing I want to do is come home and go straight into another film. That would be hard to do, and I always try to take a decent break after a film, partly to clear the air. After eleven months in another country I tend to get really tired, mentally and physically. I need time to recharge so that when the next film comes up I feel excited about doing it and I'm not fazed by the work.

But the main reason I don't work in Australia any more is because I would obviously put somebody out of work or take away a young Australian's opportunity to show his or her stuff. I don't want to do that. I am lucky to be paid well enough in the international field to be able to make that decision. I obviously do not need to work between pictures and so I stay out of commercials for the same reason. There's not much work flowing around in this country and I certainly wouldn't feel right using up somebody else's stepping stone into the film industry.

A journalist once said to me, 'What about your expertise? Why aren't you spreading that around?' But if I'm shooting a movie and I'm talking about what I do, who learns? The focus-puller, clapper-loader and anybody within earshot of the camera, and in all honesty there isn't much time to bang in a lecture in the middle of a shoot. On the other hand I've done a fair amount of lecturing and hands-on seminars at the AFTRS [Australian Film Television & Radio School] in Sydney and for the ACS [Australian Cinematographers Society] around the country. There could be 80 people per lecture listening and benefiting from what I have to say in those situations. I think that's far more beneficial than just talking to a focus-puller and clapper-loader.

Why are Australian DOPs so good?

Over the years a lot of people, particularly overseas, have asked me, 'Why are Australian technicians so good?' I think the reason is that when you come out of low-budget, short-scheduled film-making, and as long as you appreciate that's how you've learnt your skills and you maintain those skills, when you then move into bigger-budgeted films, studios and producers in America and England pound a path to your door.

The expectation of a lot of people—I know I had it when I first went over to America—is that on a $60 million picture you can just click your fingers and say, 'It's four o'clock, the light doesn't match, we're out of here.' The expectation that big budgets give you more power is simply not true. They give you more 'toys' and that's part of keeping the shoot on schedule. I've often said to American crews, when I've been shooting for twelve hours and there is still half an hour to go, that it's just like shooting a low-budget Australian picture. *Picnic at Hanging Rock* (1975) was shot on a five-week schedule, which was unheard of back then and still is today—it was an extraordinary feat resulting from the energy and enthusiasm of everyone involved.

What technicians learn in Australia is to work fast and be quite adept at using what they have at their disposal to achieve a desired result, rather than constantly relying on some technical facility to do it for them—in fact, to keep shooting when others might give up. It's a great asset, and I firmly and fully believe that the training one gets in Australia holds you in such good stead in the American situation, where you are actually paid—and paid well— to keep the shoot going. You are not paid to stop. I feel quite proud that Australians have shot two recent major film productions—*Harry Potter and the Philosopher's Stone* and *Lara Croft: Tomb Raider* (2001) in London. That says something about Australian working methods.

PART II

TAKING IT TO
THE MOUNTAIN

One of the unique qualities of national cinemas, not only in Australia but in other parts of the world as well, is the production of art or auteur films as a way to compete against Hollywood for a minuscule share of the world market. It was indeed that 'uniqueness' of voice of many Australian film-makers in the late 1970s and early 1980s that propelled the new Australian cinema into the international spotlight. In a fascinating paradox, then, a national film industry has to be infatuated with the very thing it denies for its survival, and thus the auteur is perhaps fundamentally antithetical to the idea of a national cinema. And if we add to this paradox the global trends in film-making over the past ten years, then a national film industry exhibits an even greater paradox: that is, cross-border recognition and financing appear inevitable for a film-maker to develop and maintain a voice.

We've engaged here Peter Weir and Rolf de Heer to discuss independently the notion of the director's voice, and while considering the diversity of their films and approaches, it is remarkable to discover a great degree of consistency.

Given that this series of books is a platform for film-makers, we hope the contributions of Weir and de Heer are considered tentative efforts that will provoke further thoughts, discussion and writing on the subject of the director's voice.

The director's voice 1

Rolf de Heer

I've been asked about the director's voice, how directors get to say what they want to say. For me there are two sides to the notion of voice in cinema—one is form and the other content. Form is often interpreted as visual style and as a consequence I think voice is often seen to be about, let's say, the sort of shots a director tends to use. But in my experience, style is much less important than content for the most part; when I think about how to realise a project, content comes and then I tend to work out the visual style appropriate to that particular content.

Some examples: the story of *The Quiet Room* (1996) is about the disintegration of a marriage as seen from the perspective of a seven year old girl, and so the film is shot simply, with the camera placed at the girl's level most of the time. By contrast *The Old Man Who Read Love Stories* (2001) has some very complicated motion control work in it because the story entails the memories of an old man and I wanted to visually simulate the drifting in and out of memories within the same shot.

Thus for me in a broad sense, form is only the servant of content.

*

If voice has more to do with what we want to say rather than how we say it visually, then to have voice, a director clearly needs to be deeply involved in the writing process. If not always, then at least usually.

Some more examples, from projects I either didn't write or didn't originate: I received a phone call from France asking if I'd be interested in making a film based on a book by Luis Sepúlveda set in the Amazon in South America (*The Old Man Who Read Love Stories*).[1] My first thought was that the producer must have made a hell of a leap to consider me because her call was based on having seen *Bad Boy Bubby* (1993). The producer sent me the script, which I read quickly and didn't take much notice of (because I had no time), and the book, of which I read only the first ten pages. I accepted subject to the rights of rewrite and final cut, believing the film would never happen anyway. But the film started to happen, and when I looked at the script again I realised it was a badly written, almost exploitative, pseudo-masculine action-adventure hunt piece. So I read the novel and thought it was lovely and knew immediately that was what I wanted to make. I started again from square one and completely re-adapted the book, and the film became one with something of my voice in it.

One of my problems on *Dingo* (1992) was that although I loved the script, in the first half of the shoot I tried to realise someone else's vision. I didn't, even simply as a director, attempt to make my own vision because I was quite close to the scriptwriter, Marc Rosenberg, and I knew how important the script was to him. It was a very difficult situation I got myself into, and that is why I'm quite reluctant now to direct someone else's script unless I can make it according to my own vision. The flipside to *Dingo* is *The Sound of One Hand Clapping* (1998). The script was offered to me to direct but I ended up producing the film. Obviously the script connected to my sensibilities as a film-maker; I would never have gone as far as I did with the film if the script hadn't connected. I responded very strongly to it, so strongly that I didn't feel I could direct it. The script had such a clear vision of what Richard Flanagan[2] wanted on film that I thought if he could write this clearly then he could also direct it. I could not have undertaken to make the film and be certain that it would come out the other end in the same way. My self-appointed task in that case was to try to give Richard the opportunity to realise his vision, which was what I wanted to see on film.

*

How do we get to say what we want to say? Writing, producing and directing are quite often treated as separate strands of the film-making process, though for me they are completely interdependent and I think some of the most profound creative decisions are made by producers. I find it very difficult to say what I want to say without getting involved in the producing part of film-making. In some ways the shoot is the least formative part of the process and the hardest to control—the structural elements are practically cast in stone before we get onto the set. As directors we can make a difference insofar as variables arise on location and during rehearsals, but a shoot tends to be like a runaway train that we try to guide in a certain direction and that direction has already been chosen and it's too late to change. I do not mean the script is cast in stone; I'm talking about the industrial context of how we turn the script into a film. In my case that context is generally a low-budget one.

What I tend to consider first is what I call the commercial structure of the film, which is what creates the possibility for me to make a film. How *Epsilon* (1995) evolved is a good example of how I work from the outside in. I saw some footage of the night sky that was created with a motion control system, a tracking shot where the camera shoots time-lapse while appearing to move in real time. All the stars were there, the whole galaxy was there and the images were powerfully affecting. I had never seen anything like it.

One Sunday night I suddenly had the idea for the film. I immediately started making phone calls telling people what I wanted to do and asking whether it could be achieved with the motion control system. Over the next two hours I put the film together: I knew how the film would be shot and how long it would take, even though I had no idea yet when it would be shot. I didn't know much about motion control except that it is incredibly expensive to use and that it would take an incredibly long time to shoot the film, so I guessed at twelve months (the first ten minutes of *Epsilon* took sixty-four shooting days, whereas an average feature in Australia takes around thirty to thirty-five shooting days).

All of the experimentation necessary meant that the budget had to be kept down to a certain level, which in turn meant I would work with a very small crew and cast, everybody on the same wage. The idea was to follow the motion control rig around on its various jobs. If the operators had a commercial to shoot in the centre of the city, they would set up and do their commercial and then we'd move in and shoot a scene. If they were asked to shoot material in Utah for *National Geographic*, we'd go along to Utah and shoot our next scene there. I would write the script as we went along depending on where the motion control system would take us and as a result we would have to shoot the film in sequence. The main character, She (Ulli Birve), would be an alien who can travel through time and space, which in a plot sense would allow the story to move from one place to another at the click of a finger.

With the external parameters in place, the size of the budget was decided upon essentially for commercial reasons: did the investors have a fair chance of getting their money back? I knew *Epsilon* was going to be an arduous

Rolf de Heer (right) on the set of The Old Man Who Read Love Stories

and lengthy shoot but it was still not going to cost much, and so, yes, the film could be financed on the basis of that chance. Domenico Procacci, the co-producer of *Bubby*, put up half the money and then it was a question of convincing the Film Finance Corporation to put up the other half. There was no tangible script but the investors understood there could be no real script because of the nature of the shoot. Suddenly the money was in the bank and the film was made.

*

I'm sort of schizophrenic about the question of how directors get to say what they want to say; I've learnt to apply an opportunistic and mathematical mode of thinking to the ideals and preoccupations of my work. I can talk about my projects as utter contrivances in the most commercially cynical fashion imaginable, while at the same time not care a jot for the market and be completely passionate about the content, the process and the people I'm working with. Example: I need to pay the rent in three weeks time and I have no money. The question is: how do I do that? I need to make a film is the answer. The next question is: how can I construct a film in order to get cash flow in three weeks to pay the rent?

The Quiet Room started in precisely that fashion. After about half an hour contemplating my problem I decided I'd have to make a very low-budget film—I wouldn't have been able to get cash flow within three weeks if it wasn't—and I'd obviously have to be able to write the screenplay very quickly. I had to think about subject matter I knew very well and the only things I knew well were work and family. Work was not very interesting to make films about, but I had a seven year old daughter whom I found profoundly fascinating and so I thought of making a film about the adult world as perceived by a seven year old. And I knew whom to cast in the role.

Now the project had begun to take vague shape but I still had a huge problem. I knew the seven year old was a very bad actor because I did a scene with her in *Epsilon* and it was a catastrophe. By this stage I had worked out the budget and a shooting ratio of 5:1, which is low by any standards but if I had to have a very bad seven year old actor to carry the film then no way could I keep to a low shooting ratio. One solution would be if she didn't talk, that way we might save on the amount of film stock we'd have to use. But why wouldn't she talk? Perhaps because her parents fight and she is withdrawing from their world, and so now the film is about a seven year old's perception of a marriage breakup, it has drama and is looking good. That's the cynical way of looking at *The Quiet Room* and is, in its own way, perfectly accurate. But it's less than half the story.

The non-cynical way of looking at the film is that I've always been interested in childhood. I care immensely about how children are treated and what happens to them, and how cycles of violence are repeated later in life as adults. In its own way, *Bad Boy Bubby* is about childhood, and in some way I made *Epsilon* for my children. And here finally was the opportunity to make a film directly about childhood.

I guess the example of *The Quiet Room* is instructive because it refers to a way of thinking that ultimately allows me to make films in the manner I like to make them and about subjects that are meaningful to me. The production of *The Quiet Room* had to be designed simply and the content was designed accordingly—they had to work in tandem. In fact I don't think any director can work on one in isolation of the other; I design the parameters of a film at exactly the same time as I am writing the script, a process which has always seemed to me to be the first half of directing the film.

While I'm writing I'm partly directing the piece in the sense that how a film will eventually come out is built into the script—not absolutely, but mostly. On *Bad Boy Bubby* I used thirty-two cinematographers. *Bad Boy Bubby* came into being after I left film school and I wanted to make a film, and of course nobody was just going to offer me one or the finance to make my own. I had the idea of making a film with an actor, a friend of mine, Ritchie Singer, who was in a second year play at NIDA [National Institute of Dramatic Art] in the role of an old man. His performance was so extraordinary that it became the basis for the character of Pop (Ralph Cotterill) in *Bubby*; and over the course of time our initial ideas evolved into a script from all sort of bits and pieces I had put together.

But here I am fresh out of film school and no available resources, so how do I make the film? Well, I could shoot on weekends; I knew someone with a 35 mm camera, which I could probably use for nothing, and I could work during the week until I made enough money to buy a roll of film to shoot a scene at the weekend. However, faced with the idea of having lots of week-end film shoots, I realised it was going to take a long time, maybe two years, and that the same film crew, particularly a cinematographer, in all likelihood would not be available for all of the weekend shoots. So how do I solve this problem? And this is where the final concept of the film came from: not only is the character of Bubby (Nicholas Hope) locked up and forbidden access to the outside world, I developed the character further in withhold-ing from him absolutely any reference points to what is out there—books, radio, television—other than what his mother tells him. He has no idea of what anything out there looks like and so when he eventually gets outside, the world could look like anything at all, it didn't matter. Every location could look completely inconsistent because he is seeing things for the first time, in which case the cinematographers could do whatever they wanted.

Cut to ten years later (when I actually got to make the film) and inte-grated into the script is the idea of using different cinematographers for possibly every location. I could now make the film conventionally and did not need to employ different DOPs. Yet I suddenly realised the script had been designed to take into account different cinematographers and it would be a pity to lose part of the original fabric of the script. On the contrary, it would be interesting to retain the original concept, to use it to strengthen the project, to see it as an advantage rather than a disadvantage.

So we set about casting cinematographers. There were thirty-two of them in the end, and each of them had the freedom to do whatever they wanted.[3] If they had always wanted to have a pink sun in a shot, they could have a pink sun; they could choose to operate the camera or not; they could decide on the shots or not; some got tangled up in the art direction, others just concentrated on the lighting—there were a whole range of approaches. The only conditions I imposed were that they were not to look at anybody else's material and I reserved the right to choose the shots if I felt the story was not being told properly. At first the people involved at the level of finance were edgy about the idea, but the budget was so low that they decided to give me the money and to leave me alone.

*

One of the characteristics of Australian cinema has been the contribution of the 'auteur', directors who also write and produce (or perhaps writers who also direct, and so on). Yet there is a perception in this country that the auteur is somewhat under threat from funding bureaucracies and industry groups. There is disquiet from the Writers' Guild, for example, about the lack of writers coming into the industry and being able to make a living writing because of the number of writer-directors around. For the funding bodies there have been a number of projects in a row by first-time writer-directors that were catastrophic. The issue is a real one and a matter of some concern, and the general feeling is that something ought to be done about it.

But there is an important point to be made here, particularly in the context of the director's voice. It seems there are a number of first-time writer-directors who simply want the label of director. They often don't seem to want to direct anything in particular. What sometimes happens is that they strive terribly hard to get their first feature film made and then expect the world will come to their door and they'll get to direct more films if they feel like it. They want to be directors for hire and not engage in the writing, or any other aspect of the film-making process.

Also troublesome is the expectation that any first film is going to be successful, and if it isn't then directors are seen to be no good at making films or simply unable to hack the work. Bruce Beresford, whom I believe to be an extraordinarily good director, is a great example of why that might not be the case. Some of his early films are not great films and you wouldn't have thought that he'd get to make a feature film. I'm told his first film was unreleasable. Even with *The Adventures of Barry McKenzie* (1972), although it did good box-office, it would be a long stretch to say it's a sensational film. But if you look at the body of Beresford's work over the years, one can discern an improvement in visual and narrative techniques with each successive film. By the time he gets to make *'Breaker' Morant* (1980), even prior with *The Money Movers* (1979), everything gels for him in terms of content and form.

Nowadays a second feature is hard to get going unless the first film is astonishing, and in some senses it's a pity to make an incredible first feature because the second will almost always be seen to be a failure. It takes time to practise the craft and become a good director. *Bad Boy Bubby* is my fourth feature film but many people were under the impression that it was my first. *Epsilon* was considered a failure after *Bad Boy Bubby*, but by then I had a body of work and was able to continue on to make more. Pressure on funding, however, severely restricts the opportunity to make a number of films in order to develop as a film-maker.

Ultimately a strategy I would encourage for survival in this climate is to have a compelling project. Perhaps the going will get more difficult because the hit rate at the box-office on writer-director projects has declined, but I've always found that if a project is compelling there is no law that says a writer-director-producer will not be funded.

*

Of course the rules are different since the time Beresford made *Barry McKenzie*. The international market has changed enormously, which in turn has transformed the nature of the local market. We seem to live in a period when much of our film-making is streamlined towards the global market and that means a streamlining of the type of films that can be made. In reality there is not much I can say about the situation because I exist within a peculiar little niche market, with the odd exception here and there. The issue of globalisation is certainly a reality for me, as it is for everyone else, but largely it passes me by. I would feel under threat if I were not able to make another film, but so far the only threat I've felt is in regard to my own inventiveness or lack thereof. I will feel truly under threat when I can no longer find or invent ways to fit in with the system in order to make the type of films I want to make.

I've always thought that if I ever made too many dud films in a row and people stopped financing me, I'd find a way to reinvent myself as a film-maker. In the twenty years since I first had that thought, the means of production have become very readily available. I'm a Luddite (I can turn on a computer and get on the Internet and that's about all), but depending on the project there will always be a medium appropriate to what I want to do. Technology is such that it's a lot easier to reinvent myself now than it was ten years ago, and I can control the means of production. If I have to I can own a digital camera and have an editing system on computer, and even without financial resources I will be able to invent a project that is still interesting to me and still interesting to some sort of marketplace.

Working with low budgets I can't compete with the likes of, say, *The Mummy II* (2001) or *Lara Croft: Tomb Raider* (2001), but I can provide an experience that is different. Something that drives me as a film-maker is exploring the medium of cinema. In some ways for me the process is far more important than the final product. The final product to a degree needs to conform to certain conventions in order that I get to make another film. But that's about where it sits. I may spend a year, perhaps two, making a film and if the process is no good then I'm wasting my life. But equally for me it's about exploring the question of 'what is cinema?', and I strive to create a product that in some way encapsulates at least part of an answer to that question.

I consider myself extraordinarily lucky because I get to make films with as much, if not more, freedom than almost any other director anywhere in the world. Not just once but consistently. If that is a result of having my own voice, then I'm very grateful to those who have recognised it. But I believe how I get this freedom goes back to the apparently cynical, pragmatic approach I discussed earlier. I'm part mathematician and part artist, I guess. Many might assume mathematicians and artists are in contradiction; in my case they are inseparable. It's the mathematical side that gives me the freedom to have an artistic voice.

The director's voice 2

Peter Weir

I think Alfred Hitchcock had the director's voice down to a highly refined degree. When I watched him shoot a scene in Covent Garden on *Frenzy* (1972), he only said one word, the most important word a director can say— 'Cut'. That's all he said; the first assistant director did the rest. An actor came up and knelt by his chair after a take and said, 'I think I was a little too hesitant as I crossed the street. I think this time if I stride because I know where I'm going, I know what I'm doing, blah, blah, blah.' Hitchcock would just nod, then his first assistant would set it up and off he'd go again, and 'Cut'.

Strangely, the word I don't like is 'action'. I don't know why, it's sort of a personal prejudice. I don't even like the more popular 'and...action'. I try not to say either because I actually don't know why the word 'action' was ever introduced. I think it could have been 'go', 'start', or more to the point, 'act'. In fact during the shooting of *Dead Poets Society* (1989) for some reason I was hung up on saying the word 'action'. I had the desire to shake up the sanctity of the set. So I explained to the boys that I had a prejudice against this word and that I was just going to hit a glass of water with a spoon, which would mean that the scene begins. I did that and then developed more elaborate ways of announcing the scene was to begin, ending up with throwing screwed-up balls of paper at certain actors and hitting them on the back of the head. That went on for a couple of days but then, of course, I had to go back to the conventions. I think that desire obviously came from fatigue, and also was a way of breaking down or loosening the ritualistic nature of the shoot as I got deeper into the film.

Preparing this article has caused me to look back on my career, which is not something a film-maker generally likes to do. It's always to the next project that we're looking. This was rather startlingly demonstrated when having a coffee one morning in London with a ninety-one year old Fred Zimmerman. He leant on his cane at one point, looked off into space and said, 'I don't think I'll ever make another film.'

Film-makers have two streams of time. We have real time, the world we live in, ordered and measured, and we have film time. To remember a film is really quite a different thing to remembering real time, because each film is a world unto itself and the real world recedes as you enter the film's world. Distressing world events and the petty ups-and-downs of domestic life fade. Even loved ones become strangely remote, as if viewed through the wrong end of a telescope. This film world demands all your emotional energy and so you live 'a little life'. Hence film time fractures real time because what Zimmerman's comment meant to me is that in film time he was still quite young. It's always quite a shock to me that nearly thirty years have passed since I began feature films when measured by Greenwich Mean Time.

Sometime in my early days in features—I don't quite know when or how it came about—I had a strange sort of fantasy that occurred to me as a day-dream. I think it was a troubled time for me and I think I was trying to work out how I was to be as a director. Where and how would I move for-ward? Not that I was thinking of a career; I never really thought of a career, but on this occasion I somehow felt stuck. Anyway, this perfectly formed idea came to me visually. It was set in Asia and I was going to meet the Directors' Guru, the Director of Directors, sort of Directorial Buddha. He was so famous and so completely understanding of the craft that he had actually never made a film. Which seems odd, but he didn't need to and his disciples just knew that.

There was a mountain to be climbed and there were all sorts of disciples gathered and it was very doubtful whether I would get to meet him. In fact, very few were permitted to see him. So I climbed the mountain and then I waited and waited and finally I'm led to him. All the other disciples backed away and I had to travel the final distance alone. He sat on the edge of a cliff with his back to me, and a beautiful valley down below. I sat behind him, as I'd been told to do, and then I waited again. It seemed like a long time. Then without turning around, he said, 'What is your question?' I knew I was allowed only one and I had worked it out beforehand, but it came out awkwardly. I asked, 'Master, what is a director? I mean, how must I be?' There was a silence and then, with his back still to me, he said, 'You must care and not care, both at the same time.' That was it. I backed away and made my

Peter Weir (right) on the set of Witness

way down the mountain, thinking all the while about what he had said—what did it mean, to care and not care at the same time?

I still think about that answer. 'You care too much', is what Marlon Brando said to Jack Nicholson on the set of *The Missouri Breaks* (1976). He was referring to Nicholson's acting style. Nicholson related the story years later at the Mill Valley Film Festival and went on to say how Brando's remark was the cause of a significant change in his work, which resulted in it appearing more effortless.

I was never very good at making documentary films; it's just a medium I'm not comfortable with. However, in the late 1970s I agreed to make one with Peter Rushforth, a wonderful Sydney potter who was retiring from Sydney Technical College and he really wanted his technique recorded.[1]

I thought I had a breakthrough when he told me that from a potter's point of view Japan is to pottery what Italy is to Renaissance painting. Japan is where a potter must go to truly learn the craft. He went to Japan regularly, and then he revealed that he'd been a prisoner of war in Changi. I said, 'Peter, that's the angle! I'll recreate a scene in Changi prison camp with a Japanese guard, and we'll get someone who looks like a young you. We won't do anything overly dramatic, just the guard looking at you and then we'll cut to today with you looking at Shiga, your Japanese mentor. This is how we'll get the thing started.' He said, 'Absolutely not, that's most embarrassing.' I couldn't convince him otherwise, and so I just filmed his pots turning on the wheel. It was pretty hard going until I met Shiga.

Shiga was a brilliant Japanese potter who was here in Australia on some sort of exchange program. He was living up at St Ives and we went to film him firing his kiln and offering a little rice wine up to the gods. We had to wait a couple of hours until the kiln was ready to open and so we got to talk about the different views of art between Japan and the West.

Shiga told me how in Japan pottery is the equivalent of painting and sculpture in the West, how a potter is apprenticed to a master of the great tradition for many years before they in turn become a master, how they work on utilitarian objects, their art being cups and saucers and bowls for use, how the potter never signs any of the pots by tradition, and how, every now and again, the gods would touch the hand of the potter and *that* would be a work of art. He said this view was so different from the West where we look upon the artist as a god. I found his comments to be enormously liberating because they seemed to be analogous to commercial, mainstream film-making—that film-makers do in fact produce artefacts for public use and maybe every now and again our hands are touched.

I found a reference to Shiga's comment in a marvellous book of collected interviews with Henri Matisse, in which he says: 'An artist must never be a prisoner of himself, a prisoner of style, a prisoner of reputation, a prisoner of success. Didn't the Goncourt brothers write that Japanese artists of the great period changed their names several times during their lives? This pleases me. They wanted to protect their freedom.'[2]

After *Picnic at Hanging Rock* (1975) and *The Last Wave* (1977), I felt uncomfortable with what was perceived as my style—mystical. Journalists would say, for instance, 'You always have water in your movies', as though water served to point out a mystical style. So I consciously set out to avoid that style and look for subjects as far away as possible from that area. That's when I wrote and directed *The Plumber* (1979) for television, and unfortunately water appeared again. But then came *Gallipoli* (1981) and *The Year of Living Dangerously* (1982) and so on.

For me style is to be used where necessary to help express an idea. It's simply a tool, a terribly dangerous tool, of course, in that a film-maker can become a 'prisoner of style'. Some of the greats of the post Second World War period, film-makers who have become part of the architecture of cinema, in the later stages of their careers disappointingly became prisoners of their style. I think it's fortunate to be in a position where you can write as well as draw on the material of others, as John Huston did, for example. Or if you're able to write with a partner, like Billy Wilder and I.A.L. Diamond, where you get other ideas that prevent your own little creative city-state, so to speak, becoming moribund and collapsing.

I want to talk a little bit about the idea for a story, or how a story originates. For me it always comes down to a 'feeling', whether the idea is my own or someone else's. Walking through the battlefields of Gallipoli was a feeling and I wanted to put that feeling on film. That was in 1976. In 1981 I sat with an audience and was able to assess how successful I'd been in communicating that feeling. It's never perfect, but in that case it was close to the way I had felt on a particular morning in 1976. The same thing happened when I read the book *The Year of Living Dangerously* by C.J. Koch.[3] I couldn't put the book down. I'd been to Asia and this book seemed to sum it up perfectly. It was like a smell, something that is beyond words. When this happens to me and I'm touched by something, I always try to deny it intellectually. I'll put the script or book down, leave it for days or weeks and see if it comes back to me. I have been very careful at times not to call my agent immediately after having read something that has touched me and say, 'Yes, I'll do it.' And so I wait to see if the idea comes back and sort of taps me on the shoulder, needles its way into my mind and stops me sleeping. That's the final test.

The Thorn Birds (1979) was the only time I went against my own selection process. I said yes to that film for all the wrong reasons. It was a prestigious production, the book was a bestseller, it was set in Australia and it had a world audience. The funny thing was that during the day I was able to work on the film, but at night I was seized by anxiety and knew that I'd made a terrible mistake. It was a Jekyll and Hyde situation and it was terrible for my family at night because I really became quite a monster. In the end I left the picture.

After *Picnic at Hanging Rock*, Warner Brothers offered me a film based on a Stephen King novel which I vaguely considered doing. But I had no particular desire to work in the US, even though I found the history of Hollywood fascinating, and Hollywood in the 1970s was a very fertile and exciting place. But that seemed irrelevant to me because it was also very exciting back home and I had ideas and pictures I wanted to make.

Five years and three feature films later I was ready. What a change! I was ready for fresh landscapes and stories and new people. I had exhausted my creative potential here. *Witness* (1985) was the picture I chose, a classic American genre piece but with an original element that was my doorway into the film, which is the Amish setting. The Amish are somewhat of a mystery to Americans, so in a sense I was leading them into uncharted waters. I don't think I could have taken something that was too specifically American.

When going to Hollywood you have to read 'all the books', the ones about how Hollywood can grind you up and spit you out. I was determined to start in the right way and avoid the pitfalls. So rather than saying yes to the picture over the phone, I said it depended on my meetings with the producer (Edward S. Feldman), the star (Harrison Ford) and the studio (Paramount). If all these meetings went well, then I'd do the film. The producer was fine and so was Harrison. It was a pretty tight pre-production schedule and so we were quick to agree on what needed to be done.

At the meeting with Paramount, however, I took the time to let the executives know how I intended to shoot the film. I remember at the meeting there was Barry Diller, Jeff Katzenberg and Michael Eisner sitting around a table, looking at me in a curious way. After we'd chatted for a little bit, they said, 'You've met Harrison and Harrison's called us and he's very pleased about your ideas and he wants to do it.' They were smiling and then one of them said, 'Well, we're finished, right?' I said, 'I'd now like to talk to you to make sure we're rightly matched. What I'd like to do is tell you the story in my own words. It'll take ten or fifteen minutes.' They thought that was quaint and rather amusing because here I was pitching a film they had initiated, to which Harrison Ford had agreed, which was green-lit, and I had the job. So I stood up and told them the story, which is something I've done ever since. Not only do they get to 'feel' the story in a much more effective way than is possible in the screenplay, but the storyteller discovers gaps and holes in the story along the way.

Indeed what happened later was a problem with the ending. Endings are always tricky; Americans hate ambiguity, and love to have everything explained and neatly wrapped up. That's why *Picnic at Hanging Rock* was never a great success in the US; they just thought it was a bad ending. Anyway, the ending of *Witness* was tricky. Though it was a love story between the Harrison Ford and the Kelly McGillis characters, in the end Harrison had to go back to his world and she was left with something of a second choice. But in the script were two full pages of dialogue between the Amish woman and the detective standing at the door in which each explained their feelings prior to his walking away. God, it was terrible and so I just ripped it all out. This turned into a behind the scenes drama between the producer and the studio. The producer would come to me very carefully and say, 'You should reconsider that ending; there are some lovely lines there.' Then eventually he said straight out, 'They will never let you do it.'

Sure enough, Jeff Katzenberg flew in and arranged a dinner meeting with me. At dinner he said, 'Peter, the dailies look great but the ending is a big risk. You want to shoot it with just looks?' I said, 'Yes, if I've done my job then the audience will know what's going on.' At that he said, 'Why don't we shoot it both ways?' But I'd read the books and replied, 'Absolutely not!' Then he said, 'Well, I remember you told us the story at our first meeting, tell me the story again, tell me the last two pages in your words here in this restaurant.' And so I did and he was satisfied and that was that. I never had any trouble with final cut, which is now in my contract, though I didn't have it in those days.

*

Many years ago Don McAlpine shot a documentary in Vietnam during the war and it's structured in two parts.[4] The first part is the rehearsal of a military mission and the second part is the mission itself, the sort of military operation many would be familiar with. A helicopter drops a group of soldiers into a field, they sweep through an area and then they're choppered out. In part one we see Australian soldiers moving through trees, so selfconsciously because of the camera's presence, some even have little smiles on their faces. Then a few minutes later we see the same men with the same movements in the real situation. This time the camera is a little unsteady and holds back, understandably so in an action situation. But it's the men who are remarkably different: some look directly into the camera and there is nothing between them and the lens. What we see is a human being stripped of all pretensions, not projecting anything, a pure soul in a way.

Watching footage of men in action is quite a fascination of mine because they are up against the possibility of their own death and they project nothing. The only other times I've seen that clarity, that honesty, is with little children under four or five years of age when looking into a lens, or with those nineteenth century photographs of Aboriginal people or North American Indians who stand looking straight at the camera. They don't know what it is and they don't project anything because the camera has no meaning to them—they care and not care. In some ways this is what I attempt to do when I make a film. I know a film is really working when an actor can look down the lens and remain unconsciously 'in character', when it seems that there is no camera.

To come back to my breaking the sanctity of the set, as much as I can do it without it being too contrived, my aim is to create an atmosphere so powerful that it is impossible for an actor not to be the character. Once or twice in my life I have reached a point with an actor where the words 'action' and 'cut' were insignificant and there was no artifice between them and the lens. You can't ask an actor to just do it and you can't really talk about how it happens. It just happens.

I can't talk about acting without talking about casting. It's such a mysterious process and I think one is mostly operating on intuition. I like to read with actors and I like to read all the parts, male and female. It gives me a chance to take the script for a run and to feel what it's like to be in the skin of the characters. I had this experience to an extreme degree on *The Year of Living Dangerously* when I cast Linda Hunt to play a man. There was nothing to be gained in the plot by casting Linda as a man, and everything to be lost. We had already cast an Australian actor in the role, rehearsals were underway with Mel Gibson, and the sets were being built in Manila. I looked at the videotapes of the rehearsals and they were a disaster. These two characters did not get on, they were abrasive together; yet the Billy Kwan character is a cameraman, Mel's character that of a foreign correspondent, and the two are meant to operate as a team. When I spoke to Mel, he said, 'Look, this guy irritates me, I wouldn't have him as my cameraman.' We tried rewrites but none worked. We had to pay off the actor and we had to recast. It wasn't the actor's fault; it was inherent in the character. And rewrites didn't help. I was in trouble.

We looked all over Australia and there was nobody. Talk about tough, Billy Kwan is 5 feet (1.5 metres) high and half-Chinese! He's the central character in Christopher Koch's story, and if I couldn't find an actor to play that character then I wouldn't have a film. I then read for Mel's character in various auditions in Los Angeles and New York and all sorts of odd people came to try on Cinderella's slipper. I knew all the lines, I knew Mel's character backwards, and I felt exactly what Mel had felt in his rehearsals in Australia—an abrasive tension between the two characters. It wasn't working and I was really despairing.

Then Linda Hunt appeared one day as a joke. The casting director got a good laugh from holding up a photograph that looked like a man and then revealing that 'he' was actually a woman. I said, 'We're that desperate we may as well see her.' I met with Linda and immediately said, 'I'm sorry, Linda. This is a bad joke.' But she said, 'Well, I'm interested to read for it. Any possibility of rewriting the role for a woman?' I said, 'It's just not believable that a woman would be a cameraman in Asia in 1965. Could you play a man?' I tested Linda and suddenly everything changed. The feminine sensibility suddenly connected to the male, there was a harmony, fascination and curiosity. We decided to fly with it and it worked. When people get into a state of what I might call 'recklessness', there's a sense that anything might happen, that we're all starting again. It makes you feel truly alive and probably close to the way everyone feels when making a first film.

Whatever the next project might be, I often write my own scripts or stories between films. I write scripts even if they'll never rise from the dead. It's an invaluable exercise during my 'off' periods because I become fluid in describing scenes and I gain insights into structure and character. Every now and then I get to shoot one of these scripts. *Green Card* (1990) was started in this way, as a kind of exercise. I had a picture of Gerard Depardieu, whom I admired, pinned up on my noticeboard and I wrote it for him. I had no idea if he spoke English or whether he would want to do it.

When I get a script from another writer I have to make it my own, I have to consume it in such a way that it becomes organically mine, as if I had written it myself. This approach doesn't always sit well with scriptwriters but it makes me invulnerable to studio executives, and I'm also able to personify the film to the people I'm working with, particularly the actors. I become the film, or rather the channel through which the ideas and emotions of the film are conducted. In other words I, too, serve the ideas, even though their fullest expression is always just beyond my grasp.

I begin this process by collecting visual emblems, and I think a lot of film-makers reading this probably do the same thing: cuttings from magazines, photographic material, paintings, postcards, matchbox covers, colour swatches. There's conventional research, of course, such as interviews, or visiting the location, which I find particularly stimulating. I'm very receptive to place. Then there's music, which is very important to me in the development of each film. In the words of the poet Gwen Harwood, 'Though words can never/contain, as music does, the unsayable/grace that cannot be defined/yet leaps like light from mind to mind.'[5] Much of the music I've used to inspire me, and at times to inspire the actors, has ended up in my films: Beethoven in *Picnic*, Richard Strauss in *Year of Living Dangerously*, Jean-Michel Jarre in *Gallipoli*, Henryk Górecki in *Fearless* (1993). I find music to be a key to the unconscious. It induces a meditative state that finally shows me the way to go.

It's at this point that film time begins to fracture real time—one leaves the real world behind and enters the world of the film. It's where strange coincidences begin to happen: an incidental remark from someone suddenly illuminates a problematic scene; a newspaper headline by chance refers to one of the characters; someone gives you a gift for your birthday which becomes a key prop in the film, and so on.

I'll let Matisse have the last word: 'Possession of the means should pass from the conscious to the unconscious through the work and it is then one is able to give the impression of spontaneity'.[6]

PART III

PASS ON THE HATCHET

In the absence of a film-maker's diary as was included in *Second Take*, we opted to take on an article about the making of a film by a first-time feature film director. The situation of the first-time director in Australia is sometimes comparable to a relay race in which remarkable odds are overcome, but in the last stretch the baton fumbles in their hands and the pass is missed. Getting a first feature made is one thing; the next hurdle is getting a distribution deal and seeing it up on the screen. More alarming is the accepted fact that over 65 per cent of first-time directors in Australia will not get to make a second or third feature.

The making of *Chopper* (2000) by Andrew Dominik receives extended attention here, detailing the difficulties encountered and overcome. It is worth noting at this point that Dominik had at first conceived *Chopper* as an exploitation film, or a genre picture like *Mad Max* (1979), and indeed Mark Brandon Read had a similar thought. But the film that finally made it to the screen perhaps suggests that the genre model could not accommodate specifically Australian material.

Chopper

Andrew Dominik

FROM BOOK TO SCRIPT

When I first read the book *From the Inside: The Confessions of Mark Brandon Read* (1991)[1] I was very entertained but found it to be chaotically organised; there is no chronological progression whatsoever, no attempt at storytelling, and it's full of contradictions. It didn't seem like a book you could make a movie out of. I gave it to Michele Bennett, who produced the film, and she also found the book compelling, which was encouraging. And when I re-read the book I realised that the chaotic organisation was actually the book's strength, because here is a person for whom what is true in the morning is false in the afternoon, or what strikes him as important one day is insignificant the next. The main thing that hooked me was the contrast between the unrepentant and proud killer of nineteen people and the person who has dreams in which the faces of his victims come back to him. It seemed to me that there were tensions inside him.

In the early stages of the script I spent a lot of time trying to work into chronological order the many events in the life of Mark Brandon Read, aka Chopper.[2] I think my background in commercials and music video initially influenced the writing. I didn't really have a character; I didn't know who Chopper was, and so I was just stringing together a series of spectacular set pieces. I saw *Chopper* as an exploitation film.

The guts of the script came when Michele and I started doing research. We basically went through Mark's arrest docket, which is printed in the book, and tried to contact and organise meetings with the various police officers who had arrested him. In some cases the hand-up briefs were still in existence. A hand-up brief is basically a police document written before the trial, which contains witness statements, forensic reports, that sort of stuff. It's a very detailed document, but again sometimes a contradictory picture emerges of what happened with a certain crime. I was just muddling around at the time with these very lengthy pieces of material, but it was through that research that certain elements of the film came to light—I could just see bits of the film unfolding before my eyes.

There were things such as homicide interviews, and this material had the most powerful effect on me. It's incredible to watch a person in that situation: he has just come in for an interview; he's lying and thinking he is going to get away with murder. Over the course of an hour he realises he is not going to, he is going to be charged with murder and probably go to gaol. To see a person in that situation on videotape and in a wide shot is just extraordinary because it's so different from how you would imagine it to be. How police handle criminals and the way the criminal justice system operates are just so different from the way the same procedures are portrayed in movies. I became obsessed with this material, and because of it I managed to avoid the trap of the flashy film. *Chopper* is the kind of film where the audience relates to the character not through aspiring to be him but through identifying with the weaknesses that make him human.

So what changed through this process was my perception of Chopper himself—he became a real person for me. And while the real person is a lot less spectacular than the image of Chopper the toe-cutting, one-man war on drugs, Mark Read is much more psychologically complicated and his sense of self is very tenuous. The sense I had of Mark was of someone who felt bad about his misdeeds, and generally I was attracted to the events in his life on that basis. The structure of the film then became dictated by what I wanted to show 'of Mark' and this was very much an exploratory process.

Another important aspect of the screenplay, once it was decided that the film would be a character piece, is that it's very much about language. A lot of the dialogue in the script comes from Mark's mouth, from police interviews and court transcripts of what he has said over the years. There isn't a lot of dialogue that I've made up. If you like, I just recorded what the characters would say in certain situations, but it's the way ideas are organised in the dialogue, particularly Chopper's, that is more significant than what is actually being said. What is truly frightening about Mark is the way his thought process is structured, the way he cannot leave an idea behind, and that manifests itself in his speech patterns.

Chopper. *Eric Bana as Mark 'Chopper' Read.*

Though the script didn't necessarily read that way for some people; they probably felt a wide gap between the words-in-print and the words-as-spoken. That wasn't the case for me because as I wrote down what the characters would say, in my head, the dialogue was oral rather than literary. Yet I was still amazed at the people who read the screenplay and thought it wasn't funny. Most of their objections were along the lines of, 'Well, I don't know how I feel about this. What kind of a person is this man?' I suppose they had a similar reaction to the screenplay as I had when I first read the book.

I remember having a conversation with one distributor who picked up as negatives all the things I thought were good about the screenplay. He didn't like the fact that in the scene at Bojangles, Chopper (Eric Bana) kept going over to Neville Bartos (Vince Colosimo) and bringing up the issue of having shot Neville in the leg. At first Chopper is embarrassed and apologetic, then he is frightened of retribution and finally he's calling the guy 'Hop-a-long'. And the distributor also thought it was really disturbing that when Mark stabs Keithy George (David Field), he then turns around and apologises to him.

I guess some good screenplays do not necessarily read well. The example I always use is Martin Scorsese's *Taxi Driver* (1976). I can remember being surprised by Paul Schrader's script when I first read it eight or nine years ago, thinking, 'If someone just received this in the mail, who would want to make it into a film?' Yet when you see the film, it's incredible.

MARK READ AND *CHOPPER*

Mark Read didn't have any direct involvement in the screenplay. I think his attitude was like the line in the film where Chopper says to the television interviewer, 'Anything I'd say would just be fiddling; you know what you're doing.' He didn't even read the screenplay. He refused to read it, which caused me a lot of anxiety. I don't know why he refused to read the script. I can only guess he was worried he wouldn't like it and he'd get angry, and if he got angry we wouldn't have made the film. He probably thought it would be better for the film to get made and him not like it than for the film not to get made at all.

I think that he thought the film was going to be like *Lock, Stock and Two Smoking Barrels* (1998), and that the main characters were going to be him and a character from the book called Dave the Jew. I think his idea of the film was to have lots of laughs while this toothless Jew and Chopper, the toe-cutting kings of Melbourne, ride around in a Monaro listening to Dean Martin and chopping the toes off Italian gangsters. I remember telling him over the phone one day that Dave the Jew wasn't in the film. He couldn't fathom the idea and kept asking, 'What do you mean?' I had to tell him about five times before he understood what I was saying.

And then we had trouble getting him to watch the film. I was going to go down to Tasmania with a print of the film and we were going to hire a cinema and watch it together. I didn't necessarily want to do that; it was something I felt I should do. But then I realised he didn't want to do that either, and he watched it on video. Though I was relieved that he liked the film, I was angry with him because I wanted him to see the film in a theatre. Mark did go to a cinema eventually. Somebody told me they had heard him on the radio saying that he spent most of his time watching the audience and thought they were crazy.

ON ELLE MCFEAST

Around the time we were going to meetings with government bodies, Mark went on *Elle McFeast* (axed 16 March 1998) and there was a huge backlash against him.[3] People were offended that this guy was on television making jokes about stuffing people into cement mixers. 'How dare he make a living out of writing about his crimes', was the general attitude. People thought Mark had committed the crimes to write about them and make himself famous, which is stupid. But of course political entities aren't concerned with the reality of a situation, only how it appears in the media.

I'm fairly certain we lucked out with Film Victoria because of the *McFeast* incident. They funded the development of the script and then, two days after he went on television, Film Victoria had their board meeting and decided to reject *Chopper* for production funding. Yet the screenplay for *Chopper* was commonly regarded within Film Victoria as a well-written script. Basically Film Victoria backed out, they worried about political scrutiny and coming under pressure from the newspapers. Their decision really surprised me, too, because Film Victoria has the reputation of supporting the more difficult and controversial projects.

The other issue that caused some distress was that we would never get the film up and running if Mark Read got paid for it. I think Mark had a sense of that and so he offered to donate his proceeds from the film to charity. I'm sure part of his decision was practical in that he wanted the film to be made, but I also know he feels really good about the idea of giving back to society, particularly if it's for children. Mark is very sensitive to children; like most people, he recognises that young children have not yet been corrupted, and he identifies with them because essentially he is a damaged one. He wanted to give the money to the Royal Children's Hospital, but they refused to take it, which I thought was just unbelievable—they collect money on the streets and don't ask where it comes from! Obviously they too were worried about some sort of media backlash. Yet he has served his sentence and paid his debt to society, but I guess some people don't believe he has. They believe the myth.

'TV FUNNYMAN TO PLAY OUR TOUGHEST CRIM'[4]

The casting of Eric Bana as Chopper surprised quite a number of people, me included at first. I'd not seen much of what Eric had done previously until Mark Read suggested him for the part. I don't know exactly why Mark suggested Eric other than having watched him on television one night, and thinking, 'Maybe this guy could be me'. So I watched Eric's show on television and saw this very affable, boyish-faced comedian and thought, 'This guy is not right!' But Michele insisted on testing him, and he had something.

To get Eric to be Chopper I had to work with him in two ways. One was from the outside in. Now Mark Read has a range of different personality traits, so Eric and I had to identify each trait, make up names for them, work out what those states meant, and then we would negotiate over which personality trait Mark would have brought to a particular situation. The first thing I discovered is that Eric has a great ear, so he's very good with the outer layers of a character. If I play him a tape of an anxious person, he will mimic that person's speech patterns and he'll create anxiety. Because Eric is a good mimic, initially he felt as though this was cheating, that this wasn't acting. He wanted to perform in ways that 'indicated' what was supposed to be conveyed by the writing. But in those early stages he was 'indicating' as Eric not as Chopper. So I had to work mostly on getting him to 'be' Chopper. When he was imitating Chopper he had to create different internal thought processes to make those speech patterns make sense to him and he began to think like somebody else.

Then we could work from the inside out. There is an acting 'theory' that's around at the moment, which is known as practical aesthetics. It's an approach to acting that's associated with David Mamet, with very simple and commonsense rules, and as far as I can tell it's about demystifying the acting process.

This approach doesn't really concentrate much on the affectations of character; it's more about getting an actor to perform a task but never telling the actor 'how' to perform the task. You just tell the actor what he is trying to do—and then you give him some kind of psychological obstacle which will produce the 'how'. For example, in a particular scene a director might say to an actor, 'No matter what you do, you have got to get out of the door.' Then the director might say to another actor, 'Whatever you do, don't let that other guy leave the room.' So that situation creates collision and tension, but then the director adds another layer such as, 'You want to leave, but you do not want to appear rude.' And so that creates a particular way for the actor to achieve his task—the actor is not going to head straight for the door, but perhaps cunningly manoeuvre his way out of the room.

PERFORMANCE OVER VISUALS

In my research I had watched an enormous amount of footage of the real Mark in real situations—how cops actually dressed, what interview rooms looked like, how interrogations were conducted, and so on. Then I got onto the set and everything felt a bit false. I didn't want the shoot to feel like a movie, and my only real concern was with the cast and with getting the acting part right.

I was never truly anxious about the film-making part anyway; I was always more concerned with the acting part. One of the first things I remember saying to both DOPs[5] was that I was going to evaluate everything from the point of view of performance. If the lighting was not quite right, or there was a bump on the dolly track, or even if a take was out of focus, but the performance was good, then I was going to go with the performance every time. That was pretty much my attitude throughout the whole shoot, because I knew that if I got the performances right then I'd have a movie.

I didn't completely ignore the film-making part because, for instance, the reason for the different colour temperatures of certain scenes—the red in Bojangles; the green in Jimmy Loughnan's flat—was to support the performance. But if an actor was 20 cm either way of hitting his mark and the lighting wasn't quite right, it didn't matter. I just didn't want the film-making part to overwhelm or get in the way of the performance. And, funnily enough, that style or attitude towards the shoot made *Chopper* an interesting-looking film anyway. (And just because I wasn't concentrating so much on the look it doesn't mean that Geoff Hall wasn't.) I won't have that attitude for every film but with *Chopper* I felt I had to.

THREE ACTS OF VIOLENCE

Chopper's stabbing of Keithy George

In the scene when Mark repeatedly stabs Keithy George, he knows before-hand what he is going to do: he is consumed by passion, there is a bit of a build-up and then he explodes into violence. But suddenly the scene is remarkably different to what we usually see portrayed in movies, or what we normally expect to happen next—Mark apologises. There are certainly numerous examples of that in Mark's life and I can relate to them. We sometimes find ourselves doing things in a fit of anger or passion, then the fog clears and we are left with the consequences of what we've done. We made the stabbing of Keithy as vicious as possible so that it contrasts as much as possible with the apology, but the main idea behind that scene is that when we get ourselves into those kinds of states we feel like tourists in our own bodies and it's very disturbing.

What I'm really happy with on this film is the weird, often contradictory feelings it's meant to generate—they survived the process of making the film. When I watched that scene with an audience for the first time, especially when Mark apologises to Keithy, I felt the ground below their feet just fall away. They didn't really know how to react and I could feel the audience being repelled by and attracted to him all at the same time.

Jimmy's stabbing of Chopper

In complete contrast to the scene with Keithy is the scene of Jimmy Loughnan (Simon Lyndon) stabbing Chopper. There is no build-up: Jimmy plunges the blade into Mark and there is little reaction, he plunges again and little reaction, and so on. The idea behind the scene is that when people get hurt, it doesn't register immediately. Mark doesn't know he is being stabbed because something in his character is unable to accept the idea that Jimmy would betray him. He just blocks it out and so the whole scene from Chopper's point of view is all about denial. First of all he denies that Jimmy is stabbing him and then, when he realises what is happening, he tries to be big about it by complimenting Jimmy on the attack. Mark is always trying to retain a weird sense of control, and his feelings are not present. They will follow later on. I don't think Mark realises he has been betrayed until he is in the courtroom and Jimmy is presenting a case against him.

That's the one scene I storyboarded and we rehearsed it for about five days; Eric and Simon just wanted to get in and start stabbing each other. I had to constantly hold them back because I knew how I wanted it shot and I had very specific ideas about all of their actions. So we started rehearsing the scene in slow motion and it was the most extraordinary situation because their feelings also slowed down. And Eric and Simon could sort of sit in these drawn-out spaces within the scene and I could put images in their heads or add 'melodies' on top. Just before rehearsing the scene in which Mark throws Jimmy against the wall, I said to them, 'Now consider kissing each other.' Of course they broke up in a fit of laughter and in the next three attempts they would not be able to get to that part of the scene without laughing. But on the day we shot it there wasn't much to laugh about—it was almost the first time the scene was performed in real time, and all that work we did in slow motion was there, trained into them like muscle memory.

It was Eric's idea to throw in the hug. He came to me and said, 'I want to hug him but don't tell him because I want to scare him, and let's see how he reacts.' I didn't tell the boom swinger that Eric was going to hug Simon and so we ended up having to ADR [automatic dialogue replacement] the lines, but it's magical all the same. Watching the rushes the next day I was really glued to the scene and felt like I was essentially watching footage of the real Mark.

Chopper's shooting of Sammy the Turk

There are three versions of the killing of Sammy the Turk, and that's because I wanted to show the process of rationalisation in action. I felt that Mark's decision to become a storyteller was about explaining himself to himself in order to make himself look better. The first time we see Mark shoot Sammy is the 'real' version of events. Mark is in such a state of paranoia that he desperately wants his enemy to show his face, and is at the point where anyone will do. It's irrelevant whether or not Sammy is part of a contract on Mark. Personally I don't think Sammy is part of a set-up. For Mark, however, Sammy is like a stand-in, a symbolic enemy, and so he commits murder.

The next time we see the same series of events, it is Mark telling the police his version of the story and it becomes a scenario of self-defence, justifying his actions. Then when Mark next tells the story it's like a limerick, which is the feeling you have when you read his books. His books contain so many funny stories rooted in humiliating and horrific situations; I wanted to show the process of moving further away from gravity, weight, reality or any kind of consequences insofar as humanity is concerned.

MARK READ OR CHOPPER?

Mark Read often talks about himself in the third person and sometimes he'll actually say, 'I'm not Chopper; I'm Mark Read.' He is well aware that Chopper is a character he created for public consumption. Because Mark was a stand-over man first of all, I believe he understood his reputation was of paramount importance: people gave him money because they were scared of him. His reputation had to precede him and his identity was very much a tool, and so I think he split himself off from himself long before he became a public figure. 'Chopper' was always a character.

Another thing that really surprised me about Mark is that he feels embarrassed about some of his most entertaining media appearances when he watches them later on. He sees them as circus performances and although 'Chopper' achieves public notoriety, 'Mark' goes unrecognised. The notoriety is actually denying Mark any chance of personal intimacy. He is a bit like Clark Kent and Superman in that regard: the split selves keep all people at a distance.

When Michele and I went to meet him down at Risdon Gaol in Tasmania,[6] I was truly amazed at how much I learnt that day. I don't think he formulated any opinions about us; our meeting was all about how we saw him. Most of the time I felt he was trying to work out who we wanted him to be so he could play the part for us. After we had talked for several hours, he started to 'confess', to tell about things he had done which he was obviously disturbed about. He would tell us something bad he'd done, and then when we weren't judgemental, he'd tell us something worse, then even worse, and then worse still. But he was not bragging; his stories came from the point of view of, 'What the fuck do you think of me?' 'What kind of person am I?' 'Who am I?' I had a really strong sense that he genuinely wants to know who he is. In many ways I felt my job was to answer that question and to show Mark who he is, and that was scary because although *Chopper* is a portrait made with love, it's not a flattering portrait.

CHOPPER'S POINT OF VIEW

I would have liked more scenes where there is a split between an objective presentation and a subjective one, because on the occasions when the camera does stand back from events, they somehow appear more outrageous and frightening—such as the scene at Neville Bartos's place when Chopper demands money from him: as Chopper counts down we do not cut heavily, and when Chopper shoots Neville the camera sits blankly in a wide shot. It's sort of anti-drama, yet watching this scene rather objectively produces an ugly sensation and makes the situation scarier.

But for the most part the film is a subjective presentation of events. *Chopper* takes Mark Read's feelings very seriously and doesn't really take anybody else's feelings into account at all—it's not about anyone else. The camera sympathises with Chopper's point of view because Chopper's behaviour is completely understandable to me. I had no problems with assuming his point of view, none at all, and I therefore found it very difficult to judge him. The story of Chopper's feelings is all that I believe the film is about and the camera just follows on to where his feelings propel him.

Chopper is a man apart from everyone else and there's only one time in the film when he momentarily connects with another person, with someone else's point of view, and it's with his dad, Keith Read (Kenny Graham). When you think of their first scene together, their relationship only works when there is a common enemy. In that scene Chopper's dad is having a go at him until Chopper brings up his mother to say that somebody loves him.

His father thinks Chopper's comment is hysterically funny and that's when they are brought together, by their dislike for somebody else. That's the only time in the film when Chopper is on the same level with another human being—other than that, they are miles apart.

I really wanted to explore the consequences of violence from the point of view of a perpetrator. I think the consequences come down to one thing: loneliness. You become an incredibly lonely person, and I think all of Chopper's relationships in the film, not just the one with his father, are always at cross-purposes. In his relationships with others, they never actually meet or interact on the same level. It's like they all have different assumptions about each other and most of those assumptions are wrong, and as a result Chopper is isolated in every single scene you see him in. Just in case nobody got it during the film, it's really spelt out at the end when Chopper and the two warders are watching the current affairs segment. Those two guys love his performance but as soon as the television show is over they get out of there and Mark is left alone.

*

It's a really weird set of circumstances that attracts you to a project; you can't necessarily put your finger on what they are. It wasn't like I read the book and said, 'Yeah, I've really got to do this!' I think *Chopper* is a really strange film and I would love to be able to see the film not having made it, simply because I'd love to know what I think of it. It certainly surprised me because seven years ago I wouldn't have expected *Chopper* to be the type of film I'd make.

PART IV

NEWSFRONT
RECOLLECTED

One of the central tenets of this series of books is to maintain a dialogue with the films of the past—*reculer pour mieux sauter* ('taking a few steps back to make a running leap') still holds true for *Third Take*. Our belief is that one cannot fully understand, say, *Moulin Rouge* (2001), without also understanding some of the polemical tradition(s) and history from which it springs.

A key event in Australian film history is the making of *Newsfront* (1978), a story that celebrates the newsreel cameramen who lived and worked in Australia during the height of newsreel production from 1948 to 1956. The film perfectly suits the concerns of this present volume, for the celebration of Australia's film heritage also has it flipside: *Newsfront* intimates the cultural colonisation of Australia by a marked return of American corporate power via the arrival of television in 1956.

Newsfront was also an innovative film for its time, seamlessly integrating archival footage with recreated material, and had been blessed with a controversy that continues to this day—details of its production and debate over the authorship of the film are reinvoked here undiluted.

We're grateful to Phillip Noyce and Frans Vandenburg who organised and conducted the following interviews and commentaries for the DVD release of the film,[1] and were eager to have near-complete versions published in *Third Take*.

Frans Vandenburg introduces this special section on *Newsfront* with a detailed account of the process of restoring the film and then producing a DVD version.

Newsfront recollected: an introduction

Frans Vandenburg

In December 1997 I was approached by then President of the Sydney Film Festival, Paul Byrnes, for advice on a forum event that would involve the screening of a film followed by a discussion on the creative and technical aspects of the production.

As an established film editor, the perfect candidate immediately sprang to mind: *Newsfront*. Not only is it a classic, it's also very much a work that wonderfully illustrates the art of editing. So much of *Newsfront*'s success relies on the seamless integration of black-and-white newsreel footage and recreated, fictional events of the 1940s and '50s. I was very familiar with the film, having worked on it as an archive footage researcher in pre-production, and then as first assistant editor to John Scott, the film's editor.

I realised 1998 was the twentieth anniversary of the release of *Newsfront*. What better time to stage a forum on the film? And what better place than in its hometown of Sydney at the annual film festival? It's a film many people, and festival-goers particularly, have a great fondness for. Over the years I have screened the film as a teaching guide for students of editing as well as for those interested in the technical and aesthetic use of archival material in film-making. *Newsfront* always proves to be a great favourite of those who have seen it before and those who are seeing it for the first time.

I remember a screening of *Newsfront* in December 1994 at the Valhalla Cinema in Sydney as part of the fourth Sydney Kids' Film Festival. I attended the screening with Phillip Noyce, who was in the country promoting *Clear and Present Danger* (1995). The response was overwhelming from an audience of schoolkids who clearly had not been born when the film was made, let alone during the period in which the film is set.

Paul agreed to a special forum devoted to the film with himself as moderator, and I invited key crew and cast to come and discuss their experiences of the making of *Newsfront*.

The Sydney Film Festival screening was a sell-out and the forum turned out to be a fascinating evening with myths about the making either explained or dispelled, and a good deal of argument, particularly over the sensitive issue of the film's authorship. One thing was obvious: the film had lost none of its vitality, relevance and ability to inform and entertain.

Audience responses were universally positive but—and it was a big BUT—the print we viewed that evening looked and sounded terrible. Phillip was particularly disturbed by comments from many people who believed the faded, scratched and often ghost-like appearance of the print was intentional and some highly sophisticated special effect rather than the result of extreme deterioration. Then and there Phil and I resolved to restore *Newsfront* to its former glory.

Easier said than done. In front of us was the Herculean task of locating *Newsfront*'s crucial printing materials. The print screened at the festival, the best available in Australia, had been struck twenty years ago and because of a protracted legal battle over control of the rights (held offshore by a shelf company registered in Panama), access to *Newsfront* had been frozen. This problem had been going on for some thirteen years. It was finally resolved soon after the festival event thanks to the great work of Jane Smith, the Chief Executive of the New South Wales Film & Television Office (now called the Film & Television Office [FTO]).[2] Control of the film has now returned to the production company, David Elfick's Palm Beach Pictures.

Phillip was not only convinced that *Newsfront* should be restored, he also wanted to re-release the film on the next big home entertainment format, the digital video disc (DVD). We felt we could use the DVD medium to its fullest capacity and expand on the forum idea to create a testament to the film and its makers. Phillip approached ScreenSound Australia, the major protector of our film and sound heritage, with a funding arrangement to bring the film back to life. Graham Evans of ScreenSound Australia supported the proposal, and Phil and I agreed to work together on the restoration between our other jobs.

Phillip had to return to America to begin production of, ironically, *The Bone Collector* (2000), but we managed to begin work on *Newsfront* with a series of on-camera interviews and discussions with cast and crew for the DVD commentary track. We recorded lengthy sessions at Digital City Studios

PHOTO: COURTESY OF PALM BEACH PICTURES & VILLAGE ROADSHOW

Len Maguire (Bill Hunter) and Chris Hewitt (Chris Haywood) out on a job.

in Sydney with the help of Mike Gissing and Mark Keating, who later mixed the final interview tracks for the DVD. Other sessions were recorded in Los Angeles and London.

I based myself at Island Films editing the commentaries while I began the hunt for *Newsfront* material locally, and with many film storage facilities overseas that had had any dealings with *Newsfront* twenty years previously when it first wound its way around the world. What we needed to locate were the duplicate image negatives that were made for the film's original release run and also, most importantly, the original final sound mixes in order to create a stereo remix for both theatrical and DVD release. At the time of making *Newsfront* the original sound mix was on mono and mastered onto 35 mm three-stripe magnetic film, which, when synchronised with the original final image or duplicate negatives, produced a composite print with sound.

At Preferred Media in Sydney I managed to discover some material with the able assistance of Danny Tegg. Danny's father, Tony, a well-regarded gaffer in the 1970s, had started a film vault more than twenty-five years earlier. Back then he foresaw the coming of an awareness of film preservation. A variety of interesting material there included can after can of what resembled fine pasta, which turned out to be 8 mm versions of *Newsfront* that would have been projected as in-flight movies. There were also a number of old prints of *Newsfront*, including one listed as having Japanese sub-titles. I could only guess that the Australian Film Commission had deposited this print with Tony Tegg many years ago.

These prints were more valuable as curiosity pieces and not really relevant to what we needed to restore the film: except for one very important pile of cans—of course I found these almost at the end of my search. They contained the inter-positive of the film. An inter-positive is made from the original final negative and used as the master to make duplicate negatives so as not to put the original final negative at risk. If the inter-positive was in good order we had a chance of striking a new duplicate negative for a theatrical print, and also using it via telecine to process a video master for the DVD version.

On initial inspection the inter-positive appeared to be in good condition; the reels were likely to have remained undisturbed for a long time in a relatively friendly environment. Each can even contained the various grading notes, called light bands,[3] that originally would have been determined by the film's colour grader, Arthur Cambridge. We had to ensure that *Newsfront* be given the best shot at being resurrected, and so Atlab's Peter Willard and I had established a good chain of communication and procedures while I went on with the hunt for more *Newsfront* material.

As soon as Phillip was in the final stages of post-production on *The Bone Collector*, he requested I join him for three weeks in Los Angeles to continue the search. In July 1999, a little over a year after the festival forum, I flew to Los Angeles feeling a bit like Indiana Jones.

It was with great expectation in early August that I arrived at a giant warehouse in Glendale, California, named Filmbond. With the expert assistance of its President, Roger E. Casey, I was able to navigate my way through mountains of material that resembled the final scene of *Citizen Kane* (1941). I couldn't believe my eyes or contain my excitement when I found my version of the elusive 'Rosebud',[4] almost 150 cans of film and various videotape components marked *Newsfront*. I returned the materials to Phillip's office, Rumbalara Films on Melrose Avenue, which also served as my temporary home. Like twenty years before when we were editing the film at David Elfick's Palm Beach studio, I once again was to spend many more nights sleeping alongside the film!

In the meantime Phillip had confirmed that a print he had donated years ago to Columbia University, where Andrew Sarris was still using it to teach a film course on Australian cinema, resembled a ghost of its former self. Phil was rightly concerned that Sarris's students were getting a completely wrong impression of how *Newsfront* had originally been shot. By this stage I was also beginning to get responses from some of the other places I had contacted in London and France, but all were negative. And we heard from New Yorker Films, *Newsfront's* American distributor in the late 1970s and early '80s, that they had nothing in their storage facility. But I persisted that they keep checking and rechecking.

While Phillip was sound mixing *The Bone Collector* at Warner Brothers, in a converted office I had set up film benches and at the end of each day I would take him through what was turning out to be pretty poor quality material. I discovered duplicate negative reels but these were in very bad shape from poor storage and overuse. They were heat affected and warped, heavily scratched with torn sprockets. I didn't think they would safely go through a printer. The rest of the image materials consisted of overall sub-standard composite release prints, video components, and many bits and pieces of negative material that were not much better than what I had already collected in Australia. I had never seen such a mess and it was dispiriting to look at! But each day I would carefully wind through the reels and then relabel them in preparation to ship back to Australia.

Meanwhile there was still no clue to locating the original sound mixes, yet I continued to sort through my ever-diminishing treasure trove. I was coming across 35 mm sound material but with only the M & E [music and effects] tracks, which are used for foreign distributors because they don't contain the film's dialogue. This was something, at least, because my searches elsewhere to locate original sound negatives were not proving at all fruitful.

Just as things were looking grim, a most curious thing happened. Near the bottom—again!—of a final group of boxes I found three packages that would be familiar to sound editors of a certain vintage, particularly Greg Bell, who was the sound designer for the film's wonderfully intricate soundtrack. They were three grey-fronted boxes with orange coloured sides, made by AGFA and called MF5PE 1050FT Load. Instantly I knew I was on to something because material labelled in this way was usually reserved for mastering of some kind at the time the sound was mixed. The three boxes were taped together and marked with the familiar blue and white sticker of United Sound, where Peter Fenton had mixed *Newsfront*. The most amazing thing, however, was that they were clearly addressed and marked to my attention c/o Spectrum Films in Willoughby!

I felt like I was in an episode from *The Twilight Zone* (1959–64), but as soon as I'd recovered I was disappointed to realise that eight reels of the three-stripe magnetic film were missing in action. I finished off rummaging through the rest of the material, which only turned up further warped sound negatives—though we did get a nice surprise when I discovered a wonderful cache of original American release posters.

Phil and I began to discuss what to do next. If the inter-positive was up to scratch—always a bad choice of word when dealing with this type of material—we knew the video master could be created for the DVD. We decided to go with Digital Pictures in Sydney, and Rachel Fennessy, our co-ordinator at Digital, gave Phillip a good and sympathetic deal. Atlab were saying what we already suspected: the inter-positive reels were checking out okay and they were now our best bet for an image master.

But there was still a lot more to do and my departure date loomed. I was driving everyone mad, myself included. There were eight reels of sound to find and I was convinced they were out there somewhere. The one complete duplicate negative I had found so far was dreadful, but I felt there must be one more lying around somewhere. If so, I was certain the image and sound would be together.

I was due to return to Australia on 11 August 1999. I got a call on the eighth from Jose Lopez at New Yorker Films, saying that they had found material marked '*Newsfront*' and would we be prepared to pay to have it urgently shipped to us in Los Angeles since they wanted to get rid of it. 'Yes,' we said and waited! On the tenth, while I was packing and checking through a total of twenty-one large and heavy boxes to be freighted to Australia, more boxes arrived from New York.

Collette Caraway of Rumbalara, who had been assisting me for weeks typing up condition reports, shuddered at the sight of this new pile of dusty refuse deposited in a great heap on the main thoroughfare. I waded into this heap, knowing from its weight that it had to contain sound stock. The first box did have sound but literally hundreds of broken pieces of sound negative and rolls marked 'No Good'. An understatement to say the least! There was sound material in the next box but it was two 16 mm reels that had deteriorated—I could smell the distinctive vinegary smell of film decay as I opened the cans. In the second to last box there were 35 mm final sound mixes: they were copies and one of their number, reel eight to be precise, was missing. Well, it was close but not close enough, and written on their head leaders were the ominous words 'No Good—Distorted'.

Now I know this sounds highly implausible, but here I was with one box to go and, yes!, it did contain what I was after—Reels 1–11, 35 mm full-coat, three-stripe final mixes sitting in a box distinctively labelled as AGFA's MF5PE stock. Another *Twilight Zone* moment! I only had time to do a quick check of this material. The following day I was still packing up bits and pieces for dispatch to Australia. Fortunately I was on the 10.40 p.m. flight, and I clearly remember leaving a mountain of brightly coloured taped boxes in the hallway at Rumbalara and farewelling Phillip as I ran out the door to get to the airport in time.

As soon as I was back in Sydney I reconfirmed with Atlab that the interpositive was in good enough order to begin work on the next phase. It seemed possible that, at least on video, we could get the black-and-white footage to be pure and the colour segments to be faithfully reproduced. A small army of dedicated individuals, along with the encouragement of government and private organisations, came to the party to clean up the ravages of time.[5]

By now Village Roadshow were fully involved as the distributor of the DVD, as they had been years ago as the film's distributor. I continued the recording and editing of recollections for the DVD commentary track, and began to prepare the sound reels I had unearthed in America for remixing. *Newsfront* was made before the arrival of Dolby Stereo and we had to produce a limited stereo version for both the theatrical and DVD release. Roger Savage at Soundfirm graciously offered to do a sound remastering, because we had to be careful that we didn't make another movie: Phillip is a perfectionist but one thing he was adamant about was that we always keep in mind not to use the new technology now available to us to 'remake' the film.

Some of the newsreel footage within *Newsfront* was badly damaged but I knew we could get no better than the original camera negative. We were careful not to clean up that material too much and made sure that only new scratches and blemishes were fixed, particularly in the colour material. Only on a couple of occasions were we unable to rectify damage on the interpositive. Fortunately ScreenSound Australia agreed to release the parts of original final negative for Atlab to redo the damaged areas. Jane Smith at ScreenSound's Sydney office was a great ally in helping with this. She and Murray Forrest, general manager of Atlab, along with Kodak are involved in a special recently introduced incentive to help preserve Australia's film heritage. This incentive also allows for the opportunity to do more that one print to get a result as close to the original as possible.

To cut to the chase, in December 2000 Atlab produced the first new and improved, fully completed release print of *Newsfront*. It was a great Christmas present! Then David Elfick received confirmation from Jane Smith that the

FTO would acknowledge the special circumstances and effort of all involved and would fund another print—it seemed like all our Christmases had come at once.

In 1977, when I first started researching the newsreel footage we were to integrate into *Newsfront,* so much of Australia's film heritage had already been lost through lack of care and plain ignorance. There is nothing quite as sad as opening up a poorly stored can of film, video, audiotape or disc— yes, it does happen in the digital domain if proper care is not taken—and seeing and smelling the shrunken, buckled and warped remains of decaying dreams. There is a real need to preserve the flickering delicate fragments of time that movies are. They not only show us where we've been and who we were but hopefully where we might go and who we could become.

We need to care a bit more. As Phil Noyce concludes in his contribution to this book, 'the films are fading and they need to be restored to their original glory'. Strangely, *Newsfront* is about the loss of part of our film heritage, and yet in these media-conscious times it seems that heritage is under greater threat, particularly from the complex interests of the international film world—an opinion I'm sure Bob Ellis, also a contributor here, would partly echo. More than ever we need to persist in the preservation of our national film heritage in various forms for the benefit of future generations of film-makers, scholars, buffs and the greater public. Thus the essays and interviews that follow are revised, re-edited and often more detailed versions of the commentaries made for the DVD release of *Newsfront.*

Special thanks to Natalia Ortiz-Ceberio, for whose support, patience and love under great pressure I'm forever grateful.

The director

Phillip Noyce

LIFE BEFORE *NEWSFRONT*

I was born in 1950 in a small town in southwest New South Wales called Griffith. Growing up in the 1950s and '60s there was almost no such thing as an Australian film industry; Australians suffered from what we called the cultural cringe, which told us that we needn't embark on artistic endeavours because the British and the Americans could do it better. Particularly film-making. I think I saw only three films set in Australia between my birth and the time I was eighteen years old when I saw Tim Burstall's *Two Thousand Weeks* (1969).

In my last year of high school I went to a screening of underground movies at Sydney University and saw a program of not just American underground movies, but Australian independent short films. Films made for very little money, utilising the new technology of lightweight cameras, fast film stock that didn't require lighting, and amateur actors, who were usually the friends of the director. These were movies made not as an industrialised commodity but as personal expression, and the program was organised by a group called Ubu Films.[1]

Ubu was essentially a film distribution company that collected together the short films of a number of Australian film artists, as well as a number from England and America. After talking to the guys who'd organised the screening, Aggy Read and Albie Thoms, who were themselves film-makers, I discovered their credo was that anyone could make a movie: seize the means of production, get out there and do it! And I was introduced to a new word, which wasn't 'director' but 'film-maker'. Now a film-maker, as opposed to a director, was someone who did everything: photographed, edited, sometimes acted, and certainly wrote the script. Encouraged by Read and Thoms I left the cinema that night determined to become a film-maker.

The year was 1968 and it was a time of revolution around the world, an era when my generation, the postwar baby-boomers, had just started to mature and to challenge the antiquated notions of their parents. Ironically, the baby-boomers' parents had lived through the Great Depression and fought in the Second World War, and had then given their children enough economic mobility to rebel against them. The first film I made, which was fifteen minutes long, was *Better to Reign in Hell* (1969) and it described something dear to my heart at the time: the sexual fantasies of a teenager.[2] It was financed by offering shares to anyone who wanted to act in the movie—the more money they gave me, the bigger the part they could get—and with money I'd earned digging sewerage ditches for the Sydney Water Board straight after leaving high school.

I first studied law and then arts at Sydney University, but I spent most of my time making movies, or, rather, screening movies because by then I also had the job of managing the Sydney Film-makers Co-operative.[3] The Co-operative was a company formed by a number of film-makers to distribute their films to film societies, schools, universities, or anyone who wanted to screen them. As the manager I inherited a library of 250 short films that I kept in my bedroom at my parents' house, and then at my house in Annandale in the inner west of Sydney when I moved out of home. I watched all 250 films many times over, and seeing all of these avant-garde, independent, art movies was really my initial film school, so much so that I set myself the task of making a short film every couple of weeks, sometimes editing a film entirely in camera and sometimes without sound.

The Co-op also set up a cinema on the third floor of the Third World Bookshop, a socialist bookshop in Goulburn Street, Sydney, where each Sunday night—and then, gradually, as the venue grew in notoriety, every night of the week—we screened Australian 16 mm short films to very appreciative audiences. The audiences seemed so anxious and so excited to see themselves up there on that little silver screen, because suddenly it felt like we Australians had seized the screens, we owned our own images. It truly was an exciting period.

I was very lucky in 1969—as I have been in my whole film-making career—because that's the year the Australian government legislated to kick-start a film industry. Under then Prime Minister John Gorton, a three-tiered

Phillip Noyce (centre) on set.

PHOTO: COURTESY OF PALM BEACH PICTURES & VILLAGE ROADSHOW

program of assistance to film-making was established. There was talk of a film school in the near future, but for the present an experimental film fund was initiated to give money to promising beginners, and they set up the Australian Film Development Corporation to finance, supposedly, commercial feature films.

I was fortunate enough to receive a grant from the Experimental Film Fund. With the assistance of the grant and with money I had saved myself, by the time the Australian Film and Television School was calling for applicants in 1972, I had already made twelve short films ranging in length from one minute to one hour. Together with eleven other students I was selected to attend the inaugural year of the school in 1973.

At film school we students had to make three different films—first a drama, second a documentary, and third a film of our own choice—and though the school gave me my first opportunity to make a short dramatic film with professional actors, I somehow seemed to excel in documentary. One of the films I made is a documentary titled *Castor and Pollux* (1974), which is about the contrasting lifestyles of a hippie, Adrian Rawlins, and a biker, Gus, who was head of a bikie gang. The story became well known and quite notorious within the counter-culture scene of Sydney, and somehow this movie ended up at *Tracks* magazine by accident. Actually, I'd thought

I'd lost the print but I received a call from the editor of *Tracks*, David Elfick, who'd taken the liberty of screening the movie and he wanted to tell me how much he had enjoyed it. That call was the beginning of a friendship that has lasted many decades.

When I first became involved in making short films David Elfick was already an established figurehead within the alternative culture scene in Sydney—in fact, in the whole of Australia. Around that time he had been the editor of *Go-Set*, a teen magazine, and later he had established *Tracks*, a monthly surfie magazine he'd edited for about three years. Moreover, I'd known him as a reporter for *GTK* (1969),[4] which was something of a weekly ABC youth show, and he ran a cinema theatre at a seaside suburb in the north of Sydney called the Manly Silver Screen, which programmed art and alternative movies.

David's name was also well associated with the surfie movie sub-genre, a feature-length documentary phenomenon that started with Bruce Brown's *The Endless Summer* (1966) and lasted through to the mid-seventies. David had produced and distributed a number of surfie movies, including *Morning of the Earth* (1972), directed by Albert Falzon, and then a very big hit titled *Crystal Voyager* (1973), which he produced and directed. In a way David and I had similar experiences in terms of movie-making, because while I was making and screening short experimental movies, David was producing, directing and distributing surfie movies—and by distributing I mean he was putting up the posters, booking the theatre, taking the money, running the projector, and then moving on to the next coastal town.

In the early seventies none of us who were making short or alternative films ever expected that we would be able to earn a living by making movies. There was a fledgling feature film industry in Australia, and there had been a couple of notable successes: Tim Burstall's *Stork* (1971), a comedy, and another broad comedy, *The Adventures of Barry McKenzie* (1972), made by Bruce Beresford. Still, nobody thought it would last and nobody thought that Australians would actually pay to see serious or dramatic films—the comedies were another matter. So, after graduating from the film school in 1974, like so many Australians I took off on my big journey overseas, which was like a rite of passage for everyone in those days. It was a journey along what had become known as the 'hippie trail'. One would travel up to Darwin, catch a boat to Indonesia and work your way up to India and then across to Europe, usually ending up in London before you came back to Australia, got married and settled down and disappeared into the suburbs.

I actually got to team up with David in London in 1974 when he was premiering *Crystal Voyager*. I can't remember exactly when David first told me about the project that was later to be called *Newsfront*; I guess it must have been sometime in London when he mentioned that he, Andrew Fisher and Richard Neville were working on a project that was initially conceived as a documentary compilation of footage about Australia's postwar history, and that it had evolved into a combination of documentary footage and a fictional story. I believe at that time the documentary footage was to be drawn from newsreels and television shows but did not involve cameramen: it was just going to be the story of two postwar kids. In fact, the name of the project was 'Our Time', and the idea was to take a baby born in Australia in 1948 and an immigrant boy arriving in Australia with his southern European parents in that same year, and then to follow their lives up to the early 1970s.

Unlike people of the previous generation who headed to London to make their fortunes, I just wanted to see how the other 95 per cent of the world lived. I knew I was going to come back home because, now under Gough Whitlam's Labor government, Australia seemed like the best place imaginable in the world, and certainly the best place to make movies. There was no trace of the cultural cringe I'd grown up with, and suddenly my generation seemed to have been gripped with a new nationalism and a new confidence that we could seize the reins and capture our lives in movies, music, theatre and literature. There seemed to be an incredible flame, a volcano of artistic activity that was partly sponsored by the government and partly due to the baby-boomers finally maturing.

I returned to Australia in early 1975 and started to work either as a production manager, first assistant cinematographer or editor, trying to raise money for my next film—a sixty-minute drama that I'd eventually shoot between late 1976 and early 1977. Wherever I could earn $50 I'd have a go, even though there really weren't many places where one could actually be employed to work on movies.

One of the main ones was Film Australia, then known as the Commonwealth Film Unit, the Australian government's film-making studio producing films mainly for various government departments. Over the years people such as Bruce Beresford, Tim Burstall, Peter Weir, Don McAlpine and Dean Semler had passed through this institution. Anyway, I got a job at Film Australia in 1975 and it was there that I got my first experience on a dramatic feature film. I worked as second assistant director on *Let the Balloon Go* (1976), a children's feature shot by Dean Semler and directed by Oliver Howes.

I also got the chance to direct while at Film Australia, mostly documentaries, including one called *God Knows Why, But It Works* (1976), which was conceived and produced by Richard Mason. It is the story of a

Greek–Australian doctor, Archie Kalokerinos, who had pioneered a vitamin therapy treatment for diseases specific to Australian Aborigines. This film, as conceived by the producer, was at the time an innovative combination of documentary footage of the real Archie Kalokerinos with fictional recreations of events from his past life, with an actor playing the doctor. *God Knows Why, But It Works* showed at the Sydney Film Festival in 1976, was enthusiastically received and led to me securing a grant of $25 000 from one of the film funding bodies to make *Backroads* (1977).

In late June 1976, a couple of weeks after the festival screening of *God Knows Why, But It Works*, David Elfick contacted me again to ask me to read a screenplay written by Bob Ellis entitled *Newsfront*. This was a first draft screenplay, more or less in the form that we see in the finished movie. It was the story of two brothers working for rival newsreel companies between 1948 and 1956. When I read the script the first thing that struck me was the uniqueness of the idea and how appropriate it felt to my own experience as a film-maker. It combined period newsreel footage with a recreated fictional story, for which *God Knows Why, But It Works* certainly seemed to be a springboard.

While I found the script rather long and the dialogue sometimes overblown and unrealistic, I immediately responded to the characters and, I guess, to the nostalgic elements of the piece. Although I had been born in 1950 and was therefore a young kid during most of the events described in the screenplay, it seemed to me to be the story of my father's generation and their values, a generation that had persevered through fifteen years of disrupted life, starting with the Great Depression followed almost immediately by the Second World War. It was also the story of an Australia that, even in 1976, I could see vanishing, a time before television when we really rejoiced in the tyranny of distance that separated us from the rest of the world.

But what was truly impressive about the screenplay was the way in which Bob Ellis had mapped out how the film could combine real events with a fictional story. At the same time as being an involving narrative and a history lesson, Bob produced a coherent and striking political document that described the loss of innocence and the cultural colonisation of Australia.

NEWSFRONT

Before *Newsfront* the longest dramatic film I'd made was *Backroads*. There wasn't anything I'd experienced on that film, which was shot with a crew of about six, that could ever have prepared me for the first day of shooting on *Newsfront*. I remember driving in a taxi towards the location in Market Street in the heart of Sydney, and wondering what all the cars and trucks and people were doing out on the street, thinking there must be a pageant or parade about to take place. Then it dawned on me just before I arrived at the State Theatre; they were all waiting there for me to say 'Action!' I thought, 'Oh my God! Can I do this?' I realised that everything I'd done before had been like playing—now I was a film director, I was making a real film, this was the film industry, and they were all waiting for me to tell them what to do. I was scared, to say the least.

Calling Bill Hunter

In early 1976 I was looking for someone to play the part of the white racist drifter in *Backroads*. My first assistant director and associate producer, Elizabeth Knight, suggested I meet up with Bill Hunter, an actor whom I'd not heard of previously. I turned up to an inner-Sydney pub, in Surry Hills actually, and there on the street outside the pub I asked Hunter to do an improvisation based on a description of the character I'd just told him about. Hunter immediately transported himself into outback New South Wales and captured the character I had in my mind. We went on to shoot the film, which was largely improvised, over a four- or five-week period as we travelled in convoy across western New South Wales.

I know Bob Ellis now tells the story of trying to convince me that Bill Hunter should play the role of Len Maguire and that I initially said, 'No, there's no part for Hunter in this project.' I can't say for sure whether the story is true or not, except I can say that having cast Hunter in *Backroads* and having loved the experience of working with him, I can't believe I would have been negative about the idea of considering him for the lead role in *Newsfront*. Whatever the truth may be is not important. What's more important is that Hunter was indeed cast to play Len Maguire, and as the inevitability of shooting the film drew closer, we started to discuss the character and how his character should look.

Up to this point I'd never actually seen Bill Hunter in a film, photograph or in person without a beard. About six weeks before we started shooting David and I decided finally to coax Billy down to Palm Beach where David has a studio. We were going to encourage Bill to remove his beard because we felt it wasn't appropriate for a cameraman in 1948 to be bearded, though Bill maintained that Len Maguire was a bohemian type of character. After a lot of persuasion we finally agreed that he could keep his moustache, but the beard had to go. Bill left us to go into one of the bathrooms with a razor and remove the beard. He was gone for a helluva long time and I remember David and I joking that maybe he'd used the razor to cut his throat. Then Bill emerged and for the first time we realised we'd cast someone who had, ah, more than one chin is the best way to put it. Maybe this was the reason he'd always had the beard: it had given a particular etching to his face. I think that if Hunter had come to us during the casting process without his beard we would have rejected him outright as a popular candidate for the lead role in a feature film.

Now, almost twenty-five years later, when I look at the film I see in the part of Geoff, the editor, played by Bryan Brown, who at the time was a relative newcomer to acting, a guy who was probably the obvious leading man. Yet the funny thing I also realise at this point is that Bill's very unconventionality as a leading man is what makes his characterisation very distinctive and what makes the film extremely distinctive. He is an 'ocker', an ordinary guy, and that accident of casting was a lucky accident indeed.

I remember that after we had discovered the extra chins David and I were both reluctant to admit to each other that we thought we'd made a terrible mistake. Neither realised we hadn't made a mistake at all, and that we'd stumbled onto something that would later be called genius in terms of casting. All we could think about was, 'Well, he's got to get rid of some of these chins before we start shooting!' So a guy called PJ, short for Paul Jones, who was cast in a supporting role as the assistant cameraman to Charlie Henderson (Johnny Ewart), was immediately appointed to the previously unheard-of role as personal trainer for Billy Hunter.

PJ was given the task of getting Hunter trim, taut and terrific for shooting, and Hunter had to stay at David's studio at Palm Beach for a couple of weeks while a strict training regime was undertaken. I can remember the first morning PJ set out with Hunter to jog about a kilometre along the beach and back to the studio. I was looking down at the beach and, after they'd gone a hundred metres or so, I saw one of the two figures collapse into the sand. It was, of course, our leading man, who indeed was quite unfit at the time. But over the ensuing weeks prior to the commencement of principal photography, Billy shed a lot of weight and really pulled himself together.

Having cast Hunter in the lead role we now had to look around for someone to play Len's brother, Frank Maguire. Village Roadshow, the film's distributor, kept telling us we needed visibility in terms of whom to cast, and so our first thought was Jack Thompson. Jack had appeared in a number of commercially successful movies, including *Sunday Too Far Away* (1975) and *Petersen* (1974), and was already a bona fide Australian movie star. But Jack turned us down. Of course, in Australia in 1977 there were only a couple of other actors who had any public appeal and one of them was Gerard Kennedy. Because of his parts in the long-running television series for Crawford Productions, *Homicide* (1964–75) and then *Division 4* (1969–77), Kennedy had for a long time been a favourite television actor. As soon as Thompson turned us down, and very conscious of the need to cast someone with box-office appeal, we secured Gerard Kennedy, who, when you think about it, is an unlikely brother for Bill Hunter. He was not our first choice, but at least in the Australia of 1977 Gerard was a very visible actor.[5]

When I first viewed a cut of the film I realised Billy Hunter's performance was very inconsistent in terms of his vocal delivery. Hunter operated on fear and sometimes his fear came through in the way he spoke. But, of course, the problem was that he was playing a man who never really doubts himself and is convinced of the 'rightness' of everything he does. I had heard of a concept called post-synching, which is what we now call ADR [automatic dialogue replacement]. Because of technical deficiencies, or mishaps such as an airplane flying over a scene, it's quite common on feature films to re-record part of an actor's dialogue. But we had to do more than just replace a technical deficiency; we had to even out Bill's performance. So I got him to come up and stay at the Palm Beach studio where we were editing the film and showed him the whole movie on the Steenbeck; in particular I wanted Bill to focus on the last shot of the film, which is a koala bear climbing a gum tree. I remember saying to him, 'Bill, that koala bear climbing the gum tree is Len Maguire, and I want you to now think about injecting the warmth we associate with the koala bear into the character of Len.' The next day we went into the studio and re-voiced seven scenes, and I think that had a big effect finally on the audience's identification with Len Maguire.

Newsreel against fiction, colour versus black-and-white

The production of *Newsfront* hinged on solving two major hurdles: how to realistically recreate the 1954 Maitland flood and how to combine original newsreel footage with a fictional story. The latter problem was further compounded by the fact that some of the film had to be shot in colour. The financing for *Newsfront* came principally from two government film agencies, the Australian Film Commission and the New South Wales Film Corporation, but their investment was dependent on finding a local Australian distributor.

Village Roadshow, and particularly the head of their Sydney office, Greg Coote, were constant supporters of the project and eventually released the film successfully around Australia, but their involvement was dependent on the recent introduction of colour television into Australia. Village wanted the film to be shot in colour because they figured the security for their investment would be the potential sale of the film for screening on Australian television. Of course this was virtually impossible because almost none of the original newsreel footage was ever shot in colour. Yet in order to complete the financing we had to agree on having some of the movie shot in colour. Thus evolved the idea of dividing the chapters of the screenplay into some that would be shot in black-and-white and some that would be shot in colour.

When first faced with the problem of deciding which sequences to shoot in colour and which to shoot in black-and-white, I may have given the crew an intellectual and emotional justification for my decisions. The truth was actually a lot simpler. If you are intercutting black-and-white material with recreated events you want to make the intercutting appear seamless, and so I worked out that all of the sequences involving recreated events that had to dovetail with original newsreel material, such as the Maitland flood sequence, obviously had to be in black-and-white. If using newsreel footage as archival material, such as the Anzac Day celebration sequence in which the newsreel-makers are watching a screen, even though it contains newsreel footage, this sequence could be in colour. There was really no choice, the division was made on that very practical rationale forced upon me by the simple fact that we wanted to produce a seamless reality.

In early 1977, way before principal photography began, I contacted Frans Vandenburg, who had worked with me as assistant editor on *Backroads*, and asked him to help me locate and research actual newsreel footage from the no longer existing newsreel companies Cinesound and Movietone News. I wanted to become familiar with the shooting style of the original newsreels and discovered that most of the footage was shot on medium lenses. There were very few of what we call close-ups because shooting real events on a fixed-mount camera meant the cameraman would try to stick to the one lens to shoot everything. They wouldn't have used a telephoto or ultra-wide lens; it was usually about a standard 25 mm lens, which produced a particularly 'square' shooting style. By square I mean not jazzy. A close-up was usually shot from the waist up, sometimes from the chest up. I realised that if we were going to dovetail the newsreel footage with recreated material then we had to adopt a very similar shooting style in terms of limited camera movement and the type of lenses we chose.[6]

Given the problem of having to recreate the Maitland flood, Frans collected archival material not just from the 1954 Maitland flood but material spread over a twenty-year period, because flooding in the Maitland area seemed to be an event that happened every three or four years from the 1930s right through to the sixties. Based on what Frans collected I began to imagine the sorts of images we might have to shoot to intercut with the archival material. A good example is the sequence in which Len Maguire and Charlie Henderson are out in a small boat searching for Chris Hewitt (Chris Haywood's character), and we see their various points of view. Those points of view were actually shot by newsreel cameramen, and Frans spent weeks and weeks finding all of them.

At this stage we also decided to turn to the living icon of the Australian film industry, Ken G. Hall, who was already in his mid-eighties and living in retirement at Mosman. Hall began his film-making in the early 1930s, and though Ken is no longer with us, he remains the most prolific Australian film director, sometimes having made up to four films in a year. Under the banner of Cinesound Studios and financed by Greater Union Theatres, a film distribution company here in Australia, Hall produced and directed seventeen classic Australian movies in a feature film career that ended after the Second World War with *Smithy* (1946), the story of Charles Kingsford Smith, the great Australian aviator.

Ken had also managed the weekly Cinesound newsreel, which is the inspiration for the fictional Cinetone newsreel in *Newsfront*. Although his studio no longer produced features, from 1948 Ken continued as the general manager of Cinesound, churning out a weekly newsreel until 1956 when he went to Channel 9 to oversee the introduction of television into Australia. Obviously Ken was a major resource for anyone wanting to research the reality of the Australian newsreel industry.[7] I can remember asking Ken for some ideas on how to shoot the Maitland flood sequence and he offered a really simple solution. He said, 'Well, you are not going to be able to flood half the countryside of New South Wales, like in the real footage, but you may be able to produce the appearance of a flood over a limited area. The trick is that it doesn't matter what's outside the frame, son, whatever the camera sees, that's real. So put your camera up high, point it down, and frame up what you can convince the audience is flooded area. Don't show anything else and you'll achieve the reality you're after.'

Most of the Maitland flood sequence was shot at Narrabeen Lake to the north of Sydney. David Elfick and I realised that the lake was only about one to two metres deep near the shore, and that maybe we could convincingly convert the lake to give the illusion of a vastly flooded landscape. Taking Ken G. Hall's idea of putting the camera up high and pointing it down, thereby limiting the frame over a very restricted area, the plan we hit upon was to build the façade of a street in the lake with the shopfronts three to five metres under water. Thus we only had to construct the tops of buildings and not the parts that were supposedly in floodwater, the parts we wouldn't see anyway. And to create the illusion of rapidly flowing water in the otherwise placid Narrabeen Lake, David came up with the idea of getting two or three jet boats, having them anchored just offshore, running the engines in reverse thrust and revving them up simultaneously.

When I think back it seems every frame of the Maitland flood sequence was held together by Scotch tape and rubber bands. But, of course, movies are all about suggestion, and what's important is what the audience believes they are seeing. By combining Ken Hall's idea of limiting the frame with the newsreel footage unearthed by Frans, I soon realised that we were probably going to get away with recreating a rather impossible sequence.

Musical chairs

I can remember when I first saw all the scenes strung together in their original scripted order: I came home stunned by the failure of it all, took to my bed and remained there in a catatonic state for two and a half days contemplating my future as a schoolteacher. Certainly not as a film director because, I thought, 'Well, I've been given this chance and I've messed it up and I'll never get another chance, not after anyone sees this mess.' The story didn't seem to make sense and seemed to be made up of so many disparate elements in search of something to glue them together. We were due to screen the film about five days later to our investors, and when I finally got up out of bed the first thing I did was to go into the city and search for music.

Bob Ellis's screenplay had made specific suggestions for period songs that might be used in the final cut, and so I came up with a lot of 78 records of newsreel music, newsreel fanfares, and dramatic film music from the 1940s and '50s. I went into the editing suite armed with what I hoped might be the glue that would hold the whole thing together, push the story along, provide a real emotional thread, and perhaps give the illusion of an intellectual thread.

As the editor, John Scott, and I prepared for the screening we started to lay in some of the music I'd found. It was a lesson for me because I suddenly realised how incredibly important the sound element is to any movie. I realised also that in travelling directly from the ear to the heart, sound makes an emotional connection that supersedes what we see. It's more powerful than an image because an image has to be decoded by the brain, as opposed to music that bypasses the brain and goes directly to the heart. The film we screened just five days later with a partially completed temporary music track was a completely different experience and showed signs of working. But when David investigated the rights to the songs suggested by Bob Ellis, he found that purchasing them would have used up more than the total budget of the film.

David, however, was also aware that in the 1940s and '50s Qantas and Pan Am crew members would bring in the latest recordings from America to Australia, sometimes months before the original recording would be shipped out here and records pressed. In the ensuing period Australian artists and producers would record cover versions of American hits; Australia had developed an industry based on sound-alikes, much like today's video pirates. Thus most of the songs on the soundtrack of *Newsfront*, although they sound like the originals, are actually cover versions. David was able to secure the rights to the cover versions for very little money given that they were not really sung by Frank Sinatra or any other of the original American superstars.

Catholic against Protestant

With the music problem solved, the one area that seemed to be a real downer was the ending. Bob's original script had called for a coda after the 1956 Melbourne Olympic Games sequence that ran like this: Len Maguire, having refused to sell his footage of the two communist nations fighting each other in the swimming pool at the Games, returns to Sydney to receive a special award, and on his way home after the awards ceremony he sees the newsreel theatre has been turned into a soft-core movie house showing Roger Vadim's *Et Dieu créa la femme* (. . . *And God Created Woman*, 1956), and realises that the era of the newsreel is over. This was not even a bittersweet ending, it was a bitter one. Here was a man who had fought all his life to retain his values, had achieved some degree of glory, but now, of course, realises it's all to naught because there is no longer a newsreel industry.

We persevered for a couple of screenings with that ending, experimenting with a temporary music score before eventually deciding to move the final sequence back in the story so that Len makes his discovery at a much earlier stage, and that the movie should end triumphantly with a moment signalling Len's moral strength. We then decided to cut a montage of newsreel footage that might have been shot by Len Maguire in the twenty years after 1956 through to the official demise of the cinema newsreels in 1975. And in order to give the feeling that Len would go on working through this era, I thought of the idea of superimposing an image of Billy Hunter holding a hand-held camera over the montage of newsreel clips, and then backing the images with an upbeat version of 'The Road to Gundagai'. In that way Len's moral steadfastness is not seen as foolhardy, but triumphant.

Someone who had worked on the film as a grip later accused me of turning a Catholic ending into a Protestant ending. He was probably right in as much as I suppose Catholicism encourages one to adhere to the belief that we will suffer during our lifetime only to inherit the kingdom of heaven, whereas the Protestant ideal is that life is to be enjoyed and that maybe we'll go to hell. But what I actually believe is that the rearrangement of the ending has been to this day crucial to the audience's enjoyment of *Newsfront*.

AUTHOR? AUTHOR?

From the day Bob Ellis finished the first draft of *Newsfront* I think controversy over authorship was destined to surround the project. The truth is that there were many authors with varying degrees of involvement, going back to original discussions David Elfick had with Philippe Mora, as well as with Richard Neville and Andrew Fisher, on through various outlines and drafts produced by Andrew, Richard and David, and ending with Bob's screenplay.

But it was during the pre-production of *Newsfront* that friction began, when Elfick and our associate producer Richard Brennan discussed with me the problem of not being able to raise enough money to shoot all of the scenes in Bob's screenplay. Cuts had to be made and I was given the initial task of nominating the scenes to be cut based on the responsibility of streamlining the narrative.

The suggested cuts resulted in a fierce battle that has raged to this day and will probably pursue us to our graves. When I first read the script, making *Newsfront* had maybe been possible, but not likely. When it became more apparent that we were actually going to shoot this movie, the relationship between Ellis, Elfick and myself—well, at least between David and me on one side and Bob on the other—became increasingly heated. Bob, as the man who had really cracked the problem posed by the original concept and still managed to write an engaging political thesis on a particular period of Australian history, perhaps understandably was wedded to his original scenes and their structure. I, as the director, also understandably was faced with the responsibility of delivering a movie for the budget I had been told I'd have, while trying to make the viewing experience as compelling as possible. For me there were no two ways about it, I just knew I had to make some cuts, and they were made for two reasons. The first and most important reason was economic, in that we couldn't afford to shoot all the material; the second reason was because David, Richard and I thought the story could be told more economically. That is, because of the length of the script I was to decide which scenes were necessary to still be able to tell the story effectively.

By mid 1977 we started to look for actors; Ellis had written a number of the characters with particular actors in mind, actors he'd known personally from his career as a playwright and the proprietor of the Stables Theatre in Kings Cross. So perturbed was Bob by the proposed cuts that he started a one-man battle to convince David, Richard and I to reinstate various scenes. When it appeared that failed, Bob, almost like the ancient mariner,[8] would grab anyone who would listen, including some of the actors who'd already been cast, and recount the troubles that had befallen his screenplay. No doubt Bob felt he was right, that he was saving the work from the relatively inexpert Noyce and Elfick who, as fate would have it, were truly going to be shooting the screenplay he'd written.

The whole situation became untenable. I, as a relatively inexperienced director, was completely filled with the unbearable feeling of a negative force lurking out there in the city. I still shudder when I remember the terrible feeling of inertia Bob would induce in me when I'd hear from actors something like, 'We should put this scene back in the picture,' or 'We shouldn't be doing that,' or 'We should be doing what Bob tells us.' It finally reached a stage where David severed the relationship with Bob and we decided to go it alone without his day-to-day involvement in the various decisions on what to shoot or who to cast. Although David and I argued about what was right and what was wrong for the movie, we would then reach an agreement. As a threesome it seemed that Ellis, Noyce and Elfick were not able to argue and reach agreement, but just to argue and reach a further heated disagreement, which quickly became a public disagreement that threatened to disrupt the whole process.

After I had decided on which scenes to cut from the screenplay, it became necessary to do a small amount of rewriting to provide continuity for the remaining scenes. Most of the rewriting involved the reworking of the newsreel commentaries that linked various sequences. By this stage in the production we heard threats that Bob was so disturbed by these changes he was considering removing his name from the screenplay. We eventually arrived at a decision to screen the finished film to Bob and then he could determine whether he was going to take credit for what had ended up on the screen.

The film was almost finished in late April 1978, we screened it to Bob and, although negative grunts could be heard coming from his corner of the theatrette during the screening, when the lights came up he left the screening room without saying a word. Later, at the offices of the New South Wales Film Corporation, the principal investors in the film, a meeting was held between myself, David, Bob, Jane Cameron, who at the time was Bob's agent, and various officers of the New South Wales Film Corporation, at which we received Bob's pronouncement about credit. Basically what Bob said was, 'You have changed my screenplay to the point that it's unrecognisable, the film will be a disaster, therefore you [pointing to me] can take the blame, and the credits I propose are "Screenplay by Phillip Noyce, based on a screenplay by Bob Ellis". ' He could have included 'and Anne Brooksbank', Bob's wife, who had written some of the scenes, particularly the domestic scenes between Len Maguire and his wife Fay. David and I pleaded with him to take credit for the screenplay and for it to be amongst the front credits of the film. But Bob would not agree, thus the end credit for screenplay—as it still appears on the movie—was agreed upon.

A few weeks after the meeting at the offices of the New South Wales Film Corporation, *Newsfront* had its first semi-public screening as part of the judging process for the 1978 Australian Film Institute Awards. The screening was held in Melbourne in early May and we began to get extremely positive responses from audiences, which were followed by a glowing review written by Mike Harris for *Variety*. Then in the second week of May, David and I set out for the Cannes Film Festival carrying the film on the plane with us. *Newsfront* was to be shown not in any of the competitive sections but just in the sidebar, the marketplace, where anyone can rent a cinema and screen a film. We screened it to a quarter-full house at the first screening, which was followed by four or five full houses with turn-away audiences. Here too the screenings of *Newsfront* were followed immediately by various positive reviews from around the world, particularly from Andrew Sarris and Molly Haskell in New York, and David Robinson writing for *The London Times* and Derek Malcolm for *The Guardian* in the UK.

Meanwhile, back home the film was nominated for a record number of Australian Film Institute Awards. At the awards ceremony in Perth in June 1978, *Newsfront* won a then record eleven prizes, including Best Original Screenplay, which was awarded to Bob Ellis and Phillip Noyce. But a series of rather funny incidents happened prior to, during and after the ceremony. I had flown to Perth from Europe and all of the nominees were staying at the same Perth hotel. After a long flight I went down to the basement spa in my hotel robe, opened the door and sat down naked in the spa. About thirty seconds later the door opened and in walked a naked Bob Ellis. While we were sweating away in this hot-box, I said to him, 'This is ridiculous, the film might win tonight, you and I know that you wrote the script, I rewrote parts of it and reworked the structure. But it's your screenplay, so let's just cut all the gags out here and get back to reality.' Then on the night when the award for Best Original Screenplay was announced, as I rose from my seat I felt a bolt of lightning shoot past me—it was Bob Ellis running up ahead of me to receive the award. As I said earlier, although Anne Brooksbank contributed and both Bob and I are mentioned as recipients, finally it's Bob's script.

Soon after, Ellis took out an ad in *The National Times*,[9] a newspaper that's no longer published, saying that he agreed to accept responsibility and credit for writing the screenplay, but still threatened to shoot David Elfick or myself if we ever happened to enter the boundaries of his property on Palm Beach in the north of Sydney. On that note, it appeared the fracas was finally resolved.

At the time of *Newsfront*'s release the controversy over the script was well documented in the media and anyone who was interested was aware of the whole debacle and certainly knew that Ellis had written the screenplay. But I think Bob became concerned by the fact that history may not judge him as the real author of the piece, for over the ensuing years a new generation of writers, whether journalists or film historians, have revisited *Newsfront* and, of course, based on the credits that appear at the end of the movie, they have frequently excluded Bob Ellis from receiving proper credit. The controversy was reignited in 1997 by an article written by Ian Stocks and published in the Australian film magazine *Cinema Papers*,[10] which contained an interview with Bob and seemed to suggest that he had been denied due recognition when the credits had been determined. The article also seemed to suggest that Philippe Mora had been denied credit as the originator of the idea for *Newsfront*.

TWENTY-FIVE YEARS LATER

During the early part of pre-production, Frans Vandenburg, John Scott and I visited the National Film Archive in Canberra to cull through newsreel material that might be relevant to our story. We looked at reel after reel and unearthed a lot of material that is used throughout the film, but one of our discoveries was a piece featuring Chico Marx singing 'Waltzing Matilda' with a group of Australian soldiers gathered around him. We decided to open the film with it and from this came the idea of segueing from Chico's version of 'Waltzing Matilda' into the ghost-like version as composed by Bill Motzing. It seemed so appropriate to the theme of cultural imperialism that is central to the screenplay written by Ellis. The irony is how incredibly appropriate that musical segue is twenty-five years later.

In 1998 the Sydney Film Festival held a twentieth anniversary screening of *Newsfront* at one of the Greater Union theatres in Pitt Street. Frans, assistant editor on *Newsfront* back in 1978, gathered together a lot of the cast and crew for a seminar to discuss the movie, particularly in the light of Ian Stocks's *Cinema Papers* article about authorship. Apart from Frans, cinematographer Vince Monton was there, so too were the editor John Scott, producer David Elfick, scriptwriter Bob Ellis, Lissa Coote and Larry Eastwood, production designer and art director respectively, cast members Chris Haywood and Angela Punch-McGregor, and myself. We also had the recollections of Bill Motzing, the American composer who lived in Australia during the making of *Newsfront*, but now lives back in the US.

As you can imagine, I was thrilled to see a packed house but when the movie hit the screen both Vincent Monton and myself were completely shocked. What we saw was less than half the movie—the print had faded. It killed me because I suddenly realised the integrity of the original was really an issue, a preservation issue that was compounded by another factor.

Some years ago a former member of the New South Wales Film Corporation, the principal financiers of the film, had gone private and together with some other people—who knows who they were?—started a company, which was registered in Panama but whose offices still to this day remain unknown. This company bought—well, the former officer of the New South Wales Film Corporation sold to his own corporation—a package of films that included Gillian Armstrong's *My Brilliant Career* (1979), Jim Sharman's film based on Patrick White's play, *The Night The Prowler* (1979), *Newsfront* and a number of other Australian films.

What happened was that the films were sold outright in perpetuity for a fixed sum because at the time the Film Corporation may not have thought there was any significant future income to be generated by these films, and, well, as state politics go, a windfall of $1–7 million would help the balance sheet for a certain year. But of course, as we have all subsequently learnt, the value of our then 'gargantuan-budgeted' films seems like an anthill compared to the mountain of money that can be returned to movies from all of the distribution possibilities that have emerged since the fifties. Not just television, which is probably all there was when the deal was done, but home video, cable television, laser disc, and now DVD.

But it was the fact that the company held certain printing elements that made me very worried about the certainty of making future prints of *Newsfront*. A couple of weeks after the event at the Sydney Film Festival, I really felt something had to be done about this. We—that is, Frans and myself—had to locate all the extant negatives of this film, and we had to check the original negative, which is held by the National Film & Sound Archive in Canberra [now called ScreenSound Australia].

When I got back to America I immediately recalled a print I had donated to Columbia University where Andrew Sarris was using it to teach a film course. I looked at that print and realised the students must have thought the film-makers of *Newsfront* to be incredibly avant-garde because the image had almost completely faded on that print. It looked like a cast of ghosts wandering through a desert-like landscape. It was rather interesting and certainly compelling in a different way, but nothing like the film that we had originally shot. I immediately contacted Frans and said, 'Let's not worry about the cost at this stage, I'll just pay for it, but let's get a search started.' From Australia Frans, whom I'd describe as a relentless beaver, began a long process—which lasted over the next nine months—of checking out what printing materials remained. The film archive, quite rightly, were reluctant to strike a print from the original negative because there were still inter-positives and inter-negatives around.

Soon afterwards, following political pressure from the New South Wales government, the company announced they were giving back the rights to all the Australian films they had bought in that package many years previously. That's when I decided that Frans should come over to America, because the company told us that the printing materials were housed in a warehouse in Pasadena, California.

To cut back in the story, as dismayed as I was by the fading of the prints, I thought it was very possible that the original negative of the original printing materials had also faded. In theory, and until this is also proven wrong, the most reliable original source now existing for motion pictures is a metal digital disc. Thus Frans and I decided that after he had investigated and examined what printing materials were available, along with the original cinematographer, Vincent Monton, we were to choose reel-for-reel the best possible printing source. Then as quickly as possible the best thing to do was make a digital master.

Inspired by the conversation that took place back at the festival between the various original contributors to the film, Frans suggested we should somehow compile material to develop some sort of commentary on *Newsfront*. Frans had already initiated some archiving of those conversations; off his own bat he had paid for two video cameras to record the whole of the proceedings that evening—he had an idea of making a documentary about the making of the film. I then suggested to him that since we were making a digital master, and as he had already started the process of providing a commentary, admittedly based on the recollections of people twenty years later, we should put out a DVD version of *Newsfront*.

At that stage DVD technology was just emerging in America and hadn't yet arrived in Australia. But I realised from the few DVDs I had seen in America that the whole discipline of film was about to change dramatically. Because of the emergence of this CD-sized disc, its accessibility, portability and its capacity to deliver additional audio and visual information, suddenly every home video viewer was about to become, potentially, if they wanted to be, a film buff. During the initial CD era we've seen the remastering and reissuing of great performances by singers and bands, with alternate takes and bootleg additions on the same CD. I realised there was a whole new market that had opened up in the music field and I felt *Newsfront* could have a second life. I thought we probably owed it to ourselves to seize the initiative Frans had started with the Sydney Film Festival session.

My personal dream, using *Newsfront* as a starting point, is that the copyright owners of other Australian films could be jump-started into realising there is another market for product that's been sitting on their shelves for years—they might be encouraged to remaster and reissue. And what I'd also like to do is to get one of the distribution companies interested in starting a whole new label dedicated to Australian cinema, like the Criterion collection in America. They could remarket the films by combining several titles on the one disc, like the works of one director, the work of a particular generation of actors, or different studios such as Kennedy Miller or the original Adams–Packer studio[11]—there are all sorts of possibilities. The important point is that with funds short, suddenly there is a chance to save a lot of this work and to pay for this preservation through the new commercial opportunities now available—which is as important as any film preservation issue.

We who work in cinema and have a particular passion for films of the past of course advocate preservation. To be concerned that these movies are preserved is one thing, but the beauty of the DVD disc format is that suddenly, of course, the whole population becomes potential film buff–consumers. That's very exciting because what also comes with it is a certain obligation—the audience is suddenly there again. There is a whole history there and via DVD we suddenly have someone to tell it to again, and so we should do it.

Every time I go to Melbourne I'm reminded of an event that seemed like yesterday, but I realise when I look in the mirror that it happened long ago. We finished *Newsfront*, flew the print down and carried it to the AFI Awards back in 1978 and first screened it to the public—admittedly not the general public, but a collection of film workers in Melbourne—as part of the judging process for the awards. It's funny recalling that time now because I'm always meeting young Australians who take for granted the fact of an Australian film industry. They have no idea about how it evolved, and they find it very odd when I tell them that in all my childhood I never saw an Australian movie. Then you suddenly realise that a lot of the people who were working in the late sixties and early seventies are no longer with us. It feels like time is running out in more ways than one, the films are fading and they need to be restored to their original glory—and so do the people.

The scriptwriter: an interview with Bob Ellis

Phillip Noyce and Frans Vandenburg

Can you introduce yourself and tell us a little of your background?

I'm Bob Ellis and I'm the principal writer of *Newsfront*. In 1970 I co-wrote a trail-blazing Australian play called *The Legend of King O'Malley* with Michael Boddy,[1] a war correspondent on *The Nation Review*.[2] I owned the Nimrod Theatre [now called the Stables Theatre] for ten years where many great careers were launched, including those of Angela Punch-McGregor and Lorna Lesley. I have become a speechwriter for politicians of the Labor persuasion, a political historian, controversialist, mob-orator, and sometimes a successful stage actor. I've written several screenplays and directed three feature films— *Unfinished Business* (1986), *Warm Nights on a Slow Moving Train* (1988), *The Nostradamus Kid* (1993)—and a couple of documentaries, and also I've been writing a film column for about thirty years. My career in movies would be the equivalent of what is commonly known in literature as 'a man of letters'.

What is The Legend of King O'Malley *about?*

King O'Malley is about Australian politics at the turn of the century, and about a really remarkable and eccentric American figure that was hugely influential in Australian life. O'Malley was a mountebank and a scoundrel and the inventor of his own spurious religion. The text of the play was not particularly good but the production was fantastic, and its effect was to alter and revive Australian theatre. I therefore had a spurious reputation as a dramatic writer. I also had a separate reputation as a screenwriter because of a screenplay I'd co-written with Chris McGill on the life of Norman Lindsay, which was never produced.

How did you become involved in Newsfront?

I had been a freelance writer for about four years after accidentally co-writing *King O'Malley*, and on the morning I had decided never again to work on anybody else's idea, David Elfick arrived with the best idea I'd heard. It was about the lifestyle of newsreel cameramen and the stories they covered in the years from 1945 to 1956, with the proviso that newsreels of the day would be inserted into the drama. Elfick approached me after he'd heard a speech I'd written which was delivered by Graeme Blundell for an award night at the Sydney Film Festival. He rang me saying that I was just the kind of person he needed for this project, but had not told me he had already got a script of no great value out of Richard Neville, nor that he'd been ordered by the Australian Film Commission to approach someone like me who had some street credit as a dramatic writer, rather than as a book writer or journalist.

Did you always have an interest in that particular period of Australian history?

Oh yes, it's very much my period. The best stuff I've written is always lodged in the years 1945 to 1955, and it's an era best defined by the great Robert Mitchum film, *Out of the Past* (1947). It's where I and other true believers live in our heads.

Why is that?

It's when I became politically awake. The first political event I really noticed was the Communist Referendum of 1951, and the night of the unexpected victory is still very clear to me. I also attended the 1956 Olympic Games in Melbourne, which was a big, though slightly disappointing experience for me. Of course these events found their way into the screenplay.

Also on my mind was the kind of man my father was—uneducated but smart, good but limited in the scope of his life. When writing the screenplay I came upon the phrase 'buccaneers on mortgages', which perfectly defined the kind of man who had been to war and now had a job in which there were few adventures available.

Tell us about your father.

My father was born in 1904. He was a commercial traveller and had the kind of life that involved womanising, being drunk and free roving, but he always came home to a conventional life with a wife and kids. I suspected his life was similar to the life of many newsreel cameramen.

Many of my father's sayings are in the original script, things like, 'If it was raining gravy, I'd be holding a fork.' There's a point in the film just after the bushfire sequence where Len Maguire (Bill Hunter) and Charlie Henderson (Johnny Ewart) are talking about life and getting old and then Len sings the 'Aeroplane Jelly' song. That scene was based on my father, Keith Ellis, and his mate, Bob Donaldson. They would have this ongoing routine where my dad would sing a song that is more or less one note but he couldn't sing it. There'd be a pause and Donaldson would say, 'Great voice you've got there, Keith,' and Dad would say, 'It's a gift!' That scene is a little tribute to my dad, and it's that kind of Australian irony and sense of ageless friendship that I wanted to get into the script, more so than the politics.

Interestingly, Newsfront *is a thesis on the cultural colonisation of Australia in that period of Australian history. Was that a subject you were already interested in?*

It was always on my mind insofar as the 1950s was when the Australian film industry was lost by a deal Prime Minister Robert Menzies made with the American film companies in Australia. We had a pretty good film industry in the 1930s and early 1940s, of the provincial kind but it was not at all shameful. It was extinguished in the 1950s, and the film-makers who would have been our version of Frank Capra and Preston Sturges, if they stayed in the business at all, were forced downwards into a stifling newsreel business. The character of A.G. Marwood is based on Ken G. Hall, who was such a man. Hall was our great populist auteur, but after being head of Cinesound in the 1950s he wound up as the fairly prosperous and very discontented head of news for Channel 9.

Newsfront is about how we were—and still are—repeatedly colonised by America in different ways. Whenever we seem to get our head above the parapet, it's then knocked down again. The recent arrival of Fox Studios is doing much the same now as was done back then by the deal between Menzies and the cinema distributors.

Following the surge of ambition and possibility that both war and the film industry give one, many people were pressured by their current lives into doing what amounted to an office job with some travelling opportunities. They were unwillingly stifled in the best years of their lives. That was part of the notion of *Newsfront,* as well as being about the time when television had arrived in Australia, which for a while seemed to have eradicated Australian culture from Australian screens.

Chris Hewitt (Chris Haywood) with Ellie (Lorna Lesley)

Can you tell us where you were born, where you grew up, and what newsreels meant to you?

I was born in 1942 and grew up in the country town of Lismore in a fundamentalist religion, the Seventh Day Adventist Church. My sister was killed when I was ten years old, and because my mother was going mad I was sent to stay for a while with my Aunty Jean in Newcastle. There was a ferry that I could catch to go across to the city and attend the newsreel theatrette and watch a great number of Marx Brothers films, shorts, cartoons and newsreels. I'd sometimes sit in that newsreel theatre and see the same program four or five times over, absolutely delighting in the whole experience. Of course I was mostly waiting for the Donald Duck cartoon to come on, but for a child the newsreel was still a big part of the whole experience and a dramatically thrilling way of looking at the events of the week.

At the age of sixteen I came to Sydney University on a scholarship and got involved in university drama, newspapers and politics, and because the newsreels were such a big part of my childhood I would attend the newsreel theatrette as a matter of course. I was also a fan of the stars of radio, people like Jack Davey, who were newsreel commentators as well as radio personalities. I used to attend the live recordings at the Macquarie auditorium of various shows like *The Quiz Kids* (c.1940s–50s) and *Leave It to the*

Girls (c. 1940s–1950s). I had a kind of starry-eyed view of the voices I'd heard on the newsreels and on radio. In those years, too, I befriended Mike Molloy and Howard Rubie, both of whom worked at Cinesound Studios.

So you knew both Howard Rubie and Mike Molloy long before Newsfront?

Yes, I met Mike Molloy in 1959 when I was living at the Raffles Hotel in Bondi, sharing a room with Les Murray, who is now the unofficial poet laureate of Australia and an interesting, fat right-wing man. Molloy was a friend of Murray's, and then I met Howard Rubie, who was a friend of Mike Molloy's. We used to have parties in our room and I remember a night when I had to lie between two single beds because Murray and a woman were in one bed and Molloy and another woman were in the other. They were sisters and I felt seriously left out.

Anyway, I got to know Mike and Howard and I'd hang around with them while they worked at Cinesound, watching rushes, or sometimes I'd go out with them on a job and watch them film. Howard and Mike were my first contacts in the film business, and when I first became interested in being an active participant in the industry. In 1960 I somehow contrived to have them help me make a film that I half-directed, which was called 'Who Travels Alone'. It was about a soldier who was remembering home while dying in an unknown war. The lead actor was Arthur Dignam, and it amounted to being a silent film with a lot of upside-down shots of the Harbour Bridge and things like that. We never finished it.

When David approached you with the idea, what material did he give you to work with?

Elfick originally had a vague idea of doing a film about Australian pop music of the 1950s and early 1960s. There existed then a lot of footage, principally from *Six O'Clock Rock* (1959–63) and *Bandstand* (1958–72), and by way of research into the music footage, Elfick came upon the Cinesound and Movietone newsreels and began to react to them. Then he thought of doing a documentary like Philippe Mora's *Brother, Can You Spare a Dime?* (1975). Obviously he approached Philippe Mora, who said, 'It's a good idea but why not make a drama about the men who shot the newsreels, instead of merely doing a collage film?' The idea originated with Philippe Mora and was based on two brothers called Syd and Ross Wood, both of whom worked for rival newsreel companies and had a sometimes genuine, sometimes ferocious professional rivalry between them. Elfick took that idea first to Richard Neville and then to me. That's how Elfick explained it.

I was then offered the document written by Neville and I deliberately never read it because I thought it would confuse me. I also read about two pages of a document written by Elfick and it was so dreadful that I threw it across the room, bounced it against the wall and jumped on it. I didn't get more than two or three pages into that one.

Then Elfick organised a whole day in which we researched the newsreels of the period and I worked out a hit list of newsreel items that were to be inserted into the drama. This list included such items as the great locust plague of the 1940s, Don Bradman's last Test, and the coming of the Sputnik. David had the idea that the climax of *Newsfront* should include the 1956 Olympic Games, which witnessed a bloody gladiatorial battle between two sides of the Iron Curtain.

That was David's idea?

Yes, it was his idea to feature the battle between the two water-polo teams for the ending. All of the material we watched was quite exciting, but I felt the most exciting material was left out of *Newsfront*, such as the first visit to Australia of the very young and beautiful Queen Elizabeth II. Watching this tiny beautiful girl standing up in a car with a swarm of Australians all around her I thought was a particularly striking newsreel. You would now think that she was in great physical danger. It's just a wonderful image, and I was appalled it wasn't in the final cut of the film because as far as I can remember, her visit was a big event of the 1950s.

Who came up with the title?

I think Philippe came up with *Newsfront*; Elfick wanted to call it 'Useless If Delayed'. But it was decided that the word 'useless' in the title might attract the venom of lazy critics and so Elfick settled for *Newsfront*. My summary line for the film—'buccaneers on mortgages'—was the shortest way to express the content but it was never considered as a title. It was always just a description.

At this stage was the political thesis of the script an embryonic one, or had it already formed?

The idea for the 'McCarthyist' strand of *Newsfront* was mine. I'm pretty sure of that. Partly because I remembered it so vividly from my childhood and partly because it was a moment in Australian history when we well might have become a police state. Under the provision of the proposed law, any two cabinet ministers in concert could declare you were a communist and confiscate your property and put you in gaol.

But the schism in the Labor Party, which is more thoroughly dealt with in *The True Believers* (1988), was meant only as a backdrop and the under-pinning of what happened within the Church. There were extraordinary occurrences of priests proselytising from the pulpit against the Labor Party on the grounds that they were secret communists. It was an exact parallel of the American experience. Perhaps not as ferocious, but it had certainly divided families, and it was a very important factor in the life of our nation because it's what kept the Labor Party out of government for a long time.

After you looked at the newsreel material and got your hit list, what did you do next?

I wrote a draft of the screenplay. In those days I wasn't good at stage direction, so I wrote the dialogue and Anne Brooksbank, my wife, wrote the stage directions and a couple of scenes involving Len and his wife Fay (Angela Punch-McGregor). Annie certainly wrote the scene of Len and Fay in bed talking about the children and she says, 'I gotta be mother and father to them half the time.'

This is the first draft?

No, let me go back. Before writing the first draft I consulted Howard Rubie and he told me more or less word for word and frame by frame the story of the 1954 Maitland flood, in which his experience was the basis for Chris Haywood's character, Chris Hewitt. Of course, Howard didn't drown, but the business of the chemist manufacturing the alcoholic drink in the upper room of a flooded pharmacy was true. Then I wrote the first draft and at that point Elfick found the script okay but insubstantial. He wanted more and so I went to Howard Rubie again and we wrote additional sequences, one of which had to do with photographing an erupting volcano with the cameraman hanging out of the aeroplane and being in great physical danger. I really wanted that sequence in the film but it was eventually eliminated. I felt the film needed that sense of danger—we had the 'mortgages', we needed the 'buccaneers'; we had the politics but we needed the hairy bits as well.

What were you doing professionally when Elfick approached you?

When Elfick came through the door I was the film critic and an occasional political correspondent for *The Nation Review*. I was also writing radio plays for the religious department of the ABC, as well as a moderately busy playwright collaborating with other people on works that went on at the then named Nimrod Theatre. I was a sort of minor celebrity—as I am every seven years. My wife, Anne Brooksbank, who is also a writer, was earning most of the money in the family. She was already writing soap television, as she has throughout her life, and we were living off that. She was not then my wife but my girlfriend. At that point I didn't have the tempestuous reputation I later got after moving to Palm Beach to live next door to Elfick, which may have had something to do with it.

Getting on to the subject of your tempestuous reputation—and it's absolutely fine for you to say anything you want to—from your point of view when did the troubles start?

I remember a great gloom came over me when Elfick said, 'We got the money and the film can be made, but the money is $100000 less than what is needed to make the film.' And because I had printed the script out in a silly format—it was triple-spaced and had come out to about 300 pages—there was a rumour that the script was far too long. But in fact the script was somewhere between two hours and two hours and ten minutes, which I thought was reasonable for a film that covered ten years of history. These days that's a mere bagatelle.

I also remember going into the production office at one point and noticing great lines struck through the screenplay and saying to Richard Brennan, 'What's all this? What's happening?' I remember Brennan looked at the script with an air of surprise and said, 'Oh, I didn't know anything about this!' I thought he was lying.

Was this at the office in Palm Beach?

No, first there occurred the famous incident at Palm Beach when I said, 'That's it! I'm taking the film.' I seized the script and began to run from the building, and there were workmen in the rafters cheering as Elfick tackled me and brought me down and the script's pages fluttered everywhere like butterflies.

What was the problem? That Elfick and Noyce wanted to cut the script?

Yes. The problem was that there were primal experiences in the script, and I saw the project more like a snapshot of a whole nation at a particular period of time, but what seemed to be happening was that the script was being pared back to the mere politics of the piece. There were other experiences in the script that were at least as interesting as a tedious left-wing wrangle, which had its place but needed to be supported by a number of other things.

For example, there was a family Christmas scene that made sense of the fact that the two lead characters were brothers who had a difficult and dominating father. It was a scene that depicted a classic Australian Christmas by the beach, in sweltering heat and among sandflies. These things were ill lost because of the arbitrary strictures of an arbitrary budget and a schedule that was unrealistic. I thought it was ridiculous that scenes were omitted because of the shooting schedule, and I felt that so much of the human side of the script was gone that the film would fail. I believe the film would have failed, too, if not for the geniuses of the editor and the composer, who somehow put back emotionally what had been omitted.

The script credit on Newsfront *reads 'Screenplay by Phillip Noyce based on a screenplay by Bob Ellis', which has caused considerable controversy over the years. Can you remember how the credit was arrived at?*

When I saw the film for the first time all I could focus on were the missing scenes, which to me seemed to be a travesty. Unfortunately I was with Jim McNeil,[3] a well-known 'serial murderer' and playwright, who was drunk and said it was a great film and that I should be proud of it. Of course, I didn't believe him because he was drunk! Annie was also there and she didn't like the film either. I went up to Elfick and began to say, 'You just should not have left out this or that scene.' Elfick, quite abruptly, just said, 'Well, is your name on it or off?' Because he was quite abrupt, in that moment I said, 'Off!' I was advised a few days later to restore my name because it was stupid not to do so. 'Never take your name off anything,' was the advice.

I'm not sure why, but being too clever by half I contrived the eventual credit, which is 'Screenplay by Phillip Noyce based on a screenplay by Bob Ellis'. But I didn't know the credit was going to be put on the end of the film instead of the front. I should have just put my name back on, but I guess I was young and furious and didn't realise the enormity of what I was doing. I just thought I was having a private quarrel with someone I'd come to dislike intensely for his own untrustworthiness. You just don't need intellectual dishonesty. You just don't mess around with credits because I think there's a moral bottom line—it's not fair. Life is too short and the business is too cruel.

Were you surprised by the success of the film?

I was staggered when the film was swarmed over at the Cannes Film Festival, but I was aware by then of the excellence of parts of it—in particular the music, the editing and the performances. I was also somewhat aware of the fact that *Newsfront* was quite original in form, although it did bear some resemblance to the films of Lindsay Anderson, and since it was the very first

Australian political feature film ever made, *Newsfront* had a kind of guilty impact, particularly on the left-wing movie-going community.

Newsfront had the inside track on a number of things, but that it beat *The Chant of Jimmie Blacksmith* (1978) at the AFI Awards was a little surprising to me. Although *Jimmie Blacksmith* has its faults, it's still a grand and well-wrought film, whereas *Newsfront* seems to be a bit scrappy. But I'm not an idiot and I could see the virtues in it—quite soon after, I gave *Newsfront* the accolade as the best film I'd worked on.

Why didn't the Australian film industry continue to make 'Newsfronts'? What happened?

There was a golden period in the Australian film industry that coincided with the reign of Paul Riomfalvy at the New South Wales Film Corporation, which gave us quite original films: *Careful, He Might Hear You* (1983), *Goodbye Paradise* (1983), *My Brilliant Career* (1979) and, in that era too, the quite start-lingly innovative films like *Mad Max* (1979). Then I think a man called John Howard was sold a tax dodge system by which a great deal of money could be made by almost anybody if they invested in almost anything that called itself a feature film. That would have been all right but for the fact that Howard put a June 30 limit on the production of any film. This meant that production crews were besieged by offers for the months of October and November, which, under the June 30 system, was the only time when films could go into production. So then the whole scheme spun outwards into a money-making machine and into this machine came lawyers and used-car salesmen and crooks in great numbers. The Australian film industry was once populated by people who went to small theatres, were members of small cinema appreciation groups, and made films on the weekend for the love of it, but almost overnight it went from being an industry of love to an industry of swindle money. It was a period when blue movies, bad action-adventure films and some really bad suspense and horror films were routinely made every year by a newly expanded, accountant-driven industry. It's a period from which I don't think we have ever really recovered.

When you look at Newsfront *now, how does it stand up as an Australian film?*

Newsfront is the second, third or fourth best Australian film. I'd say the best is *'Breaker' Morant* (1980) and the second best is *The Year My Voice Broke* (1987), but *Newsfront* could be the second best. It has an integrity and origi-nality of Australianness, and a level of dialogue and a kind of intellectual attack that few Australian films had in the 1970s and '80s. *Newsfront* is obviously a classic now in a way that I would say *Picnic at Hanging Rock*

(1975) isn't. It not only holds up, it declares an aggressive, confident Australian content and a colloquial dialogue that probably hasn't survived as a style. At least *Newsfront* is a measure of what has been lost.

There have been some remarkable films made in the 1990s, but I'm just not sure how they stand up or compare. There is one very fine recent film called *Praise* (1999) that gives one a sense of the *Newsfront* feel for characters, people who are working class and yet they are smart and articulate and sensitive. Maybe it's coming back.

The Legend of King O'Malley for a time started a raft of similar plays that were then overwhelmed by the Shaftesbury tradition of David Williamson, or the middle-classification of what was then a rough and interesting working-class and bohemian experience. Similarly with *Newsfront* and a few other films made around that time, a number of them by Noyce: a very fine film called *Backroads* (1977), for example, and also a lovely film by Stephen Wallace called *Love Letters from Teralba Road* (1977). But then the lawyers and the middle class got in fast—the way they always do—and what began to be manufactured was sort of a proto, mid Atlantic wank that was bound to fail. Not only because it had little to do with us, it had little to do with anything much.

It wasn't until ten years later that I really watched *Newsfront* rather more objectively, as one would, and I began to analyse its success. The writing was fine and the acting was very good but the success of it derived from two other ingredients. One of those is the accidental juxtaposition of black-and-white and colour, which always seems to add an extra emotional dimension to whatever the film happens to be. Whether it's *Abbott and Costello Meet Captain Kidd* (1952) or *The Wizard of Oz* (1939), however accidental or illogical, the juxtaposition of those two forms adds immensely to the over-all emotional effect of a film.

In fact I would say that black-and-white is better than colour because it is removed from life and so you invest more into the images than you would in colour. It is like legend. Therefore anything that is heroic or particularly zany is more convincing in black-and-white. The success of *Newsfront* partly depended on those black-and-white images as life the way it is remembered, as life turned into legend. The legendary life of Australia could not have been realised with such force if *Newsfront* had been shot completely in colour.

The music is the other ingredient. It provided the backstory for the actors. The scenes that were dropped from the film—but I thought were essential—were somehow resupplied by the music. The audience gets to know a lot more about the characters via the music than they are being told visually or through dialogue, and what I think is remarkable about William Motzing's music is that he didn't use much of his own, just occasional strings and sighs on the soundtrack. The rest of it is actual songs or echoes of songs: somehow he was able to creep in 'Waltzing Matilda' or 'The Road to Gundagai' under an actual performance.

But the best example of Motzing's musical genius is the eerie effectiveness of the music over the opening montage. Of course the opening sequence does contain a highly adequate montage of newsreel images, but it's the way 'Waltzing Matilda' seems to come in like a ghost or a distant memory that lifts the film to a point from which it never falls. I'm sure of it.

But why do you think Newsfront *was a success in Australia? Why did it speak to Australians? Was it just nostalgia?*

Newsfront succeeded because it had resonance with the erased memory of Australians. They remembered vividly the Maitland flood, which was quite a recent event, just over twenty years back, and the Olympic Games was also a great moment when Australia broke through in national pride because we came third on the medal count.

At that moment we were also coming to understand our fathers better. There was a good description of the film as being a love song to all our fathers. It's about the baby-boomers' fathers as well as about the quality of being Australian, which was also being explored in parallel ways by Barry Humphries and Paul Hogan, and certainly by the playwrights, particularly Peter Kenna and Ray Lawler.[4]

It's interesting that a film with such an unconventional structure should have been a commercial success.

The truth is that films with an unconventional structure usually always work in a way that films with a three-act structure only sometimes work. The three-act structure is not a guarantee of success and in the end is not a very good structure. The films we love are those made by film-makers like Frederico Fellini, François Truffaut, Lindsay Anderson, Robert Altman, Woody Allen, and others who do not heed to the absurdly simplistic notion that a film can only succeed if it conforms to a particular structure. It's like saying that a song can only succeed if it has five lines, an A A, B B, A rhythmical structure, which has been disproved by people like Bob Dylan and Simon and Garfunkel.

I just don't believe that a theory should precede the writing of a film. It's a silly idea. When a film has integrity in its creation of a certain 'reality' and does not stray from that 'reality', then it doesn't really matter whether the characters go on a journey or not. Nor does it matter how many acts are contained within it. With the exception of *Casablanca* (1942), everybody's favourite films disobey the rules. One of the most popular films ever made, *Gone With the Wind* (1939), has probably fourteen acts and characters that do not learn a thing. It's the most popular film ever made for very good reason: because people relate to the contents of it rather than to a journey.

In *Newsfront* Len does not go on a journey, he is the same man first and last, his brother is the same man first and last, the woman whom they share is the same strumpet first and last. Nor does anything much happen in *Newsfront*. Australia changes a bit, but not for the better. Australia is not redeemed, in fact things grow worse in Australia. These are the ingredients of a disaster but they are also the ingredients of a successful film. *Newsfront* resonated with the audiences of the time because it told of how things were no matter how harsh the reality.

Now the original ending in the script was a downbeat ending, whereas for the film the ending was changed, even though it's certainly not upbeat.

The ending as originally written was to commence with a scene between Len Maguire, Charlie Henderson and Ken (John Dease); while on a fishing boat at night they see the Sputnik come over and reflect on how the world is different. This scene was to be followed by a scene in which Len receives lifetime honours for being a fine cameraman at an event that essentially amounts to being an AFI Awards ceremony. He gives a little speech about how he was a storeman and packer and how grateful he was for having had the chance to work for Cinetone. He says something like, 'When I think of the breadth of life we witness and what good times we had, I'm glad I didn't stay a storeman and packer.' Then afterwards Len drives past the newsreel cinema, which is now showing Brigitte Bardot in *Et Dieu créa la femme* (. . . *And God Created Woman*, 1956). That was to be the end.

The scene driving past the cinema was kept, but the other two were not shot for reasons partly creative and partly due to money. Instead the original ending was re-edited and replaced by a scene at the Olympic Games, one that actually preceded those three scenes in the screenplay, and which essentially amounts to being an argument between Len and his brother about whether to go to America and become wealthy, or to stay in Australia and remain poor. To me the new ending seemed to be seriously disastrous. It gave you something of a happy ending, but also seemed to be another instance of the story having been pruned back to two or three quarrels, one about the Labor Party and one about Australia versus America. So, rather than being about a fuller experience of life in Australia, the film ends on too political a note, on some big issue about resisting American temptation where Len tells his brother to, 'Go bite your bum!' Then Len marches off like a Capra hero down a tunnel to oblivion. It was a bit gauche and adolescent for me, thrilling in its own way, but more thrilling as a film of the past rather than a film of the present. It looked too idealistic at that time. It seems okay now, but in the way that you will forgive Capra now for what you might not have forgiven him back then.

Obviously you must have been in a real funk because things became really bitter between all the participants. Can you expose to us your mindset and your feelings of betrayal?

I resented most of the film's cutting back to the mere politics of the time. *Newsfront* should have been more like a snapshot of an entire era—hot Christmases by the beach, more of the sport, the music we listened to, the way of Australian life generally. Instead it came dangerously close to being an anti-McCarthyist rancour when it wasn't intended in that way. That was what hit me between the eyes when I saw it for the first time.

But when these things happen in my life my response is one of humorous fury. I want to make mischief in the world but there's a lot of levity in that mischief. I truly was not as artistically distressed as I may have seemed at the time. I rather enjoyed writing the challenging advertisements that were published in *The National Times*, saying that I'd fight a duel with Elfick, or I'd shoot Noyce and Elfick if they came on my lawn. For me that kind of situation is like white-water rafting, it's enjoyable and dangerous. The whole situation was a battle and I don't mind being in battle.

And I wasn't frantic about what I regarded as the destruction of the script, nor frantic to have my name back on the film, as it might have seemed to other participants. I was busy doing other things and believed my life was going to be rich and full, that I would have a life like Orson Welles, and that *Newsfront* was only a chapter in my life and there would be other chapters. I'd already created a masterpiece with Michael Boddy and, as I remember, that collaboration fell apart over the matter of a missing dog. So I wasn't worried, because in my view *Newsfront* was just the next story in an ongoing saga.

But what I didn't realise then was that a sort of bombastic unruly talent, as evidenced by me, would not prevail in the film industry, and that the mediocre tenacity of clerks, bureaucrats and shifty conmen would eventually rule.

The portrait of Australia and the Australian personality is one thing that's, shall we say, unique about the film, it captures the Australian experience like no other film ever did. Can you just talk about your conception of the Australian personality and what you wanted to capture?

Michael Boddy once said that the classic Australian picture is of two quarrelsome friends bent over a fucked piece of machinery, trying to work out what went wrong and chiacking and blaming each other in a matey way. This type of quarrelsome mateship, which can quite often come nearly to blows, is the source of a lot of wit—and a lot of wounding wit—in a friendship that persists all the same. To some extent that was always on my mind with *Newsfront*: a friendship that lasts an entire lifetime of the kind of men who drink together, chiack, bait and rib one another. It was not about the kind of men who go to university and stand on stairways with scarfs around their necks, drink champagne and sally forth their wit.

Also on my mind was the kind of society where people have a lot of time on their own, they stand under vast skies and eventually say something quite brief, like, 'Think it might rain? Did once.' That sort of thing.

You wanted to capture the idiom of the Australian language?

I was trying to get in dialogue and character what, say, Edward Hopper got on canvas in America of a particular milieu of lower, working-class solitude, which can be a populated solitude. Although Len exists in a tumultuous industry, he also lives in a populated solitude: he is a lonely man at odds with his family, religion, politics, work, and his art. That kind of Australian loneliness has always been sung well by Henry Lawson, John Williamson and other great folk poets of our culture. Of course Australians have always had solitude, and I think it is their first quality. They have companionship, rather than comradeship, as their second quality.

What about the Irish strand in the Australian personality—obviously that was crucial to the characters you were presenting and your portrait of Len in particular?

The Irish have a rather unique quality of heroic self-mockery. They will often do a brave thing and mock it afterwards. Many Australians are like that. When you think about it, the classic Anzac was a very Irish kind of man. He was a man who belittled the enormously heroic thing he had accomplished, or tossed off as a mere nothing the incredibly moral or self-sacrificing thing he had done. It comes across in Australians as taciturnity, but it's very Irish at heart.

Is the purity of Len's convictions something that goes back to the Irish?

The Irish, because they were so poor throughout history, have a strong sense of self, principle and honour. These qualities have been transmitted through to the Australian–Irish, down to men like Paul Keating, who has a definite honour although it's hard to define how it shows itself. The principle for which you will sacrifice your life, well-being, job or your money is the type of Irish honour that infuses *Newsfront*.

If Len had been like his brother, who is less of an Irishman, he would have had a Hollywood life like Rod Taylor or someone like that, a man who just became an international wastrel with American wealth and American bodyguards. But Len has a stronger sense of self, a stronger sense of the kind of man he is and the kind of loyalties he owes. In those days it was believed that you should not let down the company that gave you a job, or saved you when you were broke. You owed the company your existence and therefore you stayed with it through thick and thin. It was like a marriage vow between you and the company. These days, however, companies are mere moments in the life of tawdry adventurers who, win or lose, are always gambling with other people's lives.

One of the things you took issue with in the past—which I think is totally valid—is the idea that one could watch the film all the way through and not realise that the two men, Len and Frank, are brothers. It's an issue exacerbated by the casting, and because in your opinion a crucial scene was dropped from the screenplay. Can you talk about how they were conceived?

The fact that the two men are brothers was underlined in the screenplay by a family Christmas scene, in which their old bastard of a father dominates them. If the audience didn't know they were brothers, by that stage in the film they definitely would have known. But that scene was dropped.

Moreover, I originally wrote the two brothers with the idea that they would be played by Bill Hunter and Jack Thompson, who roughly resembled one another in complexion, blondness, huskiness, and even in voice. It was a tragedy we lost Jack Thompson because two blond beasts of great charm would have been better than pairing Bill Hunter with the saturnine and curious-looking Gerard Kennedy, who was inexplicably a star at the time. If the pair looked like each other the audience would at least have sensed they were brothers. I think the film would have been better had that occurred. It didn't. Instead you had a black-haired and a blond-haired coupling, which is very unlikely for two brothers of Irish descent. And their relationship never really gelled on screen. An audience could sit through the film thinking these two men are just friends, which is a pity because the contest between two brothers for the one girl is always a different matter from the contest of two men for the one girl.

You said earlier you didn't think any one of the characters changed.

Len's wife changes, but she changes from the imperative that comes upon a woman who has been divorced or is left by her husband. That type of change is unavoidable. But it's not a journey, that's just a catastrophe.

You had written three different types of women for the film; they all seem to take different paths and represent different attitudes. Can you talk about how you came to invent those three characters?

Amy McKenzie (Wendy Hughes) is an Ava Gardner type, a tough, glamorous woman of ferocious purpose and great sexuality, who will go a long way because she doesn't mind what she does on the way up. I always tend to cast a role in my head before I write it, and in my mind for the role of Amy was Carmen Duncan, who is a very beautiful and very driven actress. In the end I think Wendy Hughes did a fine job and she looks beautiful in black-and-white, but to me Carmen had an Ava Gardner quality and she looked just like an illustration out of any *Women's Weekly* short story of the 1940s.

The absolute opposite of Amy is Fay, Len's wife, who is a puritan, sexually frightened and very much a creature of her era. She's the type of woman who exists in the blinkers of a Catholic marriage and in the blinkers of the Virgin Mary and has no idea of what is to be had by way of joy in the world. There was more than a whole generation of women like that—and probably men like that, too—who could not or did not want to see what was in front of their eyes. I thought she was an interesting type, but I had no idea why Len would marry such a woman.

Did you have a particular model in mind for Fay?

Fay was based on a lot of the Seventh Day Adventist women, whom I would describe as nervous vegetarians. They did not look outward at all but looked inward to the kitchen and the routine of being a wife. They were also the type who feared that men were wayward beasts—with some evidence and justification, of course—and they lived by the sustaining fantasy that the only wisdom needed to get through in the world depended on having the right sort of nappy wash or cleansing fluid for the dishes. Fay was meant to be that type, someone with an amazingly obtuse and shrunken view of the world.

The scriptwriter

Ellie (Lorna Lesley) is the kind of girl I remembered from Lismore, a girl who inadvertently gets pregnant after being dazzled by the pitch of a travelling salesman. She is then stuck in an innocent coat with the consequences for the rest of her life. The conception of Ellie was no more brilliant than that—with the exception of the casting of Lorna Lesley, which was my idea. Lorna seemed to me to possess those qualities straight away.

You've said that Ellie wears an innocent coat, yet you've written a woman who seems very much in control and to be taking advantage of the situation. She does say at one point, 'I wanted it to happen.'

Yes, she does. Well, in country girls such as Ellie there is the feeling for the moment when 'the' man arrives and he must be seized. He can be trapped and one of those traps can be a pregnancy. On the night Ellie spends with Chris Hewitt, she could have thought or said, 'Listen, have you got anything?' or 'I can go out to the chemist,' or 'Should we pull out?' But she didn't because she believed 'the' moment had arrived.

The sense of predestination in country girls is very big, or it was back in the 1940s and '50s. It's the idea that a certain someone will one day come along—'The Man I Love' sort of thing—and he'll be big and strong. Ellie's idea of a glamorous man is the idea my mother had of my father, who was a commercial traveller. Chris Hewitt is a very similar person, someone who is there for a moment and just maybe he can be entrapped. If not, then maybe enjoyed. It's often virgins—as Ellie is—who think that way because they believe getting their man can be that simple. But of course it can be a horror as well.

Are you saying you drew on your mother?

My mother was the daughter of the principal Seventh Day minister of the district and my father was selling Bibles when they met. She told me that when my father arrived in the doorway she looked up and he seemed to have filled up the doorway. He was so tall and lovely that she knew it had to be him. She knew he was 'the' one when she was fourteen years old and by the time of her eighteenth birthday she was married to him. My mother took a lot longer than Ellie to be married, but her focused moment is similar to what Ellie experiences.

The scene between those two characters was well performed by Chris and Lorna; there was a kind of puppy-like feeling between the two of them. There's a point when he says, 'I'm not just a pretty face,' and she says, 'You are funny!' It's a very lovely moment, and very Ellis-que, if I may put it that way.

Did you have anyone in mind when you came up with the figure of the radical, Geoff, the editor (Bryan Brown)?

Geoff was not based on anybody in particular, but on a whole generation of people who left Australia because they could no longer stand the littleness of it and could no longer stand the torpid conservatism of the Menzies era. The editor's assistant, Bruce (Drew Forsythe), was like Anthony Buckley, who I think was an editor on newsreels in those days, but I had no particular model for Geoff other than having him possess a kind of ferocious political stance, which I must admit Bryan Brown did wonderfully well. It's one of his finest performances. He gave the role an intellectual depth that he often doesn't give his characters, but that part of him is there in real life. At one point in *Newsfront*, when his character reveals he's leaving for England, he says, 'It's the best place for an aging radical.' He can just get novels into one line of dialogue.

It's a pity he hasn't done more of that kind of stuff, and it's amazing how some people have said that Brown cannot act. He's one of the best screen actors I know because he has an extraordinary intensity that is pure gold on screen. I've always said the comparison is not with Clint Eastwood; it's with Kirk Douglas. You like him but he makes you feel a bit uncomfortable and you don't want him around for too long. That's why Brown is best walked on screen for twenty minutes at a time and then shuffled off. If you've got to live with him for the entire duration of a film, it would be like living with Kirk Douglas, like living with a groin itch or a tick in the neck.

Who did you have in mind for the part of Ken, the narrator, who is played by John Dease?

I first thought that the role of Ken should have been played by Terry Deare, who had a round, avuncular personality. I used to go to the Macquarie auditorium and see Deare do things like *Leave It to the Girls* and *The Amateur Hour* (c. 1930s–1960s). There was no particular reason for my choice of Deare except that the man who actually did newsreel narrations was dead. His name was Jack Davey and Deare was someone who physically and vocally resembled Davey. But Dease was excellent, particularly with his beard and his strange beret. Ken is a wonderfully vivid character, which is not particularly due to the writing but to the performance of Dease.

How would you sum up your experience of working on Newsfront?

On occasion one is involved in a process that is combative and difficult, but also fruitful and can sometimes come out as *Newsfront*. Back in those days when it was not clear that the writer had no power over such things as the casting, I was exercising power out of sheer ignorance. The process we had endured on *Newsfront* produced a masterpiece; we just didn't know it was happening at the time. I didn't know what was happening from one day to the next.

Australian works that have many characters, what I call 'gang shows', quite often work much better than the American type of story of a single man going down a road. *Newsfront* worked precisely for the reason that it's not about one man's journey. Moreover, the 'gang show' element goes beyond the number of characters in *Newsfront*. The film is part newsreel, part documentary, part black-and-white, part colour, part drama, part history, part romance, part sibling rivalry, and so on. It had many things going into it and therefore many things going for it. It comes in at different levels, pitches, volumes, and at different colourations. We're ill to miss this variety of colourations when making movies. It's silly to imagine that a film is one thing; it is an interesting mixture of many things, and a great example is *Newsfront*.

How would you like to be remembered when you die?

I'd like to be remembered as an untidy but well-meaning renaissance man.

The producer

David Elfick

It's almost twenty-five years since I produced *Newsfront*. I'm in my fifties now and when I was a little boy my family lived in Maroubra and it always was a treat to catch a bus into town to watch the newsreels. I can remember many pleasant hours spent at the State Theatre in Market Street, which was almost like a child-minding centre that gave poor mothers an hour's respite from some nagging child. Although the newsreel format was an hour long it was continuous, and so sometimes I'd watch the program through twice, and it was always such good fun for kids because they'd also run comedies along with the newsreel.

I began my film career by making surfing documentaries and it's interesting that my first dramatic feature is *Newsfront*, which is a fiction film that leans heavily on archival footage to tell its narrative. The idea came about around the time that I directed a documentary called *To Shoot a Mad Dog* (1976), about the making of *Mad Dog Morgan*, a feature film shot in Australia in the mid 1970s with Dennis Hopper in the lead, Jack Thompson and Billy Hunter in secondary roles, produced by Jeremy Thomas and directed by Philippe Mora.

Earlier I'd gone to the Cannes Film Festival with my surfing movie, *Crystal Voyager* (1973), and Peter Weir and the McElroys [Hal and Jim] were there with *The Cars That Ate Paris* (1974), which I thought was an interesting film but not the type of film I wanted to make. Having made *Crystal Voyager*, I was keen on making something which had spectacular archival footage woven into a documentary narrative. That seemed like a more interesting concept, and of course Jeremy and Philippe had each made interesting feature-length documentaries, *Brother, Can You Spare a Dime?* (1975) and *Swastika* (1973). I suppose *Crystal Voyager* was to me what *Brother* and *Swastika* were to Jeremy and Philippe—a film that cemented my career.

On the shoot of *Mad Dog Morgan* I became very friendly with Mike Molloy, who was *Morgan's* cameraman and also a former newsreel camera-man. He ended up staying at my house in Palm Beach for a period of time after the shoot and we formed quite a close relationship. Not only is Mike a very fine cameraman, he is a good raconteur, especially with the help of a little neck oil.

At this point in time I was also a friend of Richard Neville and Andrew Fisher, both of whom I'd met in England, and I'd helped them out with their magazine *Oz*.[1] They would also end up staying at my place while Mike was there. Then Philippe would drop in on weekends and so the household became a general chat-fest about movies. Mike was always talking about the great newsreels, and of course I would remember going to see the Redex cars off at the Sydney Showground and then rushing off to the newsreel theatre a week later to see the same event up on screen.

It was on one of these weekends that I decided with Andrew Fisher to write a dramatic narrative involving newsreel cameramen, which gave us a way of working archival footage into the story and also would give us the spectacles we couldn't afford to shoot. That's the key premise or breakthrough that makes *Newsfront* a compelling film; putting our fictional characters back into real events. And one has to remember this is long before the techno-logical wizardry that ushered in a film like *Forrest Gump* (1994).

Andrew and I then received a trickle of development money from the Arts Council, thanks to Richard Keyes, and we worked on a script when-ever we could. We made a living by doing other projects but we always pushed ahead with the *Newsfront* concept, which developed over several years and included meetings with people like Syd Wood, who was a newsreel cameraman during the 1954 Maitland Flood. Eventually Andrew dropped by the wayside and then Phil Noyce became involved.

I didn't know Phil at the time, but by accident some of the experimental films he had made at the Sydney Film-makers Co-op turned up at my office in Whale Beach where I ran the surfing magazine *Tracks*. I had a 16 mm projector there and so I screened them and was particularly struck by the film about rival bikie gangs, *Castor and Pollux* (1974). This film really impressed me because here was a guy who'd gone out and basically shot a real event but turned it into a drama. Phil has always had a great dramatic sense, even with documentary.

The other thing that impressed me about the film is that Phil is not a small man, yet there he was standing between two groups of crazy bikies who were firing homemade mortar bombs at each other. He was there in the middle, getting into the action, and I thought that he must have had some of the madness of wartime cameramen like Molloy, Russell Boyd, who was also a newsreel cameraman, Syd Wood, or Damien Parer. There was a hint here that this man could direct *Newsfront*. I thought perhaps Noyce could be dangerous enough and silly enough to take on an epic idea like *Newsfront* with someone like me, who up until this time had only made surfing movies and a few scratchy documentaries.

I'd then seen *The Legend of King O'Malley* (1970), a play that Bob Ellis and Michael Boddy had written, which I thought was incredibly interesting, again, because it turned a piece of Australian history into very good theatre entertainment. I met with Bob and found him to be a lively character, but more importantly he shared a great passion for the subject matter and so that's how Bob became our scriptwriter.

Bob produced several drafts of the script but there was a long delay because this was the period of the sacking of the Whitlam government. It was always difficult getting a script from a writer who liked to make good excuses, but it was especially difficult from a writer sympathetic to the Labor Party. He just couldn't concentrate on his work because of the political matters at hand in the nation. That delayed the script for several years, yet we struggled through and managed to get some really good drafts of the script out of Bob.

The unfortunate thing with the final draft is that it was way too long and just couldn't be shot on the type of money we could raise for this film. One thing I realised early on as the producer was that it was no use spreading ours funds too much. The money was spread incredibly thin anyway, but there's a point that if the money is spread too thin then one cannot do many scenes effectively and ultimately most of them end up on the cutting room floor. We had to make the script of a manageable length. Bob produced some great writing in some extraordinary sequences. We didn't shoot them because I had to take the tough decision of having the script cut down. If we didn't then the film would have failed entirely. Ultimately we had to keep the narrative drive of the film going, and we also felt it was important that for the Maitland flood and Redex trial sequences, which were expensive set pieces, we devote a lot of money and time to make them work. We were entering unknown territory with those sequences and we had to keep a little bit of money in reserve in case things went wrong.

Len Maguire (Bill Hunter) discovers Chris Hewitt's body in the Maitland flood.

I think *Newsfront* ended up around 109 minutes in its fine cut and, as usually happens in the film-making process, some bits did indeed end up on the cutting room floor but not much, perhaps part of a scene or some lines of dialogue. It's interesting, though, that when Peter Weir did the director's cut of *Picnic at Hanging Rock* (1975) he didn't add any rediscovered material. He actually made it shorter. There were moments when we didn't have enough time or money to give Phil the opportunity to cover scenes better. Not that any scene is badly covered, but if Phil were to do another cut of the film today, I think there's a possibility *Newsfront* would be shorter by two or three minutes. We just couldn't have shot any more than we did.

When I first started work on *Newsfront* Mike Molloy was going to be our cameraman and the whole film was originally going to be shot in black-and-white. But colour television had arrived in Australia at that time and it had an enormous impact on the film-going community. We felt that *Newsfront* was going to be an even harder 'sell' if we did the whole film in black-and-white. Why would anyone pay money to go to see a black-and-white film when they could sit at home and watch a movie in colour? Of course the newsreels were all in black-and-white, but we felt that the colour films of the period had an interesting texture and could add another dimension to the story. As it turned out, colour became a very important ingredient because in terms of the period covered, at least from 1948 onwards, the country was emerging from the drabness of the war years.

Phil believed the film should be in chapters and that it should switch from colour to black-and-white depending on the emotional tone of each chapter. Our distributor, Roadshow, agreed. But Mike felt it should all be in black-and-white, and as a result he declined our offer to shoot the film. That was a big blow to us because our starting date kept on being delayed as it took us longer to get the package together. Eventually Vince Monton came on board as director of photography. We came across him through Richard Brennan, our associate producer, who knew the technicians' market better than Phil or I. Vince was young, hungry, a very smart fellow and technically adept. He fitted our team brilliantly and *Newsfront* really established him as a new breed of cinematographer.

One of the key contributors to *Newsfront* was our technical adviser, Syd Wood, on whom the film is partly based. Syd was the archetypal newsreel cameraman. While his brother Ross went on to run a very successful advertising company that specialised in commercials, Syd remained a newsreel cameraman through and through. Not only had Syd been a cameraman, he had also been an editor, and later he went on to help set up the archive of the newsreel. So as an adviser Syd was invaluable. PJ [Paul Jones], Johnny Ewart, Chris Haywood and Bill Hunter had to look like they knew how to pull up in an old Dodge car, unpack the cases, get the heavy tripod onto the roof of the car, and start shooting. They were trained by Syd, who would set up something like an accident, someone lying on the side of the road with a bicycle. The cast would then come driving around the corner in the period car, they'd have to see the accident, pull up, quickly survey the location and milk it for the best shots.

Of course working with Syd raised the extraordinary question that every newsreel cameraman had to face. If you are at the scene of a disaster, when do you stop rolling the camera and help? Or do you keep filming and maybe get footage that's going to make your career? The moral dilemma of the newsreel cameraman was something we talked about long into the night. Syd was a great trainer and he became a very good friend. I am so pleased we made the film when we did because a couple of years after we finished it, Syd, as well as his brother Ross, passed away. I feel very privileged because when we were recreating the 1954 Maitland flood, standing beside me was the man who had actually shot the original footage. If I were trying to make *Newsfront* today, it would be virtually impossible because almost all of those newsreel people have passed on.

The Maitland flood sequence is the major set piece of the movie. We knew that if this sequence worked then the whole movie was probably going to work. We chose to shoot at Narrabeen Lake in the north of Sydney because it matched Maitland beautifully and it wasn't as densely populated as it is today, which meant we could build a huge set close to the shoreline, while the newly built housing remained in the far distance. We were then able to put telegraph poles in the middle distance, as well as have a few floating roofs we could push around so that Phil could line up a shot with a roof positioned in the middle background. Of course, in the foreground was our set with the awnings of shops positioned just above the water level so that the audience would imagine that the floodwater was probably three to four metres deep, whereas in fact it was only a metre deep and we could actually walk around the set. The location really looked like a flooded valley.

But we did encounter a major problem. Our main street of Maitland was basically a very long wooden construction on steel pipes that were set in mud. At the time motorboats were allowed onto the lake, and given that moviemaking was uncommon in those days, the local residents were naturally curious. People would come up and speed past the set in their boats, which set off waves and undermined the scaffolding. Inch by inch the whole set started to collapse into the lake, and when I was called down to the set I didn't know what to do. If we had to take the whole set apart and try to reconstruct it, the cost would have been so enormous that we wouldn't have finished the film. We were running out of time and running out of money. We tried winching it but we couldn't get the winches to work. We got a local tow truck in, but it just spun its wheels and couldn't manage to pull the set up. It was quite distressing to watch our movie slowly sink into the Narrabeen Lake.

Now given that disputed ownership on ideas for this film seems to be one of its hallmarks, I won't claim that I thought up this idea, but someone had the good sense to ask, 'What happens when a coal truck breaks its axle on Bulli Pass?' It was a brilliant piece of lateral thinking. We realised they certainly wouldn't unload all the coal right there on the road, they must have some system of pulling this huge weight the rest of the way up the hill. So we rang the colliery down in Wollongong and they told us they had a 1940 model Studebaker, ten-wheel drive truck that only goes twenty miles per hour in top speed. They said that it was so strong it could pull a tank out of a ditch, and it was incredibly low-geared, so it would not lose its traction. By the time the old Stude truck got to Narrabeen Lake the set was at a critical angle and so we attached about a dozen steel cables between the set and truck. Then the old Stude slowly inched the set forward, keeping the tension even on all the cables, because if the tension shifted the set would have just buckled and snapped.

I remember this was in the month of August and it was pretty cold in the water, but as soon as the truck had pulled the set back up, the whole crew and some of the cast just jumped into the water with sandbags and pieces of wood, placed them underneath the steel pipes and secured the footing of the set. I can remember gaffer Brian Bansgrove coming out of the water looking a bit blue—he certainly did more than his fair share on the film.

And do you know what they all called for when it was over? A VB [Victoria Bitter]! It was freezing water and all that they asked for afterwards was a cold beer! Every day seemed to bring an exciting challenge and each challenge seemed to bring a great level of support from all involved.

I always believed that I could achieve good things if I had material. I think I was thirty years old when I produced *Newsfront*. It was a great idea, I had a very good script from Bob Ellis, a great director in Phil Noyce, and priceless newsreel footage from Syd Wood and many other great cameramen. I always believed I had a package that would be a great film. I'm sounding like a producer, but that film was made because I wanted to make it and because a lot of talented people were involved.

Bob Ellis was certainly one of the key cogs in the machine, but I had to make some hard decisions in order to give my director a fair shot at trying to make the film. In my mind the script had to be tightened to satisfy the director, the distributor and finally myself. That's film-making, that's the reality of the business. There's no point to this business if you don't get the film made. I'm very proud of the film and I'm very proud of Bob's contribution, but it's very disappointing that he has never appreciated my role and has spent the last twenty-odd years trying to denigrate me. Perhaps I could have handled the issue with more dignity or subtlety—I'm sure I could have—but I was young and enthusiastic and wanted to make that film.

I was really shocked when the first question at the twentieth anniversary screening of *Newsfront* was directed at me on the issue of authorship. I'm disappointed in the film historians and critics who, over the years, have perpetuated the myth that I essentially stole the idea for *Newsfront*. They seem more interested in questioning my role than giving me due credit for the work I had achieved on the film. I think that's the legacy of poor research.

Where does an idea come from anyway? I had talked about the film to Mike Molloy, Andrew Fisher, Richard Neville, Philippe Mora and others. Sure I drew on other people's input, and because of their input *Newsfront* went on to be the biggest Australian box-office film of 1978, out-grossing films like *The Last Wave* (1977), *The Chant of Jimmie Blacksmith* (1978) and *The Getting of Wisdom* (1977). I decided to push ahead and get the film made. Of that, there should be no doubt whatsoever.

The cinematographer

Vince Monton

I was cinematographer on *Newsfront* and I became involved in the production in early 1977 via Richard Brennan, who had produced a film I had photographed six months earlier called *The Trespassers* (1976) for John Duigan. Richard was production supervisor on *Newsfront* and had introduced me to Phillip Noyce and the producer, David Elfick. Apparently there were other cinematographers lined up to shoot the film, but I don't know what happened to them.

When I read Bob Ellis's screenplay I could see it was going to be a very special film. The first thing I found interesting about the story from a cinematography point of view was that it covered a period of ten years, from just after the Second World War to about 1956, the year of the Melbourne Olympic Games and the arrival of television in Australia. Period films had been done before in this country but they were always set in a period outside of people's memories. I was confronted with a situation where I had to photograph a time and place most people would remember, only twenty to twenty-five years after the events of the story.

Phil Noyce and David Elfick came along with the idea of starting the film in black-and-white and finishing in colour. They also had an enormous amount of black-and-white archival material that had been shot by newsreel cameramen, which was excellent material that not only could be used as film within a film, but could also be integrated into the drama. Having decided to start the film in black-and-white and to finish in colour, the next problem became when to switch over to colour. At first we felt we should switch over with the coming of television. There was a great sequence, for instance, in which people were watching a black-and-white television screen but the people watching it were in colour. But that didn't seem to work right because to suddenly switch over seemed to be too jarring for the audience. Also, we had some very good archival material, which would dramatically be best used later in the film.

Then Phil came up with the brilliant idea of forgetting about the chronological aspect in terms of black-and-white and colour, and just shooting it emotionally. There are some sequences that work much better emotionally in black-and-white, and some which work emotionally better in colour. For example, the early barbecue scene, in which all the newsreel cameramen come together to help Len Maguire (Bill Hunter) renovate and fix his house, is just a wonderfully light scene and looks great in glossy colour, whereas the Maitland flood segment, which contains the death of Chris Haywood's character, Chris Hewitt, dramatically works a lot better in black-and-white.

But when recreating a period people can actually remember, one problem is that a lot of the audience will be nostalgic for the period and have their own visions of it. I quickly reached the conclusion that people's memory of the past is probably coloured by the films they had seen back then. And because I'm a film buff, I felt that probably the best way to shoot *Newsfront* in terms of style was to do the sequences immediately after the war as if the audience were watching a movie actually shot in 1946, and then do the same thing for subsequent segments right up to 1956.

Having reached the point where we locked down which scenes to shoot in colour and which ones to shoot in black-and-white, I then started to work very hard on the styles within each segment or chapter. Obviously anything that was going to be intercut with original newsreel footage had to be shot exactly like the way the newsreel cameramen did it. But for most of the other sequences I used film styles from different periods as a yardstick. The work of Gregg Toland,[1] for example, was an inspiration for early sequences of *Newsfront*. There's even homage to Toland in the scene where Frank Maguire (Gerard Kennedy) and others are watching a newsreel screening—I set up and lit the scene like the 'March of Time' sequence from *Citizen Kane* (1941), which Toland shot.

In the middle sequences of *Newsfront*, the early 1950s, we went for more of a technicolour look. Now there was a very interesting transition between, say, film noir, which had reached a zenith in the early 1950s, and when colour cinematography came in, or technicolour, which was a great commercial attraction, especially to compete against television. The style of cinematography changed dramatically not only because everybody wanted colour, they wanted to see everything in the set. So for the early 1950s sequences we over-lit and tended towards creating garish colour situations. We even went to the trouble of actively forgetting about the natural light available to us because most films in those days, particularly in America, were shot on a studio set.

Towards the end of the film, which is set around 1956, I went for a photographic style that was more in keeping with the arrival of the French New Wave, and especially Raoul Coutard's work.[2] The French New Wave [cinematographers] were influenced by naturalistic lighting because they went back to filming on location, and so whatever light was available would guide them as to how a film would be lit. And so, for example, in the scenes set in the Cinetone studios towards the end of *Newsfront*, even though they're shot in colour, I tried for a more naturalistic, pastel-type colour.

I remember one day when shooting inside the Cinetone studios, the great Ken G. Hall came to visit and I was really into my Coutard phase, which was to have just a little bit of light coming through a frosted glass wall. Anyway, while Ken was chatting to the crew and going through a nostalgia kick, he must have noticed there were no lights in the room because when he eventually said his goodbyes he asked the first assistant, 'When are you guys going to start lighting the set?' It didn't occur to him that one could actually photograph a colour scene with no lights to be seen anywhere.

Considering it was a low-budget shoot I was also well supported by the art and costume departments. Again, for the Cinetone set, which was actually Ken's original Cinesound Studio in Balmain, I felt there must have been a time in the 1950s when the whole complex would have switched from incandescent lights to fluorescent lights. At a certain point in the production the art department came in and ripped down all of the tennis court shades and all the incandescent overhead lights, which gave a warm light with deep shadows. They replaced everything with fluorescent lighting, which gave the set a much softer but colder look. I felt subtleties like that were important because every time the story came back to the studio, the audience would have felt that time had moved on. That 'soft but cold' look was certainly appropriate lighting for when the film ends in 1956, which is a milestone year not only for having the first Olympic Games in Australia, but because of the introduction of television. Television meant the beginning of the end for the newsreel cameramen, and so the film ends on that note even though it ends in colour.

The interesting thing about shooting the black-and-white segments of *Newsfront* is that the film industry at the time had turned its back on black-and-white. Black-and-white was a dirty word, so much so that we had a

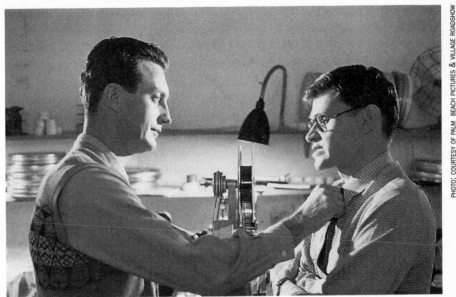

PHOTO: COURTESY OF PALM BEACH PICTURES & VILLAGE ROADSHOW

Geoff, the editor (Bryan Brown), and Bruce, the assistant editor (Drew Forsythe), in the Cinetone editing room.

great deal of trouble getting black-and-white stock to shoot with. Kodak would have made up a batch of many hundreds of thousands of feet that we needed, but we couldn't afford it. We actually ended up having to film with footage left over from different periods, made up of a number of different batches, different contrasts, and some had been lying in refrigerators for fifteen years. In the long run this turned out to be a blessing in disguise. Because the batches of film were so varied, it actually made it easier to match and intercut our material with original archival material that had been shot in different periods. I'm sure we shot with some black-and-white stock that went back in vintage to the original material shot by the newsreel cameramen.

But because of the difficulty of locating black-and-white film, I do remember there was a great deal of pressure to make the entire film in colour. To give David and Phil due credit, they stuck very strongly to their decision to shoot most of *Newsfront* in black-and-white. This also meant that we could never backtrack and release the film completely in colour, which I think was the hidden agenda of the film's distributor.

Working on *Newsfront* was really a labour of love, everybody worked so hard on it, cutting corners and squeezing the best they could out of every department. One of those areas is the Maitland flood sequence, which on screen looks like a gigantic exercise. When we started shooting the film no one quite knew how we were going to do it or pay for it. The flood sequence was definitely going to cost a lot of money and I remember sitting in one of the production meetings with everyone in the room throwing ideas around. Every idea we'd come up with, it would always come down to, 'Well, we can't afford to do it.' But to give you an idea of the level of commitment on this film, David, the producer, then said, 'It's pointless going on like this. Here is what I'm going to do. I'll somehow find the money to shoot this sequence because it's an important sequence. You guys go ahead and work out how to do it. If I can't find the money, then we can use my salary. We are going to shoot this sequence and you guys are going to do the best you can, and if it costs my fee, it costs my fee.' Up to that point I had never heard a producer say such a thing, and I've never heard a producer say it since.

Few people realise just how low the budget truly was. On the last day of filming the flood sequence we only had two rolls of black-and-white film left. That was all, there was no more in Sydney and as far as we knew nobody else in Australia had any more. The last bit of black-and-white film went through the camera when we shot the drowning of the Chris Hewitt character, and if you look very closely where Chris Haywood's hand finally sinks into the water, the film starts to have flash frames, which signals the end of the roll. I was sitting there next to the camera operator begging Chris to just drown quickly, but all actors love to work on their death scene. He would go down and then he would come back up again and grasp for life a little longer, and I was sitting there saying, 'Drown you bastard, please!' I remember just as he went down for the last time the rollers on the magazine on one side stopped rolling, which meant there was a foot of film left, and as he went down, the film ran out and Phil said, 'cut.' There was talk of doing another take, except I pointed out there was no film left—we had used all of it up. It was one take—it got down to that! Fortunately Chris was perfect on the day.

Actually, the death of Chris Hewitt is one of the dramatic highlights of the movie, and that's because Chris Haywood was unstoppable. There wasn't anything that was too much trouble for him. When we see Chris being bashed around by the current, that really is Chris being bashed into debris, half-drowning, slamming into barbed-wire fences and getting cut up by them. And when Len Maguire (Bill Hunter) and Charlie Henderson (Johnny Ewart) find his body stuck in a telegraph pole, Chris insisted on doing it. Although it's a wide shot, he held his breath for a long time in a drowned position, stuck half-suspended from a telegraph pole. That was the sort of dedication people were putting into the film. I don't think anybody thought of using a stand-in even if we could have afforded one. We couldn't just throw money at the problems; we had to fly by the seat of our pants.

The whole film grabs me emotionally but one scene in particular brings a little lump to my throat whenever I see it. It's a scene that occurs in the editing room following the Redex trial sequence. It's one of those very interesting scenes in which we begin with a close-up on an editing machine showing black-and-white footage of the Redex trial, and then we pull back from the editing machine into a colour set. And it's the scene in which Geoff (Bryan Brown), who is the editor, says, 'I'm leaving Australia, I'm going to seek my fortune in England.' Admittedly, from a cinematographer's point of view it's probably not all that interesting, but it always brings a lump to my throat because that scene is a precursor to what happened to my entire generation. Phil works overseas, most of my contemporaries now work overseas. *Newsfront* was like a premonition of what was to come and, ironically, it's also a film about a period in Australian history when our film industry almost came to an end.

Hence *Newsfront* had great resonance and a great emotional hold on all of us who worked on it because we felt like a new generation ready to be kick-started. Every film you begin work on you have great hopes for and I think everybody who worked on *Newsfront* felt that way. But I don't think anybody could have predicted just what a great film it was going to be. It was a dark horse in the pack that no one expected to bolt to the front. It made such a great impact—not only in Australia but internationally as well—and it kick-started a lot of our careers. For Phil it was his first major motion picture and he just went on to bigger and better things. *Newsfront* was very generous to us all, it paid us back many times over and it's a film very fondly remembered in Australia.

Looking back on *Newsfront* now, it's certainly the most influential film of all the films I've shot. I'm not sure if it's my best work, but I suppose if there is one film I am to be remembered for, then *Newsfront* is the one.

The actor: an interview with Bill Hunter

Phillip Noyce

How did you get into acting in the first place?

Misfortune, accident. I started out by doing stunts for *On the Beach*. That was in 1959.

Did you ever think you were going to be an actor?

No idea.

So when did you actually get in front of a camera and say lines for the first time?

Oh, it was on *Homicide* (1964–75). I called myself an actor and one thing led to another. Then I ran into ratbags like you. [Laughs]

I'd like to go back to the beginning.

Go for your life.

Because you're a very important figure in the Australian film industry, I'm sure people would love to know a bit about your life.

I'm a bush kid.

Where were you born?

I was born in Fitzroy, Melbourne. But when, at a very early age, my old man said, 'I'm going to be a publican,' I went with him obviously. Dad used to get into a bush pub, build it up and sell it for a profit. By the time I was thirteen years old I'd been to just as many schools, and at thirteen I also left school and went droving. As a consequence my education is not the type one gets at university. You had a look and a listen and you copped your lumps.

So you went from school to school, didn't learn much except?

Didn't want to know, really. Before there was a word for dyslexia, I had it. I just didn't understand and would spend a lot of time looking out the window. Didn't learn much at all, although the things they were trying to teach me were only common sense to me. It was like learning the Ten Commandments, which is easy stuff—you don't knock around with somebody's wife, you don't thieve, and if you did you got belted.

You had a hard upbringing?

Pretty hard, yes.

Was your father a tough cookie?

He was a fighter as well as a raconteur, singer of songs and teller of lies. He was a good bloke.

Can you tell me a little bit about droving?

Tim Frood lived in a tram at a place called Bald Hills outside Ballarat, with his de facto wife and eleven children. He used to drink in my old man's pub, the North Star in Ballarat. I was very fortunate to have stables at the back and a couple of horses. Tim Frood told me I had the wrong horses, that they didn't suit me. He said, 'Whatever you do, mate, do what suits you. Go for it!' I was thirteen and I went droving with him for six to eight weeks at a time. We'd bring a mob of steers down from New South Wales into Victoria, and we lived in a wagon. After that I showed a little bit of ability in the water.

How did you get into swimming?

Ballarat City Baths. There was a man called Norman Lee who was a champion country swimmer. He had won a Victorian title. I took him on when I was about fourteen years old and beat him—by that I mean I squared off with the big kids, did my best and was good enough to win. In the following year I swam in the Australian swimming championships. Frankly, I was a different man back then.

How?

By the time of my nineteenth birthday I was very close to being one of the best in the world and then I fell over just before the Rome Olympics. I had viral meningitis. I went from a sprint weight of 68 kilograms (10.7 stone) to 46 kilograms (7.2 stone) in two weeks. I couldn't compete any more and had to find something else to do. I was deranged for a long time.

Because you gave up swimming?

I didn't give it up, I wasn't allowed any more, and as a consequence there was a desire to be quenched. I had to try something else.

So in 1959 you were living in Melbourne and you heard about this American film, On the Beach. *Just tell us the story.*

My old man was in charge of security and they were looking for a stunt double—a maniac, really, because there was no skill involved. It was all balls and guts. Fred Astaire, Gregory Peck, Ava Gardner and Tony Perkins came to see me swim one night. In fact, Tony Perkins rang up my father and that's how I got to do all the stunts.

Tony Perkins rings your father and says what?

Actually my sister answered the phone and Perkins said, 'I'd like to speak to Bill Hunter,' and my sister said, 'Junior or senior?' 'The one I've just seen swimming,' says Perkins, and that's how it started.

Do you remember the type of stunts you had to do?

Yes, I drove a Ferrari for Fred Astaire. I crashed that rather spectacularly. I rode a tricycle for Tony Perkins. Crashed that too, but not deliberately. And I swam, which was a snap. I was getting about £30 a day, which was quite extraordinary in those days. My old man was on the basic wage, I think he was getting about £15 a week.

And did you learn anything of the craft on that film?

No. But I did see Fred Astaire do twenty-seven takes for a two-minute scene and I thought, 'Fuck! I can do that.' I think I just fell short, didn't I? I once did twenty-five takes for you. [Laughs]

146

Bill Hunter (right) and John Ewart during a break on the set of Newsfront.

Okay, so you finished On the Beach, *your swimming career is more or less over, and we're in the early sixties. What happened next?*

In 1961 I went to London and by that time I started calling myself an actor. I was still, for want of a better word, deranged, and so I just hit the road and did repertory theatre for a while in London. It took my brother two years to find me. He didn't know where I was and my parents were very worried.

Tell us about being an Australian in London in the early sixties.

Bloody amazing! Ray Barrett and Rod Taylor were there, you had the arse out of your pants, living with Irishmen and sometimes sleeping on the embankment of the Thames, over sewerage grates because it was warm there. It stank, but it was warm. You inhaled a culture made up of actors like Jeremy Kemp, Peter O'Toole and Albert Finney. You'd drink where they drank and you became imbued with an attitude of what it takes to be an actor. It takes a lot of courage, especially if you don't say much and you're a shy person by nature. In order to pursue it, you've got to be a bit bold.

I ran into those people some time later, O'Toole and Finney, and they reminded me of things I'd forgotten, like my fighting in London pubs. Don't get uneasy, this is the truth. I was knocking around with Irish and Scottish actors and the same belligerent attitude was prevalent among them as it is among Australians. They were all outrageous men. I think Trevor Howard made a salient point about me back then. He said to me one day, 'My dear young fellow, nobody can do it like you.'[1] I can remember getting into the Pickwick Club one night and I had about three and sixpence in my pocket. I walked out with about £400 from playing pennies against the wall with John Lennon.

London in the sixties was quite extraordinary in that it was the capital of the world and you felt yourself in the middle of it. I don't remember much of it but I do know I was in trouble a lot.

Was your accent a problem?

To me the acting game is not about accent. It's intuition and it has to do with instinct. You can only play what you recognise and I recognise quite a lot.

So why did you go to London?

I had to go somewhere. I had to get out and I thought I had something to say, though I wasn't quite sure what that was.

Could it also have been because you didn't see much of a future in the acting game in Australia?

There was no future at all in Australia then. That's why Peter Finch and Chips Rafferty and a lot of great Australian actors all went overseas. But when I went I was just kicking around, I wasn't deliberately setting out to become an actor.

When did you come back to Australia?

I think I came back in 1968 or early 1969. I'd worked with some really good people and though I really hadn't hardened up, I came back and just waltzed into television. I worked for Crawford Productions and tried everything that was going around—albeit, ignorance breeds fear, I brought that to my acting, and fear's a great stimulus, isn't it?

So when did you start in movies in Australia?

I think it was your film, *Backroads* (1977), or perhaps *27A* (1974) by Esben Storm. I did some good television work prior to that, but not a feature film. I didn't have a clue of who you were—and neither did you. [Laughs]

I'd like to thank you for giving me that opportunity.

We had a script on Backroads *but most of it was improvised. Can you describe that process?*

I think the process started when you introduced me to Gary Foley. You thought you were introducing us but we'd known each other for some time and so we stacked on a bit of a scene for you. I was the first lead, one of the very few I've played. You paid me respect, I gave you my best, and it was a process of 'just have a go'. That's what has brought me to this point, really.

Can you remember shooting some of the improvised scenes?

Yes, but we did them best in rehearsal. [Laughs] There's something that happens in a performer—I'm calling myself a performer now—when they reach a point and they 'just go for it'. As a director you should know that. There's something electric in just turning the actor loose. I remember the opening scene of *Backroads* because it's so extraordinary: the furtive look of Foley, the down-and-dirty look of me, and you can tell something's going to happen. It was lovely. I think 'turning the actor loose' is very important and you gave us the opportunity to do just that.

Do you remember the old Pontiac? It was in pretty good shape. I wanted that car when we started the shoot.

You know what I did with the Pontiac, don't you?

I don't know.

I used it for a publicity stunt. I towed it out onto the front lawn of Sydney University and then as a stunt to raise interest in the movie I brought along six sledgehammers and invited the students to wreck the car.

Do you mean that I could have bought it cheap?

Real cheap!

I remember at one point Foley and me screaming along in the Pontiac and for no reason at all a mob of Friesian cattle start coming across the road. Now Friesians are black and white. I said to Foley, 'Jesus, look at this!' He said, 'Don't hit the black bits.' He's a bad bugger. I have very fond recollections of Foley. I know some fine black actors in this country but I think Foley was the first one to have the courage to really pursue acting.

Okay, you did Backroads *and so now tell us how you got the part in* Newsfront.

You know how I got the part.

I know, but for posterity.

It was at a pub called the Gladstone on the corner of William and Palmer Streets and it was a strange sequence of events because I think *Newsfront* was the first time I had refused to do an audition. Halfway through *Backroads* you said to me, 'I've got a part for you,' and I said, 'Ease up, Phil, I've heard that all my life.' You walked into the Gladstone Hotel, threw a script at me and said, 'You can play one of the brothers.' Without having read it, I said, 'No, I'm going to play "the" brother and I won't screen-test and I won't audition.' That turned me around a bit because it was a huge punt for me, but I felt it was the right time to assert myself. I didn't do the audition and you still gave me the part.

Then Elfick asked me to read in for people at Palm Beach. I really thought I was secure, that I had the part. I'll read in for anybody, I don't care, but I didn't realise the reading at Palm Beach was in fact an audition.

I can remember you weren't too fit at the time. Do you remember your trainer PJ [Paul Jones]?

Yes, poor bugger. I love him, I really do.

Tell us about getting you ready for the film.

I had a bit of a reputation, the man was engaged and didn't drink and he was assigned to me for a couple of weeks. I don't know whose idea that was, but at the end of the film he called himself an actor and his engagement was off.

Remember when we had you shave off your beard?

There was a hidden agenda, wasn't there? And it also caused a bit of a dispute, too, because apart from the fact that I've got no chin, I had a really cavalier attitude, and still do insofar as what you see is what you get. You wear who you are and I didn't really want to change the way I looked. David Elfick, I think, insisted that I shave. I remember him saying, 'Listen, I'm the producer and I don't give a fuck who you are!' I remember that worked. He was right, I was wrong. Forgive me.

As I remember it, David said you had to shave your beard off and you said no way. Then I remember you disappearing into one of those side rooms at David's studio.

You have to realise that I was hiding at that point in my life. I was never happier than when I was playing somebody else, which I suppose is what acting's about. But to take the beard off and show myself to the world was a major step. It would have been like taking my clothes off in Martin Place. I felt that exposed.

I remember you coming out of the side room looking like you were naked and you were wondering what our reaction would be. Now I can reveal what it was that we didn't say to you. We thought, 'Oh, Jesus!'

So what did you rely on then?

Well, that's why we decided to get you a trainer to take a little bit of weight off your face. Obviously your beard was covering the chin and so we thought we'd better try to get you in shape, firm you up.

Didn't know what you were dealing with, of course. [Laughs]

The first day you were put with your trainer, he set you to run from one end of Palm Beach to the other. I think you got about 100 metres before the session was over.

Well, I probably knew more about fitness than PJ. What you don't know, sir, is that I had a massive heart attack and Sandy Beach—God love her—took me to an acupuncturist two days before we started shooting.

You had a heart attack! When?

Two days before we started shooting.

You went to hospital?

No.

How did you know it was a heart attack?

I stopped breathing for a while.

Where were you?

Down on the beach with PJ and Sandy.

You mean the training we set you caused a heart attack?

Virtually. I'm not telling you a fib. This actually happened. PJ knew, Sandy knew, and I certainly knew. Nobody else did. I still saddled up for the part, though.

What was your reaction when you first read Bob Ellis's script for Newsfront?

Bob's script really had nothing to do with what I actually did. Though I do remember Ellis trying to out-sprint you down the aisle for the AFI Award. [Laughs] What I do know is that *Newsfront* looks like a $4 million picture and you brought it in for about $500000, didn't you?

What do you remember after all this time about the character of Len Maguire?

Don't ask me for any theory on acting. What you see is what you get. I do remember Syd Wood and his approach to just about everything, and that somebody was silly enough to give us a few bob to go have a drink and get to know each other. That has stayed with me.

So Syd Wood, this former Cinesound cameraman, was an inspiration for you?

No, I knew who I had to play. Syd brought his craft, for want of a better word, and I just thought, 'Well, that's the way to play it.'

Syd allowed you to find the character?

I can play Prospero in a minute, but I don't think you can put it that simply because Shakespeare is almost a foreign language. Whereas Syd Wood, for me, was somebody I knew and good at what he did. But for the advent of television, he'd have been there with the big ones, hitting hard and often.

Do you remember some of the rehearsals we did in preparation for the shoot?

Yes I do, but I didn't take much notice. I remember one session with Christopher [Haywood] and the lovely Lorna Lesley, and the young Steven Bisley and Bryan [Brown] were there as well. It was wonderful to watch them. I was having a beer, you know?

Hang on, I missed that.

I was in the electrics truck having a beer. I wasn't taking the film seriously enough until I realised I was in fact playing the lead.

John Ewart played Charlie, the cameraman for Newsco. Can you tell us a little bit about your relationship with him and your recollections of him as an actor?

I remember the first day of shooting on *Newsfront*, lunch was called and John and I thought we had an hour and so we hit the pub. We only had half an hour—you tight bastard!—and you had to come looking for us. We were half an hour late in your terms and there was a moment of angst there. That was okay, though, it was your first major feature. But we didn't deliberately stay out longer; we genuinely thought we had an hour for lunch.

Johnny Ewart, I miss him.[2] Yes, I do. He was much like me. He didn't act; he reacted. I think that's an important difference. I'd sooner be called an actor than an Actor—good actors react. It was our attitude too. John Meillon[3] shared that, and I think all the good ones do react.

What does 'react' mean?

Like I said before, I'm doing Shakespeare at the moment, *The Tempest*, and I can't come to terms with that. I'm playing Prospero and that's being an Actor, but Prospero has nothing to do with me. The really good actors bring something else to a great role—themselves.

Were you surprised when Newsfront *was a success?*

No, the film was something I believed in. I'm not sure of the degree of success *Newsfront* actually achieved, but for me, selfishly, it was a turnaround. I didn't have to play any more the heavy who doesn't say much standing on the left-hand side of the screen. *Newsfront* gave me a look at the 'rabbit' and I grabbed it. I was fortunate because you trusted me. I'm also very proud of the film in as much as it was on the school curriculum for about eight years, and I believe that it sustained a particular Australian ethos. It was significant for me for that reason and I'm grateful.

Do you remember anything about the working methods on Newsfront*, such as the way we shot it?*

No. I was flat-out doing what I had to do, you were doing what you were doing, and Vince Monton was doing what he was doing. That stuff had nothing to do with me; I just wanted to play the role.

Have you changed as an actor over the years?

I hope I've become better.

In what way?

I know what not to do. Less is better, I think. I'm not looking for another *Newsfront*, but because I have more respect now, I would approach it in a different way.

Respect for what?

I want to be as good an actor as the great ones I've worked with.

You haven't achieved that?

Nowhere near it. I think there's a point where you say, 'Okay, I'm a good actor,' and then you find that you can go further and be an even better actor. No result so far.

I'd debate that.

You can if you like, but on my terms. Not yours.

I think one of your greatest performances is in The Dismissal *(1983).*

I got a letter from a man in Los Angeles who I really respected. The letter was an affectionate acknowledgement—he wrote I had given the greatest performance by an Australian actor anywhere, any time. That letter was from Byron Kennedy shortly before he died.[4]

Referring to?

Rex Connor. Francis Xavier Connor.[5]

I have to agree with Byron Kennedy that your portrayal of Rex Connor is one of the greatest performances ever seen in an Australian film.

Well, thank you, sir.

It was a brilliant characterisation that brought tears to one's eyes—the tragedy of the man's ambition, his love for the country...

And he came within three weeks of bringing it off. Without ambition there are no great influences, no great directors, no writers, and no great actors. Unless you can emulate those you habitually admire, you're fucked.

So who are the great actors you've worked with, the ones you would like to be as good as?

Albert Finney, John Hurt, Trevor Howard, Peter O'Toole. O'Toole bemuses me because he's just one of those wonderful people who have an innate ability. The rest of us have to work for it. There are people still running around, like Dennis Hopper and Timothy Roth, who have a wonderful, belligerent, gutter attitude that I like. I'm privileged to have squared off with those people.

We're skirting around a bit, I guess that's just because I've a low tolerance for detail.

Oh, rubbish you've got a low tolerance for detail. You're fucking fastidious.

Whatever. How did you prepare for each of your scenes, or did you play them instinctually?

React; don't act.

Were you thinking about the whole film?

No.

One scene at a time then?

I read the script, I knew what it was about and so it was like, 'What do I have to do today?' That was it. I didn't take the film home with me. It was: 'That's a wrap, I'm out of the joint. What time tomorrow?'

Have you always worked like that?

Yep, because I didn't have the ability to get into NIDA. Not that I really wanted to. The whole thing was an afterthought.

You didn't have the ability, so therefore?

Oh, come off it! There's no ability. You know that getting the job is harder than doing it.

Has it always been like that?

I think it always will be. I'm amused and bemused by young actors that do a lot of training. They receive respect—and deservedly so—which I've never had. On the other hand, if you have the opportunity to work with great actors then you better measure up. But 'measuring up' cannot be taught.

No it can't. But your process must have changed over the years. Surely for Rex Connor it was a little different?

No, Rex Connor was only common sense when it comes down to it. I've done fifty-eight films now and out of those films I think I got away with Rex Connor, I got away with the major in *Gallipoli* (1981) and I just scraped through with *Newsfront*. What else have I done? I think I was quite good in *The Hit* (1984). Then there are the frivolous things like *Strictly Ballroom* (1992), *Muriel's Wedding* (1994) and *The Adventures of Priscilla, Queen of the Desert* (1994). But, then again, I owe those performances to you.

Why?

You showed faith in me in the first place.

You may not remember this, but Elizabeth Knight, who was the first assistant director on Backroads, said to me, 'You've got to meet Billy Hunter.' I remember going with her to a pub in Surry Hills in Sydney to meet you. You came out of the pub and we stood on the footpath for a moment. You gave me about two minutes of your time. I don't know whether you'd read the script or whether we had a script at that stage, but I told you what the character was like and you did an improvisation for me there on the spot. The improvisation lasted about twenty seconds, I explained it to you for about thirty seconds beforehand, and I can remember looking into your eyes and there was a fire in your eyes I'd never seen. I thought, 'What the Jesus is that?' That's when I decided, 'I've got to have this man in the movie.' It was a fire I've not seen before or since until this moment with you sitting here opposite me.

And do you know what that's called, Phillip? It's called fight, fuck and feed.

That goes back to the pubs in Victoria?

Yes, and courage is telling yourself that you're frightened. I've been frightened all my fucking life.

You think you've fed off fear all your life. Is it a good thing to be afraid?

I think it has more to do with running into people that you really have no other option but to admire. You say, 'Jesus, he did that well!' Anything less makes you a bit frightened. I'm not talking about acting skill here. I'm talking about panache and about innate ability. I've seen it a few times. So what do you want to talk about now, Phillip?

We're talking about it.

Any danger of getting a beer?

[Long pause]

Obviously you grew up in the era during which Newsfront *is set. Do you have any particular recollections that helped you when doing the film?*

I remember the 1950s very vividly because that was a part of my life when I was training as an athlete, and I was also working with the Melbourne Sports Depot, which was a chain of outlets around Victoria that catered purely to sport. I was a sports salesman all of fifteen or sixteen years of age. The newsreels would come out weekly, so at least once a week I used to duck across the street in my lunch hour, pay my shilling and see the newsreels and short films. I loved watching them, though of course I never dreamed I'd end up in a film about the newsreels.

Do you see Australia in that time as being different from today? Do you think we've changed as a nation?

I heard an absurd remark the other day: that Bob Menzies would have been in favour of a republic. I'm fiercely Australian and I find that there's still a defiant attitude or spirit, if you will, that encompasses our migration policy. I think it's a wonderful thing to walk down the streets of Sydney, or anywhere in Australia, and see Asian faces and Aboriginal faces. I think the migration situation right now is helping our own indigenous people because nobody looks the same any more. If 'Pig Iron' Bob were in power we'd still have a white Australia policy, thank you very much. We're too good for that.

What appals me now is that we were defeated in becoming a republic despite the fact we've fought other people's wars and that we were sent out here as the idiot sister in the attic in the first place. I lent my name to the republican cause, I did commercials and political campaigns for it, I did everything I could for it, but we got beat because of a silly little quirk, a question that wasn't cloaked in the right way. I'm a bit ashamed and I think it's about time we stood up on our own two feet. Apart from that, I have no opinion whatsoever.

How about the values of the country, have they changed from the fifties?

When I was growing up Australia had a population of about nine million. We are now around eighteen million but I think there's still a defiant spirit. Your mum and your dad were not dissimilar to my mum and dad, but I also think the people who have come from elsewhere love this country because of that attitude.

That attitude being?

A freedom and a licence to behave as you will, in that this is possibly the last bastion of a free democratic society—although we're still licking up to the Americans.

So you very much identified with the values espoused by the film?

Certainly. When I met you and Peter Weir and a whole lot of other film-makers, the film industry was pretty fiercely Australian. And I didn't do anything that wasn't—I've never played an American.

Would you ever?

I don't think I could.

How was it working with Chris Haywood? Where did you first meet him?

I did a play with him at the Nimrod Theatre with Tony Llewellyn-Jones, but I had never worked with him on a film set before. He was a mischievous little bugger and he reminds me of Timothy Roth in lots of ways. Christopher has a wonderful personality and he brings that to whatever he does. He's fervent and for that I admire him.

I know you're going to ask me about Angela Punch-McGregor and Wendy Hughes. They blazed a trail for Australian actresses, and I insist on the term 'actress'. I'm sick of being castrated because I'm a male. All the good ones I know take pride in the term 'actress'.

When you're working opposite another actor, what is it you look for in them?

Exactly what we've got here. If you can't look at a man, then you can't look at a man. Simple.

You look in the eyes?

Of course. It's like squaring off with a good fighter—the eyes tell you.

So you will try to make contact. What do you do if the other actor is not contacting you?

Ignore it and run the race. This may sound like elitism, but fortunately I don't work unless I know who I'm working with. That's because I'm a bit bristly, a bit fragile, and I don't want anything less than what I can give.

Don Crosby[6] played your boss in the film, A.G. Marwood. When did you first meet Don?

It might interest you to know that *Newsfront* was the first film for Don Crosby and John Dease. They'd never done a film before. They were scared shitless.

How do you know that?

I talked to them.

And what did they say?

'It is a whole new world and it's a mistake.' It was just a lack of timing; they should have been doing it all their lives because they were very wonderfully talented people. They were radio stars I grew up listening to. They thought I was used to it; they didn't know I'd never really done it before either.

And Wendy Hughes?

I've never seen anybody, male or female, as luminous as Wendy was in that scene at the bar in *Newsfront*. I've worked with some of the best but Wendy on that day, at that moment in time, was just sublime. Why hasn't somebody realised and truly utilised the Wendy Hugheses, or the Punch-McGregors and the Lorna Lesleys of this country? They can act the pants off any Hollywood star.

I took my woman to the opening of the Fox Studios, against my will. She wanted to go; she doesn't get out very much. I found myself saying, 'Oh God, I'm in the lion's den, I'm sleeping with the enemy.' It was awful until I ran into Paul Keating, who gave me a big hug.

You think Australia is special?

I think it's very special. I've watched this country becoming something that America failed to achieve. I actually wept because the republican issue was cloaked in such oblique terms.

Did it matter? Isn't it about the people?

It's precisely about the people. That's what I'm saying.

What is it about the Australian people and the Australian temperament that you really feel proud of?

I'll tell you straight, it's no coincidence or accident that the Australian of Irish stock has an affinity with the Australian Aborigine. Because they're both persecuted races, exploited to the nth degree, and it's about fucking time we stood up and said so.

And what is your heritage?

Well, my mama's name was Eileen Frances Burke. You can't get more Irish than that. My father's name was William Watson Hunter. You can't get more Scottish than that. When I first arrived in Naples I felt completely at peace. Years later I told my mum and she said, 'Well, it's not surprising, Bill, because your great, great grandmother was Dimontina from Naples.'

What do we believe in as Australians?

I'll tell you, Phillip, we believe in the fact that we weren't here by choice. We shouldn't be here and we have to respect the people who were here before we were.

Did you go to a Catholic school?

I went to all schools.

Do you believe in God?

No. Do you?

Yeah.

Why?

I'm not saying it's the God that's taught by the church...

Well, which god are you talking about?

The one in you.

What about him?

Back to Newsfront; *what about Gerard Kennedy?*

Kennedy was well established and I really liked watching him. It's like what we were talking about before—Actors or actors—I'm an actor and so is Gerard Kennedy. I have great respect for him; he taught by example and I'd like to think that eventually I would do that too. He's a man of high integrity and I like him because he has done it tough. I think we both realised that when we squared off as brothers. Unlikely casting, though.

To be playing brothers?

Yes.

When did you first work with Gerard Kennedy?

Probably in *Division 4* [1969–77].

You were playing...?

Oh, the third heavy from the left. He was playing the lead.

Was he someone you looked up to at that time?

No.

The actor

Why?

With remarkably few exceptions, I don't look up to anybody. Because I know most of the acting game is bullshit anyway. If you can adapt to that you're halfway there. But I did admire Kennedy as a man. I've watched him behave in a way that I would like to behave—and he had an appeal.

What do you think your appeal has been?

I'm not sure that I have any appeal. I'm just telling the truth. Maybe that's appealing.

Phillip, I applaud you.

Thank you, and mutual applause because you started me.

I applaud you because you're one of three or four directors I can pay a compliment to. While a lot of other directors have no conception what an actor is about. No idea at all.

What is an actor about?

An actor wants to be considered. An actor wants to be there because he's the only one to do the role. I don't want to be second choice; I don't want to be third choice. That's why I refused to audition for *Newsfront*. Otherwise I could have been a coachbuilder for the Victorian Railways.

Are you glad you weren't a coachbuilder for the Victorian Railways?

I'm not sure. This might be a shocking thing to say, but I look at people who I grew up with, they're married and they're grandfathers and grandmothers and I don't think I could have done that.

Phillip, I understand you're a bit of a party animal in Los Angeles?

I am? Who said?

That's the word.

Must have been my publicist.

I don't think so. We get a bit of feedback occasionally. I don't think I could survive in LA. I think I may live in Europe for a while. I think Europeans are better actors. Do you not agree?

Some, yes. Different style.

Style is what we're talking about though, isn't it?

Different market, different everything.

Let me ask you this, where was the first film studio in Australia? Come on...

Where?

In Glebe Point Road, Glebe. Two French brothers set it up and it's now a fish and chip shop.

Looking back, do you wish you'd had more opportunity?

No. I don't think lack of opportunity has anything to do with lack of ability. It has to do with being as good as you can and want to be. The type of people I run in tandem with are Max Cullen, an extraordinary talent out there called Ric Carter, Paul Chubb, who has survived a near-death situation, and Dennis Miller. They're all sort of low-profile people but they are supreme actors. They're wonderful and they can't help themselves but be wonderful. I prefer to be in that company.

Do you remember the arguments that you and I and other cast members had about alcohol? Because alcohol was a part of the making of the film, it was a part of the culture.

Well, that's also how I grew up. If you didn't drink and didn't smoke, you weren't considered much of a man. I should have been more intuitive in that role. But we've laid the bricks; we can't change it now.

Any regrets about Newsfront?

There are none.

None?

I'd like a poster.

Okay, I can arrange that.

The American poster or the Australian one?

I can get one for you.

It'll be under glass.

Okay, you want it under glass.

No, no, no. You give me the poster; I'll put it under glass.

You said earlier you should have taken Newsfront *more seriously. What did you mean by that?*

To me the time was in the job.

It was just another job?

That's what people think, but I knew that *Newsfront* was more than just a job. You have to remember that I had a certain cavalier attitude because I was frightened. But I think I might have pulled it off for you, son.

You did and you've never looked better.

'You're a bit old-fashioned, that's all.'[7] [Laughs]

The inspiration

Ken G. Hall[1]

In 1976, I believe, two young men came to see me at my home at Mosman. I had not met them before, save for a telephone conversation with one of them to make the appointment. They said their names were David Elfick and Phil Noyce, producer and director respectively of a film they were about to create and which was to be called *Newsfront*. They sought my help, which I said I would be glad to give. They brought a bound script with a well-illustrated cover—good showmanship for a start, I thought!—and said it had to do with the 'war' between Cinesound and Movietone in the forties and fifties. In an immediate reaction, I said, 'Don't make it.' When they asked why, I said I did not think anybody in this day and age would be very interested in what Cinesound and Movietone may have been doing in the forties and fifties. How wrong I was!

I took an immediate liking to these two men, who had never made a feature film up to this point. Although they were frankly perhaps a little wide-eyed in their approach to the immense problems I could see in what they proposed to do, their enthusiasm was contagious. I responded and I am glad I did. Their storyline involved using perhaps 1000 to 1500 feet of the very valuable newsreel library material. They knew all about it and had already viewed vast amounts of the footage available. I pointed to the immediate problem of integrating the old black-and-white footage with the colour of today. How were they going to get in and out of it? They weren't exactly sure at that stage—another point I liked about them. There was nothing cocksure about their approach. They left the script with me so that I could digest it and said they would be back in a week.

I didn't like the script—or to be more exact, I didn't like a good deal of it. A film should build to a climax. This script built to a climax…and anticlimax after anticlimax! Another glaring error was that the authors had sort of stood off and flung handfuls of four-letter words, willy-nilly, at the dialogue. This was stupid, I said, because the cameramen of the period were mature, intelligent men who did not behave like street-corner louts and just did not talk the way off-target authors had them talking. If someone dropped a camera case on a foot of one of them, he would undoubtedly have sworn like the proverbial trooper (depending on how heavy the case was), but to have them effing their way through life was both ridiculous and to me, on their behalf, libellous.

Further, and again vitally important, here was an action picture in the making which should have strong appeal to the younger generation. Leave the four-letter words in and the film would almost certainly get an R Certificate. Therefore, from purely commercial sense alone, they should come out.

They came out.

There were a good many other weaknesses and in my opinion the script, as written by Bob Ellis and Anne Brooksbank, would not have made a good film. But because the enthusiasm of these young men got me in I took the time out to type up two or three pages of suggestions as to what might be done with the script so that eventually it could become a playable motion picture. They thanked me and said that what I had written was the most constructive criticism they'd had.

Among the highlights of the action the script contained the black-and-white newsreel coverage of the Maitland floods—several of them in fact since they happen all too regularly. The script had modern live action in colour woven into the black-and-white newsreel coverage—colour mingling with black-and-white. How did they propose to do the flood scene? Frankly they weren't too sure yet, they said, and again that honesty and frankness impressed me deeply.

All my film-making life I had been improvising, using makeshift, creating illusions. With that background it is not very difficult for me to say, 'If I were you I'd go down and have a good look at Narrabeen Lake which is handy, sandy-bottomed and shallow.' (I knew the lake well, spent a lot of my youth in and on it.) 'I would get a blow-up from the original newsreel negative of Maitland's main street in flood (a character in *Newsfront* was called upon to row up that street in a small boat in the middle of the flood). I would build a section of that street, mainly of 'flats', and have in the foreground the edges of perhaps two other buildings which would indicate that the camera was looking across the street.'

I pointed out the obvious fact that most coastal floods, and certainly Maitland floods, usually involved madly turbulent water rushing downstream to the sea. What to do? Well, I felt I would get two or three boats with extra powerful outboard motors on their sterns, lash them to supports just out of camera range and set their propellers churning at nearly flat-out revs. Then I would have a prop man, or two, also out of range, tossing debris into those rushing waters (a dead cow would add enormous realism, but they didn't go that far!). Since this was all being done in shallow water it would be so much easier to get the turbulence, and the prop boys, cameramen and others would be wading around in, at worst, only waist-deep water—knee-deep if they wanted it that way.

Well, they did it, bless them, and I for one was delighted with the effort they came up with, as was the vast mass of the people who stormed the theatres to see it, not to mention the critics. I am not claiming any credit. I made some suggestions; *they* made it. Nevertheless they put my name in the credit titles and producer David Elfick went on air on three or four occasions and spoke very generously of the help he said I had given them. Phil Noyce was overseas at the time, accepting the many awards the film won at film festivals. I mention it here because that kind of appreciation does not happen very often.

The two newsreel parent companies have had, over the years, a small gold mine in their libraries which has long been used by TV news services, commercial makers, documentary producers and other people—at around twelve dollars a foot! They struck a financial bonanza with *Newsfront*. Their royalties must have amounted to many thousands of dollars—which is not bad since they did not have to work for, or even raise a finger to get it! But that was a mere bagatelle compared to the rich pickings from the thirty-seven television episodes of the highly successful *This Fabulous Century* (1976–77).[2] All previous returns, good as they were, must have been made to look almost like a deficit! *This Fabulous Century* certainly produced a fabulous revenue. And to the cameramen and others whose sweat, blood and tears made it possible—naught! Well, who knows? Some day the companies may decide to give some of those royalties back to the nation to help finance the heavy cost of all those transfers to 16 mm.

Immediately after the premiere of *Newsfront* in Sydney, Walter Sullivan, a friend who is not only a front rank actor but also a newspaper television critic, raised quite a question when he said, 'What is it like to be part of history?'

Len Maguire (Bill Hunter) and Chris Hewitt (Chris Haywood) while shooting.

I said it was a thought which had never occurred to me, but since the excellent *Newsfront* made it clear how much of Australian contemporary history and way of life had been encapsulated on film, I supposed that those who played a part, great or small, in making that record were perhaps part of history. But no more so than the journalists, the novelists and the painters of the period. These people engaged in the past in recording events, trends, social comment and happenings which have become important to the historical records—with the obvious exception of war correspondents—would not have given that aspect of what they were doing a single thought, I am sure. It was a job to be done and you did it to the best of your ability and that was that.

Viewed in retrospect I realised the great importance of what my associates and I had put into the Cinesound library—just as the executive and staff of Movietone had put their historic material into their library for posterity. The men and women who are the television newsgatherers and presenters of today are far more conscious of the importance of what they are doing because they often have recourse to the Cinesound and Movietone library for footage of the past to illustrate the story they are currently preparing. The library *they* are creating is already vast. But to date these immense footages are held in the libraries of the television stations. No doubt a large amount of footage from them eventually will go into the National Library storage so that the citizens of the future may know something of the people who made up the twentieth century Australian men and women.

In the drive to get the television library really off the ground I used an illustration which was colourful enough, I think: 'Suppose,' I said, 'we could reach into the library and come up with the moving picture of Captain Cook landing at Botany Bay *and hear what he said*!'

Posterity can never hear James Cook, or Shakespeare or Nelson or any of the greats of the past. But it *will* hear what Neil Armstrong said when, as the first man to do it, he landed on the moon!

PART V

IN THE MARGINS: DOCUMENTARY

C risis might be too strong a word to apply to documentary film-making, for the documentary has always been commonly regarded as a second-class form or the poor relation of the feature film. But since the release of *Second Take*, the hunger of global broadcasters has become insatiable and appears to have pushed the observational documentary deep into an area it was never comfortable in: mass-market entertainment, as exemplified by such television 'reality' programs as *Big Brother* (2000) and *Survivor* (2000).

Yet unlike most other national film industries, Australia has a strong documentary tradition and many of its practitioners are highly regarded overseas, if not at home. Despite the growing global and institutional challenges, many continue to artfully forage—termite-like, independently and unpredictably—for new documentary 'truths'. Two of those termites are Curtis Levy and Dennis O'Rourke.

The painter, the president and the piano player

Curtis Levy

How many of us would agree to having our life examined by a documentary film-maker? In the unlikely event that I was approached, I would want to know something about the boundaries and the ethics of the film-maker's approach. My most recent subject for a biographical documentary film, Abdurrahman Wahid,[1] the President of Indonesia, set no such boundaries when I set out to make *High Noon in Jakarta* (2001), although he and his family wanted the right to see the film at fine cut stage, so that if there was anything that would cause them undue embarrassment they could ask for it to be deleted. In return for that compromise, I was given pretty much unlimited access to the President's activities and personal conversations. This access was, as far as I know, unprecedented. To my knowledge, no other leader in the world has allowed a film-maker to share their lives, to the extent that Wahid, popularly known as Gus Dur, did.

Despite the fact that Gus Dur was blind and had had two strokes, he kept to a punishing schedule. Luckily I was able to live in the palace for four months. I had to be there in order to be around from four-thirty every morning until around eleven or twelve at night, when he turned in. Early mornings were the times that I was able to film the most intimate and telling sequences. We would start off with a half-hour walk round and round the palace in the dark. I had a light on the camera, which I would use when I thought the conversations or the songs were interesting. Gus Dur loves to sing, especially Janis Joplin and country music. Luckily he's not at all self-conscious about his performance. After all, there was always an audience of security men, adjutants, doctors, and me. Perhaps the fact that he is blind makes him less selfconscious than are most subjects of documentaries. But I really don't think he gave a damn whether he was being filmed or not—in fact I believe he actually likes the idea of having every moment of his life recorded.

My theory is that because Gus Dur is blind, he wants to have his life visually recorded so that when he regains his sight he will be able to see the events of his life in a way that he is unable to at present. Gus Dur is ever the optimist in his belief that he will one day regain his sight. Luckily my friendship with him was started when he still had his sight, so unlike most people he meets, he has an image of me in his memory bank. The fact that we go back a long way almost certainly contributes to the trust he places in me. I first filmed with Gus Dur when he was an opposition figure to the then dictator, Suharto. At that time Gus Dur was leader of the largest Islamic organisation in the world, Nahdlatul Ulama, with around 35 million followers.

In his capacity as Islamic leader I made a film with Gus Dur called *Invitation to a Wedding* (1996). This film became somewhat of a comedy of errors. In terms of the filming, everything that could have gone wrong went wrong. I had spent a couple of months researching the film and arranging a very detailed schedule with Gus Dur. We were to visit Islamic communities in exotic outlying islands of Indonesia, and I would be able to see him in action wooing hundreds of thousands of followers towards a spiritual and democratic alternative to Suharto's cruel dictatorship. But when the crew arrived, Gus Dur had been called into military headquarters to be interrogated about his plans for democratic change, and I could not get any access to my subject.

Instead of panicking, or should I say, as well as panicking, we decided to film the process of trying to make a film about someone who is not available to be filmed. Fortunately my Indonesian location manager, Fakhri Amrullah, was trying to organise his daughter's wedding just as we commenced filming. So the film became a kind of Islamic comedic road movie. While I was trying to make a film about Islam and democracy, our location manager was trying to organise his daughter's wedding. The film demonstrates, in a way which is sometimes personally painful and embarrassing, the pitfalls of documentary-making in a foreign country.

Fortunately there are some who appreciate the jokes, which are largely at my expense. But there were others, in particular the Australian Broadcasting Corporation (ABC), which had commissioned the film, who were not amused. The ABC had expected a formal portrayal of a revered Islamic leader. They

PHOTO: COURTESY OF OLSEN LEVY

High Noon in Jakarta.

were even disappointed in the few sequences I was able to shoot with Gus Dur, because he looked nothing like the preconceived image that people have of an Islamic leader. Wearing colourful batik shirt and sandals and no ceremonial costume, Gus Dur did not pay off as the outside world's idea of an exotic Islamic leader. In addition, they had not expected to be witnessing the persona of a somewhat desperate film-maker relating to the unravelling of an increasingly chaotic and unpredictable narrative.

I am always conscious of the need to create a sense of normality around the people I film, even if, as is the case with Gus Dur, he exists in an atmosphere that is both manic and bizarre. Gus Dur may be a Sufi mystic, but he still loves to listen to country and western music and when he was sighted he adored French movies, such as François Truffaut's *Les Quatre Cents Coups* (*The 400 Blows*, 1959). Perhaps this is one of the reasons foreign cultures tend to remain foreign to Western audiences. Outside observers tend to concentrate on the exotic, rather than the familiar. As a film-maker I tend to look for the aspects of my subjects' lives that I can personally connect with, or which can help me to interpret and make sense of that life to a wider audience.

The tendency to concentrate on the exotic was certainly true of most films about Australian Aborigines that were being made at the time when I first began making films. In the early 1970s I was working as a production assistant with the then Commonwealth Film Unit, which later became Film Australia. I was given the task of rewriting the narration on an early film made about the Aboriginal artist Albert Namatjira.[2] On researching the true story of Namatjira, I realised that this early film greatly romanticised and sentimentalised his life. In fact this is what a lot of documentaries do with their subjects. There is a belief that the ordinary and the normal will not hold an audience. I wanted to make a film which did justice to the real situation of Namatjira's life, a life which was neither that of a total victim of white society, nor was he some kind of legendary hero. The story I uncovered created Albert Namatjira as a man who was far more complex than the simplistic labels of victim or hero.

It was this early research into the life of Albert Namatjira that taught me the danger of clinging onto any kind of preconceptions when telling the story of people's lives. Probably what helped me to come down to earth was to meet and get to know the sons of Albert Namatjira, who were living the same kind of life their father had been living by a water hole in the hills just outside Alice Springs. I realised that it hardly made sense to attempt to recreate Albert Namatjira's life on film, when his sons were living out a similar story, a story which could be filmed in the present rather than attempting to recreate the past. This is the background to how I came to make *Sons of Namatjira* (1975), which centred on the story of Albert's son Keith.[3]

Like his famous father, Keith Namatjira made a living from painting landscapes of ancestral homelands. These paintings were usually sold to art dealers who visited the Namatjira camp from time to time to encourage the Namatjiras to increase their output. One dealer had bought the family a car, which the family had to pay off in instalments with paintings. When the artist wanted instant cash they would sell to passing tourists who were always asking for a cheap painting. Although there was obviously some exploitation going on, it was not all one-way. Keith was well aware of the strategies of dealers and tourists who were only too willing to rip him off. This awareness enabled him to be able to play games with those whites who wanted a Namatjira on the cheap. The relationship of Keith and his brothers with the transient white society that hovered around their camp seemed to me like a parable of black–white relations in Australia.

It could be suggested that white film-makers spending a few weeks at an

Aboriginal camp are just as exploitative as the other whites who visited the camp to obtain Namatjira paintings. My rationale is that *Sons of Namatjira* is a film that attempts to dissect the problems of communication that bedevil white society's relationship with Aboriginal society. In terms of biographical film-making, there are obvious cultural differences which make real intimacy difficult to achieve. For example, I believe there is reluctance on the part of Keith Namatjira, the main character of the film, to engage in personal introspection. It's been suggested to me by an anthropologist that Aborigines generally are reluctant to verbalise emotions. For me as a film-maker it has meant that any emotional exploration of character must arise from what is happening in the immediate present. Therefore in *Sons of Namatjira* Keith develops as a sympathetic and complex character through the interactions we observe him having with white society.

In some respects this reluctance to indulge in emotional introspection was shared by Gus Dur, the Indonesian president, who believed that revealing emotions was akin to revealing personal weakness. In fact one of the reasons Gus Dur continually tells jokes is to make everyone around him aware that his enemies are not getting the better of him. An outsider may see both Keith and Gus Dur as living in desperate and untenable situations, but both men survive and to some extent thrive through their dreams. Gus Dur's ultimate dream is to diminish the power of the military and transform Indonesia into a true democracy. Keith's dream is to own an art gallery of his own, so that he will be able to receive a more just return from his efforts as an artist. Unfortunately Keith's dream was never realised. Not long after I finished filming, some bikies rode through his camp in the middle of the night, hurling firecrackers at the Namatjiras' tents. Keith decided to move to the Todd River bed in search of peace and quiet, but the move from his ancestral home must have been a traumatic experience, as he died not long after from a heart attack. Keith's ancestral home, an area known as Morris Soak, is now a shopping centre.

Filming people's lives always creates an issue regarding how much a film-maker intrudes into the personal life of the subject. With Gus Dur there appeared to be little separation between his personal and his public life. With me he seemed to want to allow total transparency. The Indonesian media were always trying to dig up dirt on their president, frequently accusing him of corrupt behaviour and even infidelity, which is a serious charge against someone who is an Islamic leader. But in my four months of filming, I never came across any situation which placed me in a dilemma as a film-maker. I never had to consider destroying my relationship with the subject for the sake of truth. While I was constantly in a situation that journalists would have died for, I never felt I had to be overly protective in what I filmed or what I included in the final cut, although there were situations where off-the-cuff remarks were made which, if included in my film, could have endangered the delicate balance that existed at that time in Indonesian politics.

Basically the issue of what you reveal about a subject's personal and private life is a matter of trust and sensitivity on the part of the film-maker. I want to make strong and honest films which give a real insight into the subject. To achieve the intimacy I need, I have to build a high degree of trust between myself and the subject. In the case of Gus Dur, we had known each other for more than ten years. He knew that I was unlikely to take unfair advantage of the access he gave me when he became president. On the other hand, I am extremely aware of the danger of making a hagiographic film, and believe that the film reveals Gus Dur as a flawed human being, just like the rest of us, who is doing his best in a practically impossible situation. There are sequences in the film which show Gus Dur as prevaricating and inconsistent, especially in his relations with the media. Sometimes it is difficult to know if these inconsistencies, labelled by the media as 'erratic behaviour', are manifestations of an intricate strategy or just naive mistakes. The point is that, as a film-maker, I never felt that it was my role to judge. I would rather the audience make up its own mind about the character I am portraying.

Of course it is all very well for me as a film-maker to state that I am allowing the audience to make up its own mind. In truth, I believe there is no such thing as objectivity. The moment you choose a subject, the moment you point the camera, the moment you make a cut in the edit—all are subjective decisions which affect the audience's feeling for and against the subject of the film. This is where how private space is treated becomes so crucial. The films about Gus Dur and Keith Namatjira are at extreme ends of the spectrum in terms of their position in society and the way in which they manage their private space. Gus Dur is a much-maligned president living in a palace. Keith is a revered artist living in a tent on the outskirts of town. While filming with Gus Dur I lived at the palace. While filming with Keith I stayed at a nearby motel and visited the camp each day. Despite this separation from Keith's camp, in terms of living away from the location, Keith was always open and welcoming to us moving around the camp. We filmed domestic scenes as well as interactions with the white world. There was always an understanding of what we could or couldn't film. For example, if Keith felt too tired or wanted to be alone, he would either tell us or I could sense that he needed space. But most of the time Keith, like Gus Dur, seemed

PHOTO: COURTESY OF OLSEN LEVY

Hephzibah.

happy to be filmed in domestic situations. As I alluded to earlier, the respect for the private and domestic aspect of people's lives is always a contentious issue in documentary film-making.

The issue of how far it is acceptable to delve into people's lives is perhaps even more contentious when the subject of the film is dead, as was the case with my feature documentary *Hephzibah* (1998), a film which examines the life of Hephzibah Menuhin,[4] the celebrated concert pianist and human rights activist. When I was researching this film I had unrestricted access to an abundance of intimate and personal material. I read hundreds of Hephzibah's letters to friends, and more than 100 letters she wrote to Paul Morawetz, with whom she was having an affair whilst living with her sheep farmer husband. I decided to choose those passages which would further our under-standing of Hephzibah's personal story. Naturally these letters, especially the letters to her lover, were never intended for the eyes of others. In fact the letters to the lover were not even entrusted to the postman. They were deliv-ered by a mutual friend of both parties, as both Hephzibah and her lover were married and secrecy was crucial.

Sifting through reams of such intimate, and at times passionate, material potentially positions the documentary film-maker in the role of voyeur. It is the way such material is selected and included in the film that determines whether or not our power as film-makers is used in a salacious or constructive way. Hephzibah's letters formed the narration for the film. It was as though Hephzibah was telling us her own story. An actor, Kerry Armstrong, read the passages I chose, using an inflexion that we felt was as faithful as possible to the way the real Hephzibah would have expressed herself. Our concentration was more on replicating her emotional expression than on trying to imitate her unique accent. Fortunately those who knew her well felt we had captured her in a way that gave her a palpable presence in the film.

In telling Hephzibah's story there were relatives and children who were still sensitive about some of the things she did. For some, the fact that she had extramarital affairs and that she left her children behind when she left her husband was still extremely painful. Fortunately, Hephzibah's immediate relatives, such as her brother, Yehudi Menuhin, the famous violinist, her sister Yaltah, also a concert pianist, and her four children, all felt that it was a good thing to tell the whole story. So in the telling of the story I encouraged various members of the family to give their version of what happened, so that the resulting portrayal of the persona of Hephzibah is drawn from a variety of disparate and contrasting sources, like a number of mirrors reflecting different truths. It is the selection and the editing of these sources that determines whether justice has been done to the subject. In this film, it would have been so easy to inadvertently increase the pain and, in some cases, bitterness caused by Hephzibah's actions. In the end, I believe that the film had a kind of therapeutic effect for those who were close to Hephzibah. I like to think that the film helped those who were left behind to understand and even respect the decisions she made at the time.

All of these characters lived a precarious life on the edge. Keith Namatjira, like his father, straddled both traditional Aboriginal society and white society. Gus Dur could easily have remained a respected Islamic leader, but he chose to take on the military, at great personal cost. Hephzibah could have remained living in the lap of luxury as the wife of a wealthy farmer. She chose to leave her family and work full-time for human rights. It is perhaps the dilemma faced by each of these characters that made their situations so fascinating for me as a film-maker. As film-makers we too are often faced with a similar dilemma: whether to stay with things that are tried and true, or to make a leap into the unknown. Certainly making films about people such as Keith, Gus Dur and Hephzibah has enabled me to share some of their aspirations.

I believe films that look deeply into other people's lives can help us to better understand the human dilemma. Unfortunately, these three incredible characters were never able to see the films I made about them. Keith Namatjira died prematurely of a heart attack before I could take the finished film back to Alice Springs for a screening. Hephzibah died twenty years ago, and Gus Dur, who is blind, fell asleep during the screening of the final cut at the palace. So I will never really know what the subjects themselves felt about the films I made about them—unless, of course, falling asleep during the screening is the ultimate comment. I like to believe that the president was too tired from running the country to enjoy listening to himself singing along with Janis Joplin.

On the poetry of madness: an encounter with Dennis O'Rourke

Martha Ansara

If any man come to the gates of poetry without the madness of the Muses, persuaded that skill alone will make him a good poet, then shall he and his works of sanity with him be brought to naught by the poetry of madness.[1]

Every time I meet with Dennis O'Rourke, we're in Kings Cross and I step into the melancholy dissolution of other voices, other rooms. Sometimes we're in a gin-mill powdered with the ghosts of standover merchants and American GIs, or a Korean cafe watching red-faced white men eat alone, or a room that belongs to Dennis for a week or a month or a year. Following a screening of *Cunnamulla* (2000), we meet in the lobby of the Gazebo Hotel, somewhere in Asia twenty years ago. We sit in a dim corner and Dennis persuades the staff to turn the music way down low; I turn on my tape recorder, and he turns on his. He pays me compliments and fixes upon me the same watchful, vulnerable gaze that I know he fixes upon the subjects of his films, and I too become strangely complicit in his search.

It's a momentary shock, sitting with him in the gloom of the pot plants, to recognise that semi-unconscious state of self-manipulation, that blurring of the boundaries between documentary film-maker and subject, that courtship that lures us where 'the film' wants us to go. This is what I also experience when looking through the camera. And Dennis is, of course, a superb instinctual cameraman. I know that he will run the interview the way he wants to, just as I would try to do, if I were his subject.

Dennis orders soda waters and says he doesn't want to start drinking alcohol too early—but at a certain point in the conversation, we find we want a beer. I stop then and look at him, and he looks back at me, not knowingly, with little pretence of innocence, and I see a certain familiar woundedness. He's one of those strawberry blond men you meet in hotels like this, perhaps a foreign correspondent, the last of a dying breed—going, going, gone with the old Australia. It's an encounter which triggers in me a sort of self-mocking nostalgia for the heroes who used to dominate the glittering 'imaginary' which once constituted—at a sanitised fictional remove—my vast red map of the British Empire. And I recall going around for early morning chats with banished Australian correspondent Wilfred Burchett in 1980 and 1981. At 6 a.m. Wilfred would be up and well into his workday. I'd find him in his Hanoi hotel room, wearing a white singlet, drinking whiskey and tapping away at a portable typewriter, writing about places and people far from home. One night at the Rex Hotel in Saigon, despite his age and the late hour, he out-danced us all.

For men like Wilfred, adventure heroes who never really settled and certainly never stopped, the kaleidoscope of new people and distant places represented, I suspect, some sort of outward manifestation of their particular psychic home—or was it a discomfort with home? But Wilfred was a man of another generation and, unlike Dennis, his world was strictly out in the world. His decades-long attack on imperialism was launched from within a paradigm that has now all but vanished. Dennis, although for many years inhabiting an exterior territory not dissimilar to Wilfred's, by comparison has been drawn into an interior marked by the complicated consciousness of self and subjectivity so characteristic of present-day thought. Over the past fifteen years, Dennis's work has moved far from documentary journalism towards a more pure form of expression. Nor is this movement without consequences for him.

This interview is in part about these consequences. To quote Edward Lucie-Smith, 'The position of the artist as a kind of favoured outcast in our society creates many difficulties for [Dennis] in [his] attempt to define his role. Perhaps the most logical way of dealing with it is to…see the man who makes art as one who offers a challenge to the rest of society and at the same time accepts a kind of bet with existence'.[2]

DENNIS BEGINS:

The Good Woman of Bangkok (1992) was a watershed for me, not just in terms of subject matter or content, to use the jargon terms, but also in terms of my motivation in making such a film. As you know, *The Good Woman of Bangkok* was an attempt to, *inter alia*, critique the praxis of documentary film-making, particularly the notion of the relationship between the documentary film-maker and her or his subjects.

When it was finished, sadly, although I knew it was a provocation, I thought—naively now, as I understand it—that the film would be its own defence. I wanted to convince people, particularly other film-makers and critics, of a new possibility of creating cinema that is about real events but doesn't suffer the limitations of most documentaries. But you'd have to say, in retrospect, that I didn't succeed and that my expectations of the ability of the film to bring about a revolutionary change in the way people would think about making a documentary were not achieved.

There's a quote from [Bertolt] Brecht, which I love: 'The government is unhappy with the people; then let the government elect a new people'.[3] I wasn't an adequate messenger when I made *The Good Woman of Bangkok*, and a lot of people out there wanted to shoot me. So, basically, I lost faith; I wasn't motivated to make another proper film for years after that. I also had personal things to deal with, the kind of crises that all parents have. I was divorced and had children growing up and I had a lot of work there. I do my best but I'm no perfect parent; my mind's always somewhere else. So I was depressed and paralysed in terms of working.

You have to have a certain sort of energy for documentary film-making?

Energy would probably not be the word. It's a force, something that's inside you. It sounds pretentious to say 'creative force', but it's a sort of qualified madness and you just absolutely feel you've got to do something. It's all intuition for me. I believe that it's no good being rational. You have to be irrational, because if you're rational then the true beauty of any idea will escape you.

I remember thinking recently that it's about passion, not about form. But how do you talk about the soul of the film? How do you say what allows a film to have soul and what doesn't?

I don't want to be hard on individuals because everyone does the best they can, I suppose, and probably they know what their deficiencies are, but let me just try to get this out here: when you meet film-makers and get to

PHOTO: DENNIS O'ROURKE, COURTESY OF FILM AUSTRALIA

Cunnamulla.

know them, just by the way they generally practise their lives, you can see in someone's personality and the things they're attracted to whether or not they're interested in a career or their practice. The nature of careerism is sickening when it comes to what we do. There's no such thing as a career, if you're really an artist.

Everyone thinks now that you go to a prestigious university and become a prestigious film-maker or a prestigious visual artist and that's your career! And it's all about money, about making a consumable product and 'networking' with the doctors and lawyers and politicians. Well, fuck that! I'd rather 'network' with the people in Cunnamulla than the crowd who attends the Opera House in Sydney. There's something about documentary practice that seems to attract a certain kind of clever, politically committed—in a theoretical sense—but retentive person. It's a refuge for a certain kind of artist *manqué*. I look for the madness. If the madness isn't there, then I'm pretty sure they can't quite get it. Joseph Conrad says, 'Before all, to see.' To see, before all else. That's a maxim I carry with me. Like all maxims, it's very economical.

I'm only critical because I wish for something better. I don't want to be mean-spirited to individuals, but they get very good press, they get awards and they get standing ovations at the Sydney Film Festival, and they may be convinced of the achievement of their films, but there's often a certain hollowness.

The fact is that there is a fundamental crisis in the critical understanding of the potential of documentary film-making which seemingly cannot be properly addressed. These days the word 'documentary' has almost lost meaning. It has so many different meanings. The term 'documentary fiction' that I invented for *The Good Woman of Bangkok* is somewhat misleading also. It stresses the fiction too much. As adjectives, 'documentary' or 'non-fiction' are good words. I like 'non-fiction'. It's understood in book publishing what non-fiction is. Although it might mean a cookery book or instructional manual to some, it also means serious writing.

I'm still trying to get at this sense of working with the observed reality, and changing it fundamentally. But at the same time as it's changed, it still remains the same. The notion is to try to transfer the experience, the recorded reality, to make it totally different. I tried to make every scene in *Cunnamulla* this way, to take something that seems to most people to be unprepossessing, almost banal—someone sitting on a bed talking, or sitting around a kitchen table talking. It's just what it is, there's no movement, there's only that. But something happens in the process, in the tone of the recorded moment, such that it changes fundamentally while staying the same. It acquires a meaning, a deeper meaning, which is pretty much universally understood. People don't miss it.

The only two things we've really got to work with in all film are *mise en scène* and montage. But how film works, what gives it the extra dimension of meaning is what puzzles people when they say to me, 'How did you get people to be so intimate?' I can't give the answer. I don't think the people in my film actually are being so intimate; I think they're just being how they would be at any time with anybody. They're being themselves, really. But there's a transformative effect if it's recorded and photographed in a certain way and then placed in a certain context. As my hero Joseph Brodsky, the Russian poet, says, what matters in telling a story is not the story itself, but what follows what.[4]

Except on a few occasions in Cunnumulla, *it seems you haven't edited for 'meaning' or to make obvious links.*

When I say 'what follows what', I'm not meaning 'cut from eye looking through keyhole to keyhole-framed shot of naked woman in bed'. I'm talking about 'what follows what' in terms of the totality of the meaning of the previous moment. Every scene has to have some level of transcendency before I use it.

But don't think that I've lost my sense of this film's deficiencies and that my ego is out of control. Quite the opposite—I know what its deficiencies are. Well, I don't know, but I know that it is deficient. It's what Mallarmé said about poetry: a poem is never finished; it's merely abandoned. That's true of film: you run out of time, you run out of money and your film's abandoned and you send it out there and that's the end of it. It's quite imperfect.

But talking about the montage now, what I'm striving for is best described as a symphonic effect. There are ten major characters in *Cunnumulla*: Arthur and Neredah, Jack, Marto and his girlfriend Pauline, Cara and Kellie-Anne, Herb, Paul, and Ringer the dog-catcher. There are ten people and they're supported by fifteen minor characters: the man who does the classical music program, the man who announces Slim Dusty, the concert pianist, Paul's sister, the mother of Cara, and so on. You can't rely on a tightly constructed script to connect all those people together. They're just disparate, really. You've got an elapsed time of eighty-something minutes for the whole film and it's happening in a non-specific time frame, although there's the conceit of Christmas to create a movement and to try to universalise the specific, because that's what I'm attempting to do. So these ten characters are basically just living. They're living and these are just the moments that are there, with their stories and their concerns: will Marto get a job? Will Marto marry Pauline? Will Cara and Kellie-Anne get pregnant? Will they be able to get away? What the hell is Ringer doing shooting a dog one day and burying a man the next? How wounded is Herb, living alone and hating the council? And then you get to understand a little bit. They're just there and they all exist in a certain time and place, and that's the basis of the symphonic effect.

While each of these individual stories is respected, in the sense that these people are living and they're sharing some of their life with me, I'm making a film. Their autonomy is respected but then they're all there to serve a larger idea and the larger idea is this: that the film is about nothing and, one hopes, everything. That it is about life. That's what I'm striving for, and increasingly I'm drawn to the most unprepossessing of situations. I find more meaning, a more fertile environment, to have the things that are inside me come out in these more banal situations. I used to be attracted to more exotic scenarios where the gloss was already in place, but I'm moving away from that now. I wish I'd discovered that earlier.

I'm thinking about some of the decisions you made about the photography of the film and its steady gaze.

A lot of it, again, was not thought through. In the beginning, my films were pretty much all hand-held. With *Half Life: A Parable for the Nuclear Age* (1985) I began to realise how much pure cinematic power could be obtained just from the landscape of the human face talking. It all depended on the quality of the conversation. And I discovered the notion of the absolute static frame. If I ever do use movement, like when there are two characters, you notice the movement. There is quite a lot of panning and that's just bringing time into the space. It's not done in any way that's mechanical, where the pan seems to be motivated the moment you expect it. It's happening in a different moment, a moment that's actually going on in the other person's brain and there's something like telepathy being sent to my head to say, 'move at this point'. It's not call and response; it's not action—reaction. Those movements are done through an intuitive process: Marto and Jack having the fight about the drugs, or Cara arguing with her mother across the kitchen table with Kellie-Anne in the middle; why you move at a certain time and why you don't move when in theory you should be moving. This creates the extra level of tension. It creates a sense of a word I keep harping on about: verisimilitude, the semblance of something being absolutely true. And it's only true because of the actual process of making the film, that synthetic process. You have to tell lies to get at the truth. Not really lies, but illusions.

By the very act of making the frame rock solid, locked off, and letting things happen outside the frame as they would, you get an advantage that you can never get if you're just doing it hand-held, because even if you don't go there and actually change the frame, the way that the audience reads film, they're getting the sense that at any moment they could go there. In my film, they know that mostly they're not going to.

I'm sitting here and I'm really looking at you. I'm not interested in what's over there. But if it were relevant, I would look.

Well, and if it were relevant to me, I would do it too. Where I pan, I pan. But, you know, the other thing is that there are only 220 cuts in this film. A normal ninety-minute film would have a thousand or more. There are only 220 event changes in the picture but it doesn't feel that way. It's something about the energy within the frame, but it's ineffable. You cannot pin it down.

But there's an abstract something in cutting that has to shape the film too.

It's ineffable. You cannot pin it down. If you do pin it down, I think you're fucked.

That's what I'm saying: if you cut for 'meaning' too much...

Oh, I'm cutting for meaning. But it's a meaning that I don't fully comprehend. I don't know it, but I have faith that it's there. That's my god. I don't believe in God, but I believe that there's this level of possibility of meaning, of exploration, of each other.

Do you believe in a higher power?

No, I don't actually. All of these mysterious things and all of this emotional, sexual energy that drives us all, which can be explained through genetics and some people want to explain through religion, I like to channel all those things to the point of just living, just knowing when you're there and doing it. I've had experiences as much as anybody: I have five children, I've had three wives, and still fall in love all the time, and still drink too much, and whatever.

You talk about the banal circumstances in which you can 'let the things inside me come out'. But it seems all documentaries that are supposedly about the outside world are most freely the reflections of the feelings, obsessions even, of the people who make them.

They would be if they were made well. But so many film-makers don't go there. You cannot expect to create any good work of any kind unless first of all you completely go inside. As a film-maker, whether I'm making a fiction film or a non-fiction, I reject the notion that I can pretend to represent something, especially other people's ideas and, in part, their lives, without first of all placing myself completely within—insofar as I can. This always involves very deliberate strategies, sometimes dangerous strategies, in terms of my emotions and what it might do to other people around me. For example, finding Aoi [the prostitute in *The Good Woman of Bangkok*] as a customer and not finding Aoi as a film-maker was absolutely essential to the project in order to collapse all that normal, comfortable, insulating distance.

Cunnamulla is really not that much different. You're still making the film but you've got to align yourself emotionally as much as one can. You're still in this other space, but you work to emotionally and physically and intellectually see it through other people's eyes—or try to. But at the same time, for them to understand and to take you on, to love you—while knowing what you're doing—is something beyond that. They don't see you as the film-maker who turns up with a crew and says, 'Okay, now just show me how you live your life today and we'll film. We've got two days and then we're out of here.' I need many days with anyone I'm filming. I make myself vulnerable to them, as they are vulnerable to me. I have all sorts of strategies for this.

In *The Good Woman of Bangkok*, Aoi could always only remember me from the first time we met, when I paid to have sex with her, and then buying the rice farm for her before any filming took place. I'd already worked it out that as a very good woman—and she is—she would not be able to abandon me. But she then had power over me and that's what I needed, the complete inversion of what you'd expect. I needed her to have power over me in order to get to where I wanted to get, and in order for me to say something about her condition in the way I did. The strategies are always different depending on who the person is, but it's exactly the same in *Cunnamulla*.

I don't think we should talk about this in an interview; it's so easily misunderstood. Besides, it's 'secret film-makers' business'.

Why not? What I say is there's one thing, above all: you've got to be totally engaged. If there's one word that sums it up, it's engagement. Now that word 'engage' can mean different things to different people. For me, it means that when I'm not with Neredah or Arthur, they might be thinking about me and I might be thinking about them. I might be somewhere else and we're dreaming about each other. I'm turning up in their dreams and they're turning up in mine. Or someone, man or woman, might have sexual desire for me, and I'm aware of that and they're aware of that. Or we have an argument about something. It's that complex.

It's as if you make yourself fall in love with each person, in a way, each time, and you're completely convinced of it and yet you have a distance. It's too weird and people don't understand it.

Well, we're all frightened and we all want to be loved, and we are part of the Judeo-Christian tradition. There's a lot of repression, and for me having being brought up a Catholic there's a lot of baggage. I seem to have been shuffling it off more and more, which is good. For me, what you just described is just a new, more refined form of privilege. But there's another element to the scenario: the characters I'm filming also have an understanding of my extra role. They're not film-makers. They're the taxi driver or a kid who breaks-and-enters for a living and is in trouble with the police, or a scrap merchant. They can't make the film. But—and I hope it comes through in *Cunnamulla*, I think it does—their recorded moments are as true as you could hope to have in terms of the realities of their lives as recorded and represented within the frame of cinema. That's not just because I was clever enough to get it; they also understand that I'm getting it. In a way, it's another form of contract. Week after week they understand that whatever my process is, I need to do it in order to properly tell their story.

And you need to do it for reasons that have nothing to do with their story and nothing to do with film.

That too. One of the marvellous advantages of the new digital technology is that you can keep rolling and you only have to break the mood every forty to sixty minutes. I think of the cameras and microphones as my recording angels because they're silently there and they're non-judgemental. They're doing my bidding. They understand me like I understand them. I've set them up and pushed the button, made the frame and adjusted the technical stuff, but from that moment they're doing something beyond my control. They capture something that's in the air. It's not just the image, it's something else they capture: the moment. The notion of a moment is a beautiful one; a moment can be quite long.

But remember also that people like you make films in order to be able to embark on an exploration. It's not as if the end is the end.

No, of course not. Each film is a project to connect your past experiences, all of them, of all kinds, with the present and the future. Most people only do that in their private lives because their work is drudgery; they don't have that privileged situation. But there are other people who do. I talk about my atheism but priests, for instance, have what artists have. They're connecting all the time the past and the present and the future and their beliefs. It's all fused and it's gorgeous. Artists have it if they're real artists, as opposed to artists who are really just careerists.

Let's not lose sight of the fact that you've gone to a place in Australia that's usually only treated in terms of victims, but there's a huge underclass, if you want to call it that, hundreds of thousands of people...

Millions!

...who live the lives that you describe, but who never appear in our films as themselves. They appear as victims...

Stereotypes.

Or not at all.

Stereotypes of failure, which we feel comfortable with.

Whoever the 'we' are.

Well, that's the elites.

And in the cities.

Absolutely. People who just cannot connect with the wider world, and cannot keep up for whatever reason.

Or don't want to.

That's right, and why they should they?

You seem to identify very strongly with these people in your films. I think Cunnamulla *rejoices in their strengths and deeply shares their sorrows.*

That's very nice of you to say. The film is called *Cunnamulla* and that happens to be the name of a town. I could not have called the film *Cunnamulla* if the film was simply about a town. It's not a portrait of a town. If you want to call it a portrait at all, it's a portrait of ten characters. The locus is Cunnamulla but Cunnamulla is not the subject. The subject is just ten people who know a little bit about each other—I refer back to the symphonic effect.

But people like the characters in my film—and I suppose it can be extended to most people who live in these remote places—are considered from the perspective of the city as marginal. We deny it but it's nevertheless true: we say 'marginal' about people who live west of a certain line in Sydney. In Sydney, particularly, there's an obsession with postcodes. Where you live defines you in a particular way, and there's sociological information to back it up: 'Oh, you live in a place like Cunnamulla, so probably your education is low, probably you're not attractive physically, or you've got right-wing politics.' The implication of all this is that somehow these people are marginal and their so-called marginality means they have less humanity. It's implied that somehow they would not be able to, say, care about the environment or care about politics or feel as eroticised as someone who lives in a nice house in the eastern suburbs in Sydney. But these people are not marginal in their own heads and they're not marginal to each other. People like the people in *Cunnamulla* are always represented in the media at one remove. They're always spoken of as a sociological class.

As an object.

And not as individuals, but as a stereotype and as a statistic and we accept it. When we say, 'Oh, the bush,' the bush means people who don't like classical music and don't have erotic feelings or whatever else. There are 20 000 towns like Cunnamulla in Australia. We see nothing. Who would imagine that in this town, as you've driven through, there's Marto and Cara and Kellie-Anne and, of all people, Neredah. They're there and they're so vibrant and full of humanity and longing and love.

So my project with this film—as with all my films from now on, there's no doubt about it—is to get inside and then look out, not be on the outside looking in. The opening scenes in *Cunnamulla* are set up that way as a metaphor. The first moment is with Neredah conspiratorially talking to me about something that's already going on outside. I'm already in. Our relationship is clearly one of intimacy, and that I'm on the inside is the all-important tone for the whole film. Mercifully, somehow I've got myself there. And how do I do it? You said before that we should not tell people, but even I don't know how I do it. I've sat watching my own films and how I make my films is truly a mystery to me. I'm not bullshitting you. I've already spoken to you about all the strategies I employ, of which a lot are automatic. It just comes out. It's like a sort of courtship and there is manipulation, I'm not denying it, but there's mutual manipulation, and when you come back to it, it's called engagement.

I'm searching for something and so I was drawn to people like Paul, Cara and Kellie-Anne who can speak with such eloquence about their condition. Cara and Kellie-Anne speak for all young girls like this in all country towns of Australia—and cities for that matter. The first time we see Paul he just talks about chasing girls and getting drunk and smoking dope and breaking into houses, and he's on the screen for a minute and a half. The next time we see him, he talks about the lack of culture. And in so few words, through this transcendental moment, just one shot, slightly easing back, and the pauses, suddenly he sums up everything about the condition of Aboriginal youth more eloquently than even Noel Pearson could do. And he's a marginalised person within a marginalised place. He's the marginalised of the marginal.

You know you're going to get into trouble for not showing that other layers exist in the town, and for revealing the sex life of the girls.

Good. I wouldn't want it any other way. I believe that if I'm not provoking people, then I'm not doing my job because my job is to reveal certain realities no matter how troubling they are. How can we progress if we don't address these things? The prurient types who want to save the world are just wrong and they'll be proven wrong.

Not that I think the film-maker's job is to show a balance.

But there is a balance in this film. For whatever bleak picture of Cunnamulla it shows, I don't think that it's totally bleak. In fact I believe the film is about redemption in the end. The girls do go away to Brisbane. Paul maintains his autonomy to the end. Herb does get a letter saying that the sister he's never seen is coming in four and a half years. Neredah is pleased just to get vegetable oil and seaweed soap, even if she's opening her present alone and Arthur is out cruising the streets. She's still making the best of it. And Marto and Pauline, they may be at the end of the railway line, but they're still in love. A bleak picture of Cunnamulla would have detailed all the incest cases that went on while I was there, all the murders and the bashings.

Which are merely the symptoms.

That's the *60 Minutes* version. In the early days of this film I thought I'd be filming a lot more of the graziers. They were very cautious, because they're paranoid about the ABC and they thought this was an ABC film. Eventually, the man who was acting as the representative of the graziers' association was calling on my mobile asking, 'When are you going to film us and get our side of the story?' He thought the film was going to be an 'Aboriginal versus whites' story on land rights. In the same way, there's none of the Aboriginal activist in the film because he was not able to drop his mask of being official. But while he couldn't, Paul could. It's not a sociological profile of Cunnamulla. It's about people.

And it's a film about you.

Well, it's always that too. And it may be that they're all about me. *Half Life* is about the death of my father; *'Cannibal Tours'* (1987) is about my leaving Papua New Guinea. But so what? This is not news! A film-maker carries these things with him all his life.

And if the film-maker doesn't invest the exploration of how they feel into the film, the film remains in the realm of the exterior.

If people don't get the idea that *Cunnamulla* is just the title of the film and that it's not about Cunnamulla, then they're in trouble. But I'm not going to let it get to me like it did with *The Good Woman of Bangkok*. It's water off a duck's back. If people want their truth as fantasy, I can't help that and I'm not going to give it to them. If I want to make a film about ten characters, the film is its own defence. There's no other defence. I'm not interested in what's not in the film. That's somebody else's film, and they can go ahead and make it!

I shot 100 hours of film. I could have made that other film, but it wasn't the one that I wanted to make. And I have that great privilege. I can make the film I wanted to make. If I couldn't, I wouldn't make anything at all. I repeat: I'm not a careerist.

As I say, my recording angels were just collecting it all. As I'm looking through the viewfinder, I know where the performances are transcending and where the performances are official. Eventually I was more and more drawn to the characters who were opening up to me, who were revealing not just themselves, but were emblematic of all the conditions that affect people who live in marginal, remote parts of Australia.

I want to ask you about the sadness in the faces of Paul, Pauline, Cara, Kellie-Anne and the girl who plays the piano. What's the word?

The sense of anomie.

That's not the word I'm looking for, but that's part of it.

I've often thought an appropriate term to describe something about the Australian character in general is 'to be desiccated', like desiccated coconut. You're dried up. This is not contradictory to all the things that I've been saying about these people being vibrant and full of love. It's something in the Australian character in general, a kind of deep emotional woundedness.

Woundedness?

A sense that life's possibilities are more restricted. That's not everybody, of course, but if you want to take the national character, I think that's even happening with, say, Italians who migrated here or the second generation of Lebanese or Vietnamese migrants. I'm struck by it every time I travel to other countries like Papua New Guinea, Mexico or Laos, for instance. Although we are supposedly so vibrant and free and young, blah-blah-blah, there's an emptiness, a void. I'm going to offend a lot of people when I say this, but it's almost like the huge, gorgeous, wide blue skies somehow suck up some aspect of our sensibilities and make us less—and the poetry of life is reduced.

People cannot speak their feelings but it comes pouring out of their faces.

That's just what it is. Everyone is emotionally constricted somehow.

And why are you so interested in this?

Well, you'd have to be. I don't understand why you ask me that, because generally I'm desperate to be loved and I always want more. I'm like the character in that Saul Bellow book—

Henderson, the Rain King[5]—the character travels through Africa crying out, 'I want! I want!' Because in the film we see some people who have a strong edge of depression as part of their make-up, do you think your feeling of depression prior to making the film was worked through in any way?

No, it was very much the other way: I was very much a working man in Cunnamulla. It was very hard to get through. The only two characters I imagined would be in the film before I commenced filming were Neredah and Arthur, as essentially fulfilling the role of dual unreliable narrators, as it were, as constant points of reference from beginning to end.

I actually filmed a lot more of the interaction of the characters in the film, but I found that didn't serve the purposes of the story I was trying to tell in the editing. Those moments when all the characters are together lost certain energy and, using the word in its literal sense, were confused through the montage of the film. For example, Herb comes down to see Neredah and give her some eggs from his guinea fowls and Neredah brings out this old broken jaffle-maker and says, 'Oh, Herb, I was going to throw this on the dump and then I thought you might have it.' It's a very funny scene and it works a treat. But there was something of a hermetic quality I was trying to get in the film, and those scenes somehow broke the mood. Those sorts of scenes somehow diluted the level of subconscious tension I was trying to keep there all the way through.

On the idea of the depression, I have to say that after several years of not feeling confident to go out and make another film like *The Good Woman of Bangkok*, the light went on and I saw in my head the film that we're now talking about. It does sound like I'm up myself, but you want honest answers and I have to say I just had the film in my head. It's a film that I've imagined from my own childhood memories, from reading literature, from reading the newspapers, from watching politics in Australia, from travelling in the bush, from working there as a young man, and knowing that they are being badly served by the way the bush is represented. So the film I've made is the film I already saw. I didn't know who was going to be in it, I didn't know what town it was going to be. I had no idea.

What do you mean when you say 'saw it'?

What I saw was the effect the film would have on me when it was finished and—as much as I can know this—in my contract with the audiences, the effect it would have on the audiences of the film. Then I had to just find it, find the town and find the people. And I found Cunnamulla.

The story of settling on Cunnamulla is interesting too. I was just coming out of the years when I was feeling very low and I was asked to give a talk at the National Library of Australia at a rather highbrow seminar on biography. One of the other speakers was Sister Veronica Brady,[6] whom I'd never met but I admired. I wasn't so sure she was going to admire me. I had to talk about *The Good Woman of Bangkok* and I was conscious that Veronica Brady was going to talk after me—and I was very insecure. Then she spoke and it was a great relief. She spoke beautifully, in the way a great teacher can speak, and she said something about what I'd said. I forget what it was, but at that moment I thought, 'My God, she's with me and I'm with her!'

Then when we were having drinks, some of her friends brought her over. She's this wiry, diminutive feminist nun and I was feeling a bit worried, but she comes over and shakes my hand and says words that I cherish: 'I thought *The Good Woman of Bangkok* was a very moral film, Dennis.' Finito! And I thought, 'Jesus, these fucking Phillip Adamses of this world and those holier than thou characters that want to pillory it—thanks, Veronica!' Then she said, 'What are you doing next?' And I said, 'Well, I've been feeling a bit low for a little while but I've just got this idea about this country town.' I told her how it had to be black-and-white and about all the issues I wanted to deal with. She said, 'Oh, come to Western Australia!'

When you're talking with somebody as formidable as she is, you really have to engage, like I'm engaged talking to you now. And because she's asked me the question and I owed her an answer, I stepped up a gear in terms of my own cognitive process and it just hit me straight away. I said, 'I think I have to do it in Queensland because that's where I grew up.' And you know what she said? She put her hand on my shoulder—she had to reach up—and said, 'That's right, Dennis, that's your country.' And she was right. So then when I got some money to make it, I went to about thirty places in Queensland over a month, looking for the right town, just anonymously coming into town, checking into the pub, and starting conversations. Cunnamulla was the first place I went to and I came back to it again. Intuition plays a big role. Then when I started filming, I started filming with all those official-type people, but what happened in the process of just being there was that I got to meet the characters that now are in the film. I've been saying this for twenty years: you don't so much make the film; the film makes you.

Notes

N B: All notes provided by the editors are distinguished from those of the contributors by the notation '[eds]'.

THEM ARE FIGHTIN' WORDS

1 Thomas Friedman, *The Lexus and the Olive Tree*, HarperCollins, London, 2000. Taken from the robotic construction of Lexus car by Toyota, the Lexus is a metaphor for change and improvement, the continual modernising, streamlining and privatising of economies that is necessary for the new system of globalisation. On the other hand the olive tree represents all the things that anchor and identify us—such as family, religion, nation and so on—and can be resistant to change and new systems.

2 ibid. See in particular Chapter 12, 'The Golden Arches Theory of Conflict Prevention', pp. 248–75.

3 ibid, pp. 240–1. Friedman covered the efforts of then Secretary of State Robert A. Baker's mission to form a coalition of allied forces as well as raise funds to pay for the Gulf War.

4 Naomi Klein, *No Logo*, Flamingo, London, 2000; Noreena Hertz, *The Silent Takeover: Global Capitalism and the Death of Democracy*, Heinemann, UK, 2000.

5 See Umberto Eco, *Faith in Fakes: Essays*, Secker & Warburg, London, 1986. See in particular Chapter 4 'Reports from the Global Village', pp. 133–74.

6 Friedman, ibid, pp. 325–64. The two chapters form Part Three 'The Backlash Against the System'.

7 Arnold and Philip Toynbee, *Comparing Notes: A Dialogue Across a Generation*, Weidenfeld and Nicolson, London, 1963, p. 32.

8 In the Internet journal, *Senses of Cinema*, the editors of a symposium titled 'Terror, Disaster, Cinema and Reality', wrote of September 11: 'All distinction between screen

fantasy and the crises of history seemed to disappear in a flash.' Although not the subject of *Third Take*, a book exploring the relation between cinema and reality would certainly be timely. In the immediate aftermath of September 11, reality and movie 'reality' became artlessly homogenised, as was evidenced by reports of the entertainment industry shelving films deemed too insensitive, in particular the Arnold Schwarzenegger vehicle *Collateral Damage*, or mainstream commentators comparing the catastrophe at the World Trade Center with action blockbusters like *Die Hard* (1988) or *Independence Day* (1996). See Fiona A. Villella and Adrian Martin (eds), *Senses of Cinema*, issue 17, 2001 (*www.sensesofcinema.com*).

9   A sample selection of commentators includes Shimon Peres (*The Age*, 15 October 2001), Leon Davis (*The Age*, 15 November 2001), Thomas Friedman (*The Age*, 19 November 2001), Malcolm Fraser (*The Age*, 28 December 2001).

10 Noam Chomsky, *September 11*, Allen & Unwin, Sydney, 2001, pp. 30–1.

11 Friedman, ibid, p. 248. [emphasis Friedman]

12 From *Wit and Humor from Old Cathay*, Panda Books, Beijing, 1986.

13 Raffaele Caputo and Geoff Burton (eds), *Second Take: Australian Film-makers Talk!*, Allen & Unwin, Sydney, 1999, p. 91.

SELLING NUTS AND BOLTS [EDS]

1   American writer-director born in 1930, best known for his first film *Bob & Carol & Ted & Alice* (1971) and also credited as co-creator of popular teen program *The Monkees* (1969); he recently made a brief appearance in the HBO series *The Sopranos* (1999).

2   Alan J. Pakula, producer-director born in 1928, formed a highly productive association with director Richard Mulligan in the 1960s. He made a number of successful films in the 1970s and 1980s, including *Klute* (1972), *All the President's Men* (1978) and *Sophie's Choice* (1982).
Martin Ritt, director born in 1920, began his career as a theatre director, moved into television directing production for CBS, but was blacklisted in 1951 when charged with donating money to Communist China. He taught acting at the Actors Studio until 1956 when he got to direct his first film, *Edge of the City* (1957).

3   The McCarthyite era, or McCarthyism, is often confused with the House of Un-American Activities Committee (HUAC) hearings of 1947, but the two events are distinct; the McCarthyite era refers to Senator Joe McCarthy, who led an investigation into 'communist infiltration' of the television industry in the 1950s.

4   The film is, of course, an adaptation of the book by Nene Gare, which was first published by Heinemann in 1961.

5   Russell George Drysdale (1912–81), famous Australian artist who was born at Bognor Regis, Sussex, England, the son of Australian pastoralists.

6   McAlpine is obviously referring to Russell Crowe's Oscar-award winning role in *Gladiator* (2000).

I'M NOT AN ARTIST; I'M A TECHNICIAN [EDS]

1   Seale is probably referring to *Deathcheaters* (1976), which featured John Hargreaves and Australia's premier stuntman Grant Page in the lead roles.

2 K refers to degrees Kelvin, a unit for measuring heat and colour temperature.
3 Seale is simply referring to a fill light, which is used to fill in or remove shadows that are cast by the main light source.

THE DIRECTOR'S VOICE 1 [EDS]

1 Luis Sepúlveda was born in Chile in 1949. His novel *Un Viejo que leía novelas de amor* (*The Old Man Who Read Love Stories*) was first published in the US in 1993 by Harcourt Brace, New York
2 Flanagan directed the film and also wrote the script from his own book, *The Sound of One Hand Clapping*, Macmillan, Sydney, 1997.
3 Ian Jones is credited as the principal cinematographer; the others were Paul Dalwitz, Kim Waiteklis, Rick Martin, Clive Duncan, Ross Blake, Steve Arnold, David Burr, Gerald Thompson, Richard Michalak, John Chataway, Jeff Morgan, John Ogden, Barry Hellepen, Tibor Hegedis, Paul Ammitzboll, John Armstrong, Ernie Clarke, Brian Bossito, Brigid Costello, Brendan Laville, Lisa Tomasetti, Harry Glynattis, Walter Holt, Geoffrey Simpson, Steven McDonald, Roger Lanser, Simon Cardwell, Richard Rees-Jones, David Popemann and Max Pepper. Apart from using thirty-two DOPs, *Bad Boy Bubby* is also unique for its use of binaural sound, a pair of miniaturised radio microphones and transmitters that were built into the wig worn by Nicholas Hope.

THE DIRECTOR'S VOICE 2

1 *Head, Heart and Hand* (1979), commissioned by the Crafts Council and Crafts Board of the Australia Council.
2 Jack Flam (ed.), *Matisse on Art*, University of California Press, Berkeley CA, 1995. First published by Phaidon, New York, 1973.
3 Christopher J. Koch, *The Year of Living Dangerously*, first published by Thomas Nelson, Australia, 1978.
4 This documentary was actually shot for a *Four Corners* program; see interview with Don McAlpine in this book.
5 Gwen Harwood (1920–95). The quote is from the poem 'Impromptus III', which was first published in the collection *Poems: Volume Two*, Angus & Robertson, 1968. Harwood also studied music, was a church organist and wrote numerous librettos for operas, including Larry Stisky's *The Fall of the House of Usher* (1965) and *The Golem* (1989).
6 Jack Flam, op. cit.

CHOPPER [EDS]

1 *From the Inside: The Confessions of Mark Brandon Read* was published by Sly Inc. (John Silvester) just after his release from Pentridge Prison in Melbourne. The book became an immediate cult classic and continues to sell steadily ten years later, making Read one of Australia's bestselling authors. His ninth book in the *Chopper* series was published in May 2000. His other titles are: *Chopper 2: Hits and Memories: More Confessions of Mark*

Brandon Read; Chopper 3: How to Shoot Friends and Influence People; Chopper 4: For the Term of His Unnatural Life; Chopper 5: Pulp Faction: The Revenge of the Rabbit Kisser and Other Jailhouse Stories; Chopper 6: No Tears For a Tough Guy; Chopper 7: The Singing Defective; Chopper 8: The Sicilian Defence; Chopper 9: The Final Cut. Read has also released two music and voice-narrated CDs, *The Smell of Love* (1997) and *Get Your Ears Off* (1998).

2 Mark Brandon Read was born in the inner-Melbourne suburb of Carlton in 1954. Police files record his first arrest in late 1971 at the age of seventeen, and he has spent twenty-three years of his adult life in prison.

3 Mark Read appeared as a guest on the ABC chat show *Elle McFeast* (hosted by Libby Gore) in March 1998. His appearance sparked a volley of complaints from viewers and the media, and is considered the reason for the show's axing.

4 Part of the headline for a *New Idea* story on the making of *Chopper*.

5 Midway into the production of *Chopper* Geoffrey Hall was replaced by Kevin Hayward.

6 Mark Brandon Read was released from Hobart's Risdon Gaol in January 1998. He currently lives on a farm outside Hobart with his wife Mary-Ann and their son Charlie.

NEWSFRONT RECOLLECTED

1 The DVD of *Newsfront* was released by Roadshow Home Entertainment in June 2001.

2 The FTO also appointed George Mannix, a man long experienced in trouble-shooting for them. It was hoped that, along with *Newsfront*, other films that had been tied up all this time could be repatriated from an agreed holding facility in Los Angeles.

3 Light bands are hole-punched paper rolls that trigger the printer lights to change colour.

4 Charles Kane's last word before his death, which sets the newsreel makers in *Citizen Kane* on an odyssey to discover the meaning of 'Rosebud'.

5 Apart from those individuals already mentioned in this introduction, this army comprised *Newsfront*'s original grader Arthur Cambridge, cinematographer Vince Monton, and associate producer Richard Brennan. Then there were Simon and Kerry Dibbs, Adam Sharman and Supriya Naidu-James at Island Films; Jan Thornton and Olivier Fonteay at Atlab; George Mannix of the FTO; Laura Burrows and Jonathan Goldman, who were then at Rumbalara Films; Ruth Jones, former Chief Executive Officer of the Australian Film Institute; Annalie Chapple and Roy Andrews at Digital Pictures; Gethin Creagh and Ian McLoughlin, both award-winning mixers; Liz Wright, Michael Thompson and Luke Dunn Gielmuda at Soundfirm; Ruth Evatt and Roen Davis of Visualeyes; Brian Rollason at Digital Video Mastering; Simon Drake of ScreenSound Australia; Al Thompson, Geoff Thomson, Roslyn Wilson and Michael Brooks at Village Roadshow; Kerry McGovern of Clever Types, who does great transcriptions; Leilani Hannah and her crew, who videotaped the festival forum, and Leo Sullivan who recorded the sound, and Ned Lander for kindly lending a camera; Emma Hay, who kept things in perspective; all the original cast and crew of *Newsfront* who happily gave of their time to record their recollections for the DVD commentary track; and finally my mother Joyce, whose stash of *Newsfront* reviews and memorabilia had even amazed David Elfick and Phillip Noyce—she was happy to lend it to us as long as she got it back!

THE DIRECTOR

1 Ubu Films was formed in 1965 by Albie Thoms, Aggy Read, David Perry and John Clark with the express purpose of producing avant-garde films. The company also had its own magazine–newsletter, *Ubunews*.

2 Noyce ran foul of the police, who alleged the film was pornographic.

3 The Sydney Film-makers Co-operative was formed in 1966 by the co-founders of Ubu Films with the express purpose of distributing avant-garde films.

4 *GTK* stands for *Get To Know*, a ten-minute pop culture ABC program that was aired four times a week at 6.30 p.m.

5 Another important role to cast was the part of Ken, the voice of our Cinetone newsreel. We were lucky enough to discover a voice that was well known to all Australians in the 1950s and '60s, the voice of John Dease, who had been the compere of a very famous radio program called *The Quiz Kids*. Although John had never acted before, he seemed to possess both the voice and the dignity that perfectly captured the character he played. His most memorable scene is when he argues with Geoff, the editor, and that's because of the emotional intensity Dease brought to his characterisation. When he said the line, 'When you're sixty-four and you've had your first heart attack, you'll know how it feels, Sonny Jim,' at times his expression was so intense, he had thrown himself so much into the conflict, that I really thought he might collapse. It was almost like he was living out his own life, his own feelings, like the character was no longer being acted but that Dease had been possessed.

6 One of the few times we used a telephoto lens is on a close-up of Angela Punch-McGregor, who plays Fay, Len Maguire's wife. It is during a very crucial and emotional time as her husband is moving his clothes from their bedroom into a spare room. I chose to disobey the rules we'd set for ourselves because I felt this one moment encapsulated so much about the personal and political story the film describes. That one moment mirrors the schism that occurred in Australian society as a result of the Communist Party referendum, wherein two people lived together under the one roof, as one family, but no longer lived truly as man and wife. In a way I chose to make that one image of Angela Punch-McGregor the most indelible in the whole movie.

7 A boon of Ken's association was the discovery that in Balmain in 1977 the original headquarters of Cinesound was still standing. A large number of the film's scenes are set in the headquarters of a fictional newsreel company called Cinetone. Well, Ken's Cinesound studio was deserted, but with a lot of the original equipment, old arc projectors, a lot of the original rooms, including the screening and mixing theatre, editing rooms, conference rooms, the foyer and corridors. The real thing was actually sitting there intact and we were able to just walk in, take over what was once a thriving newsreel company and turn it into our standing set.

8 *The Rime of the Ancient Mariner*, a poem by S.T. Coleridge which first appeared in 1798, tells of an ancient mariner who meets three gallants on their way to a marriage and detains them to recount a story of woe.

9 *The National Times* (1971–86), a national weekly paper of business and current affairs, was first published by W & F Pascoe, Milsons Point, New South Wales.

10 Ian Stocks, 'Newsfront', *Cinema Papers*, no. 115, April 1997, pp. 20–5, 46–7.

11 A production company formed between Phillip Adams and Kerry Packer. Films include *Lonely Hearts* (1982), *We of the Never Never* (1982), *Fighting Back* (1983) and *Kitty and the Bagman* (1983).

Third Take

THE SCRIPTWRITER [EDS]

1 *The Legend of King O'Malley* was formed from a short workshop season at the Jane Street Theatre, Sydney, in 1970. The play was first published by Angus & Robertson in 1974.
2 *The Nation Review* (1972–81), published by Incorporated Newsagencies Co., Melbourne.
3 Jim McNeil was born in Melbourne in 1935, the youngest child of a Scots–Irish working-class family. By the time of the *Newsfront* screening, McNeil had served a seventeen-year sentence for armed robbery and the wounding of a police officer. He wrote his first play in Parramatta Gaol, outside Sydney, in 1970 titled *The Chocolate Frog*; other plays include *The Old Familiar Juice* (1972) and *How Does Your Garden Grow?* (1973).
4 Peter Kenna was born in Balmain, Sydney, in 1930. He first came to prominence as a playwright in March 1959 when his third play, *The Slaughter of St Teresa's Day*, opened at the Elizabethan Theatre in Newtown. Other plays include *Talk to the Moon* (1963), *Muriel's Virtues* (1966) and *A Hard God* (1973).

Ray Lawler is, of course, the writer of *Summer of the Seventeenth Doll* (1955). He was born in Footscray, Melbourne, in 1921. Other plays include: *The Piccadilly Bushman* (1959), *The Unshaven Cheek* (1963) and *A Breach in the Wall* (1967).

THE PRODUCER [EDS]

1 Australian *Oz* (then London *Oz*), a magazine of Australian satire, was started in 1963 and published by Oz Publications Ink Ltd., Sydney. It ceased publication in 1969.

THE CINEMATOGRAPHER [EDS]

1 Gregg Toland (1904–48) was a distinguished American cinematographer who worked mostly on films produced by Samuel L. Goldwyn. Apart from *Citizen Kane* (1941), Toland shot *Nana* (1934), *Dead End* (1937), *Wuthering Heights* (1939), *The Grapes of Wrath* (1940) and *The Best Years of Our Lives* (1946).
2 Raoul Coutard is a French cinematographer born in 1924. The 'phase' Monton is referring to is the period in which Coutard shot films for Jean-Luc Godard and François Truffaut, which include *A bout de souffle* (1959), *Tirez sur le pianiste* (1960), *Jules et Jim* (1961), *Vivre sa vie* (1961), *Les carabiniers* (1963), *Pierrot le fou* (1965) and *Made in USA* (1966).

THE ACTOR [EDS]

1 Howard and Hunter appeared together in Lewis Milestone's 1962 remake of *Mutiny on the Bounty*, with Marlon Brando in the role of Christian Fletcher.
2 John Ewart, 1928–94.
3 John Meillon, 1934–89.
4 Byron Kennedy, 1952–83.

5 Rex Connor [Reginald Francis Xavier] (1907–77) entered federal politics in 1963 as the Labor member for Cunningham and had aligned himself with Gough Whitlam, who gave him the new portfolio of minerals and energy after the 1972 election. Connor had a vision for a fully Australian-owned resources industry, but he was sacked as minister in 1975 over his unorthodox method of raising capital via a middleman, Tirath Khemlani, to exploit alternative energy sources. His sacking was one event that led to the dismissal of the Whitlam Government.

6 Don Crosby (1924–85) was a radio personality who actually started acting as a child in both radio and theatre, and later studied at the Royal Academy of Dramatic Art in London (1946–48). He was also known as a director of numerous radio shows, including the very popular *Blue Hills* (c. 1970s) in his last years. Apart from *Newsfront*, other film credits include *Moving On* (1974), *The Fourth Wish* (1976), *The Picture Show Man* (1977), *The Chant of Jimmie Blacksmith* (1978) and *Heatwave* (1982). In 1980 Crosby was awarded the Order of Australia for services to media and theatre, and in 1985 received the Raymond Longford Award from the Australian Film Institute.

7 Hunter is paraphrasing the last line of dialogue from *Newsfront*. When Hunter's character, Len Maguire, marches away from his brother's offer to buy an exclusive piece of news footage, Amy (Wendy Hughes) turns to Frank Maguire (Gerard Kennedy) and says, 'He's just a bit old-fashioned, that's all.'

THE INSPIRATION [EDS]

1 Ken G. Hall died in 1994. We've wanted to provide a fairly comprehensive picture of the making of *Newsfront*, and especially given that Hall and his Cinesound Studios are in large part an inspiration for the film, we believe the reader will be interested to know Hall's thoughts on the making of *Newsfront*. Hall's article is an extract from his book *Australian Film: The Inside Story*, first published by Lansdowne, Melbourne, 1977.

2 *This Fabulous Century* was produced by former current affairs personality Peter Luck for the Seven Network.

THE PAINTER, THE PRESIDENT AND THE PIANO PLAYER [EDS]

1 Abdurrahman Wahid lost Indonesia's presidency to Ms Megawati Sukarnoputri in July 2001.

2 Albert Namatjira (1902–59) was born at the Lutheran Mission of Hermannsburg in Central Australia, where he took up watercolour painting. He held his first solo exhibition in Melbourne in 1938, and since then has been the most well known of Aboriginal artists.

3 Keith Namatjira died in 1975. He is not as renowned as his father Albert, but is still considered one of the finest of the Hermannsburg group of painters in Central Australia.

4 Hephzibah Menuhin (1920–80), an American pianist, was the sister of celebrated violist Sir Yehudi Menuhin, with whom she toured widely as a recitalist in the US and Europe.

ON THE POETRY OF MADNESS

1 Plato, *Phaedras*, translated by R. Hackforth, Cambridge University Press, Cambridge, 1972.

2 Edward Lucie-Smith, *Late Modern: The Visual Arts Since 1945*, Praeger, New York, 1976.

3 The quote by Bertolt Brecht is famous. I recall that it is inscribed on a monument somewhere in the former East Germany; and I read it on that monument as I was given a tour by the organisers of the Leipzig Documentary Film Festival in 1986.

4 Brodsky (1940–96) said it and I registered it—that's all I know. The quote could very well be in his book of essays *On Grief and Reason*, Farrar, Straus & Giroux, New York, 1995.

5 Saul Bellow, *Henderson, the Rain King*, first published in the US by Viking Press in 1959.

6 Veronica (Patricia Mary) Brady was born in Melbourne in 1929. She became an English tutor at the University of Western Australia in 1972, a lecturer in 1974 and associate professor of English in 1991. A Catholic nun and academic, Brady speaks out on issues of land rights, racism and media monopolies. Her books include: *Crucible of Prophets* (1981), *Playing Catholic* (1991), *Polyphonies of the Self* (1992) and *Caught in the Draught* (1993).

Contributors

MARTHA ANSARA is a Sydney documentary film-maker.

ROLF DE HEER is one of Australia's foremost writer-producer-directors. *Bad Boy Bubby* (1993) won the Grand Special Jury Prize and the International Film Critics Prize at the 1993 Venice Film Festival, as well as five Australian Film Institute awards. *The Quiet Room* (1996) and *Dance Me to My Song* (1998) were selected for Official Competition in the Cannes Film Festival. De Heer's other films include *Tail of a Tiger* (1984), *Incident at Raven's Gate* (1988), *Dingo* (1992) and *Epsilon* (1995). He is currently working on *The Tracker*, which stars Gary Sweet.

ANDREW DOMINIK was born in New Zealand and moved to Australia when he was two years old. Following graduation from Swinburne Film School in 1988, Dominik was selected by advertising firm McCann Erickson to direct commercials. He also joined Cherub Pictures and directed music videos for major Australian artists including Crowded House, Jenny Morris, Diesel, James Reyne, The Cruel Sea and The Church. *Chopper* (2000) is his first feature.

DAVID ELFICK began his film-making career as a writer-producer-director of short films and documentaries, including the feature-length surfing documentaries *Morning of the Earth* (1972) and *Crystal Voyager* (1973). After the success of *Newsfront*, Elfick produced *The Chain Reaction* (1980) and *Star*

Struck (1982). He also directed and produced the features *Harbour Beat* (1990), *Love in Limbo* (1993) and *No Worries* (1993).

BOB ELLIS is a colourful Sydney identity who dabbles in a number of mediums or professions—freelance film critic, playwright, broadcaster, political speechwriter, songwriter, theatre owner, regular journalist, screenwriter and film director. His screenwriting credits include collaborations with Paul Cox on *Man of Flowers* (1983), *My First Wife* (1984) and *Cactus* (1986). Apart from writing many other Australian films, Ellis has also directed three feature films: *Unfinished Business* (1986), *Warm Nights on a Slow Moving Train* (1988) and *The Nostradamus Kid* (1993).

KEN G. HALL (1901–94) was Australian cinema's most commercially successful film-maker. A long association with Union Theatres led Hall to directing *On Our Selection* in 1929 and the formation of the Cinesound studio, which was guaranteed a steady stream of film production. The studio also produced a weekly newsreel titled *Cinesound Review,* which won Australia's first Academy Award in 1942 with the newsreel special *Kokoda Front Line.* Hall's feature films include *The Silence of Dean Maitland* (1934), *Grandad Rudd* (1935), *Orphans of the Wilderness* (1936), *Tall Timbers* (1937), *Dad and Dave Come to Town* (1938), *Mr Chedworth Steps Out* (1939) and *Dad Rudd M.P.* (1940).

BILL HUNTER is a Sydney based actor who was also a former champion swimmer. He began his film career in minor or support roles in such films as *Mutiny on the Bounty* (1962), *Ned Kelly* (1970) and *Stone* (1974). His association with director Phillip Noyce catapulted him into lead roles with *Backroads* (1977) and *Newsfront* (1978). His other credits include *In Search of Anna* (1979), *Gallipoli* (1981), *Far East* (1982), *Heatwave* (1982), *The Dismissal* (1983), *Street Hero* (1984), *An Indecent Obsession* (1985), *Rikky and Pete* (1988), *The Last Days of Chez Nous* (1992), *The Custodian* (1994) and *Road to Nhill* (1997).

CURTIS LEVY is an independent film-maker who has made several films in Australia and Asia for television and cinema release. His documentaries have won many international awards. In 1998 *Hephzibah* won several awards, including the AFI Award for Best Documentary, the Silver Wolf Award for Best Video Documentary at the International Documentary Festival in Amsterdam, and the Australian Film Critics Circle Award for Best Documentary Film. *Riding the Tiger* (1991), a three-part series examining the origin of authoritarian rule in Indonesia, was nominated for the AFI Award for Best Documentary and won the ATOM Award for Best Television Series. *Breakout* (1984), about the mass suicidal breakout of Japanese prisoners of war in Cowra, won the award for Best Television Documentary at the Chicago International Film Festival.

DON MCALPINE is one of Australia's most influential cinematographers. He began his career at the ABC and the Commonwealth Film Unit (CFU), becoming that organisation's chief cameraman in 1968. McAlpine's first feature, *The Adventures of Barry McKenzie* (1972), was shot while on leave from the CFU. He shot his first American feature in 1981, and has recently completed work on *The Time Machine*. Other film credits include *Patrick* (1978), *The Earthling* (1980), *Puberty Blues* (1981), *Now and Forever* (1982), *Moscow on the Hudson* (1984), *Romeo + Juliet* (1997) and *Moulin Rouge* (2001).

VINCE MONTON is one of Australia's most talented cinematographers, whose credits include *Street Hero* (1984), *Stalked* (1993), *Lucky Break* (1994) the telefeatures *Double Sculls* (1985) and *The Hijack of the Achille Lauro* (1989) and the mini-series *The Dunera Boys* (1985). Monton is also a director: *Windrider* (1985), *Fatal Bond* (1991) and *Point of No Return* (1995).

PHILLIP NOYCE, born 1950, was among the first intake of students when the Australian Film and Television School opened in 1973. He wrote, directed and produced an extensive number of short films and documentaries while also managing the Sydney Film-makers' Co-operative from 1970. The critical and commercial success of *Dead Calm* (1989) secured Noyce his passport to Hollywood. His credits include *Heatwave* (1982), the mini-series *The Dismissal* (1983) and *The Cowra Breakout* (1985), *Patriot Games* (1992), *Clear and Present Danger* (1995) and *The Bone Collector* (2000). He recently completed *Rabbit Proof Fence* and *The Quiet American*.

DENNIS O'ROURKE started his film-making career in 1970 as a cinematographer for the ABC. In 1974 he became a documentary producer and director for the government of Papua New Guinea, where he made *Yumi Yet: Independence for Papua New Guinea* (1976) and *Ileksen: Politics in Papua New Guinea* (1978). In 1990 O'Rourke was the recipient of the Australian Film Institute Byron Kennedy Award. His other credits include: *Yap...How Did You Know We'd Like TV* (1980), *The Sharkcallers of Kontu* (1982) and *Couldn't Be Fairer* (1984).

JOHN SEALE spent many years at the ABC as an assistant cameraman. He went freelance in 1968 and soon established himself as a seminal camera-operator. He is regarded as one of Australia's world-class cinematographers with many awards and nominations to his name. Credits include *Picnic at Hanging Rock* (1975), *The Survivor* (1981), *Careful, He Might Hear You* (1983), *Silver City* (1984), *Goodbye Paradise* (1983), *Witness* (1985), *Rain Man* (1988), *Dead Poets Society* (1989), *Lorenzo's Oil* (1992), *The English Patient* (1996), and *Harry Potter and the Philosopher's Stone* (2001). Seale has also directed one feature film, *Til There Was You* (1990).

FRANS VANDENBURG is an editor whose credits include *Romero* (1989), *The Sum of Us* (1994), *Blackrock* (1997), *Sample People* (1999) and, as co-editor with John Scott, *Map of the Human Heart* (1993). He was archive footage researcher and first assistant editor on *Newsfront* in 1977, and a driving force behind the recent restoration and DVD release of *Newsfront*. He recently completed a documentary on Phillip Noyce titled *Better to Reign in Hell?*, which is a slight variation on the title of a short drama made by Noyce in 1969 that police alleged was pornographic.

PETER WEIR is perhaps the most distinguished of the generation of Australian film-makers to have emerged in the early 1970s. *Picnic at Hanging Rock* (1975) is regarded internationally as the film to have marked the rebirth of Australian cinema. Weir was a former actor and writer for radio; his films include *Three to Go* (1971), *The Cars That Ate Paris* (1974), *The Last Wave* (1977), *The Plumber* (1979), *Gallipoli* (1981), *The Year of Living Dangerously* (1982), *Green Card* (1990), *Fearless* (1993) and *The Truman Show* (1998).

Index

Index

Index

Index

Index